Rhetorical Philosophy and Theory
Series Editor, David Blakesley

WITHDRAWN

Other Books in the Rhetorical Philosophy and Theory Series

Kenneth Burke and the Conversation after Philosophy
Timothy W. Crusius

Breaking Up [at] Totality: A Rhetoric of Laughter
D. Diane Davis

Seduction, Sophistry,

and the

Woman

with the

Rhetorical Figure

Seduction, Sophistry,

and the

Woman

with the

Rhetorical Figure

Michelle Ballif

Southern Illinois University Press
Carbondale and Edwardsville

Library of Congress Cataloging-in-Publication Data

Ballif, Michelle, 1964–
    Seduction, sophistry, and the woman with the rhetorical figure / Michelle
Ballif.
        p. cm. — (Rhetorical philosophy and theory)
    Includes bibliographical references and index.
    1. Women in literature. 2. Women and literature. 3. Rhetoric—History.
    4. Woman (Philosophy) I. Title. II. Series.

    PN56.5.W64 B28 2001
    809′.93352042—dc21
    ISBN 0-8093-2333-8   99-086609

The paper used in this publication meets the minimum requirements of
American National Standard for Information Sciences—Permanence of Paper
for Printed Library Materials, ANSI Z39.48-1992. ⊗

to D. Diane Davis
for Everything

and Victor J. Vitanza
for Nothing

Contents

Acknowledgments

I was first seduced by rhetoric in the fall of 1985. It was a mis/taken and serendipitous seduction. I was working on a master's program in English and had completed most of my required course work in the various periods and genres—in Naturalism and the novel, in the Renaissance and poetry. The program required, however, that in addition to courses in literary studies I take a course in the study of language. Because I was not particularly passionate about all things morphological and syntactical, I avoided the obvious grammar courses and enrolled, instead, in Professor Greg Clark's ENGL 521R, "Studies in Language and Rhetoric." That is, I remind myself with incredulity, I enrolled *by default* in *the single course* that forever altered the trajectory of my personal and professional life. Through readings of wonderfully strange texts such as Plato's *Phaedrus,* Greg Clark seduced all I knew, all I had assumed, all I had hoped to know.

Once seduced, I was not abandoned. I would like to acknowledge the role that my mentors at the University of Texas at Arlington have played in the construction of this text and its presumed author. Through their discourses, they have constituted me as such and, thus, have provided the very conditions of possibility for this text. I thank Luanne T. Frank, C. Jan Swearingen, Hans Kellner, Robert Reddick, Charles Chiasson, and especially Victor J. Vitanza—contra to (as in alongside) I'm Nothing.

Of course, lest I risk cement shoes, I cannot forget to mention the "Humanities Mafia" of the University of Texas at Arlington: Diane Davis, Phil Doss, Bob Cook, Rebecca Sabounchi, Jo Suzuki, Cynthia Haynes. Special thanks is due to Bob Cook for much more than Quark.

I thank, also, my colleagues in the field(s) of rhetoric and composition, especially Susan Jarratt, Kris Ratcliffe, Steve Mailloux, Cheryl Glenn, Mike Rose, Jorie Woods, Sharon Crowley, John Poulakos, and Takis Poulakos, who have served as exemplary models both personally and professionally and who have befriended and supported me in significant ways and in key moments, kairotically.

Thanks, too, to Dave Blakesley and to Karl Kageff of Southern Illinois University Press for making so much so possible.

With profound gratitude I acknowledge my parents, Jae R. and Carma F. Ballif, for continued love and support, as well as my siblings—Michael, Cydne, Gregory, Stephanie, Bryan, and Blake—for food, fire, and friendship.

The University of Georgia has afforded me every available opportunity; I thank supportive administrators Wyatt Anderson, Hugh Ruppersburg, Anne Williams, as well as my students and my colleagues, especially Christy Desmet and Michael G. Moran, and—it must be said—John Vance, who mis/took me for Helen of Troy. Thanks also to Bill Provost, Chuck Platter, and Naomi Norman (the latter for emergency Greek). I am appreciative of a University of Georgia Research Foundation award, which allowed me a summer to work on significant revisions. And thanks to all my Athenian friends who remain innumerable and unnamable, including Kevin Young, Adam Parkes, John Murphy, and particularly Barbara Brickman.

But especially I would like to acknowledge Larry Nackerud, the man who seduced *me*—turtles all the way down.

I also thank the publishers of the following articles of mine for graciously allowing use of the material in the preparation of this book:

"Writing the Third Sophistic Cyborg: Periphrasis on an [In]Tense Rhetoric." *Rhetoric Society Quarterly* 28.4 (fall 1998): 51–72.

"Seducing Composition: A Challenge to Identity-Disclosing Pedagogies." *Rhetoric Review* 16.1 (fall 1997): 76–91. Copyright 1997 by *Rhetoric Review*.

"Mothers in the Classroom: Composing Masculinity via Fetal Pedagogies." Originally published in *Pre/Text* 16.3–4 (fall–winter 1995): 288–314.

"Extricating Ethics from the Ego: Liminal Subjects and the Discourse of the Other." *Studies in Psychoanalytic Theory* 1.1 (spring 1992): 103–13.

"What Is It That the Audience Wants? Or, Notes Toward a Listening with a Transgendered Ear for (Mis)Understanding." *JAC: A Journal of Composition Theory* 19.1 (winter 1999): 51–70.

Seduction, Sophistry,

and the

Woman

with the

Rhetorical Figure

Introduction: A Pre/Script Regarding the Subject of Woman, A Pre/Face Regarding the Figure of Woman

> There is, after all, a difference between really attempting to think differently and thinking the Same through the manipulation of difference.
>
> —Alice Jardine, *Gynesis: Configurations of Woman and Modernity*

> For one must be able to lose oneself occasionally if one wants to learn something from things different from oneself.
>
> —Nietzsche, *The Gay Science*

> Finally, it . . . is our business not to supply reality but to invent allusions to the conceivable which cannot be presented. And it is not to be expected that this task will effect the last reconciliation between language games.
>
> —Lyotard, *The Postmodern Condition: A Report on Knowledge*

Prefacing his analysis of a case of hysteria, Sigmund Freud claims all the rights and privileges of a gynecologist (*Dora* 23). Once so legitimated, Freud lays Dora on a couch and, in the words of Philip Rieff, "pushes the protesting girl back through her inner history—of which she is largely unaware—descending ever deeper" (Introduction to Freud, *Dora* 9), probing her repressed desires, in search of the truth.[1] Freud is the "psycho-gynecologist" *par excellence* who desires to know: what is it that Woman wants? What is the truth of Woman?[2] In contradistinction to Freud, I have no desire to probe nor to reveal in any way what the truth of Woman is, although my subject, as was Freud's, is Woman[3] (but not Woman-as-subject). I have undertaken an examination of

1

Woman insofar as she has been the subject of discussion for several on-going conversations within our postmodern age. Feminism has concerned itself with the category "Woman," its parameters, its constitution, its experience. French feminists, such as Hélène Cixous and Luce Irigaray, have examined Woman's writing or the *jouissance* of *l'écriture féminine*. Philosophers, such as Jacques Derrida, Félix Guattari, and Gilles Deleuze, have taken the name of Woman as a point of departure for a line of flight from the excesses of rationality and phallic thought. Indeed, Woman has become the central point of entry into postmodern thought.

As the discipline of rhetoric and composition studies currently borrows from, answers to, and inhabits a postmodern world, it has, likewise, employed the conceptual figure of Woman for various purposes. The work of Cheryl Glenn, Krista Ratcliffe, and Andrea Lunsford, for example, has sought to revise the history of rhetoric by "reclaiming" women in the tradition. Additionally, composition studies, hugely influenced by feminism and gender studies, has concerned itself with the "feminization" of composition, focusing on manifestations of Woman in the form of the Mother, female experience, and—most recently—the Cyborg. My examination of Woman will explore these various representations in order to identify whether they are complicit with the Western metaphysical tradition—that is, do they represent Woman as the dialectical antithesis of Man, as that which is Not Man? Or do they figure Woman differently as, I will argue, do Gorgias of Leontini, Friedrich Nietzsche, and Jean Baudrillard? This "different" figuration is, in Alice Jardine's words, a difference with a difference (*Gynesis* 17). That is, this difference is not the negative, the opposite, the "other" of Man. Rather, this different figuration of Woman is that which confuses the traditional binaries of Man/Woman, truth/deception, being/not being and therefore embodies the discursive form known as sophistry—a form condemned by philosophy and by most of the rhetorical tradition as effeminate and deceptive.

The use of the figure Woman has been denounced, alternately, as an act of essentialism and as a figuration that ignores the lived experiences and oppression of "real," "flesh-and-blood" women. These criticisms, valid within their respective registers of feminism and modernism, are concerned with representing women accurately or truthfully and, therefore, presume Woman's being, the standard of truth, and the efficacy of representation. It is not my purpose to attempt to reveal in any way what the truth of Woman is, nor is it my intent to demonstrate how Woman has been falsely imaged heretofore, for such a move would be a Marxist one of demystification, which suggests that Woman is governed by a "false" consciousness and that we have, in effect, been "deceived."

Rather, I want to interrogate what makes it even possible for us to speak of having been deceived; for it is the status of truth, or in Baudrillard's terms, the "principle of the real," which is precisely what is at stake in the question of Woman. It is the philosophic impulse to refute sophistry and/as Woman because its relationship to truth is suspect, just as it is the philosopher's desire, above all, as was Descartes', to "learn to distinguish the true from the false" (see Lacan, *Four Fundamental Concepts* 222). What motivates this desire? To know the truth? To know the truth of Woman?

I propose, therefore, to move in a genealogical manner by investigating what wills are and have been operative in the signification of Woman. I intend to explore how Woman has been represented and what purposes that representation serves, following the trajectory of a postmodern genealogy—a tracing of the will-to-knowledge that creates Woman as an object of study and desire—by asking the Nietzschean question, "what does the one want who seeks truth?" Deleuze explains that this question "is a matter of showing that [one] could not say, think or feel this particular thing if [one] did not have a particular will, particular forces, a particular way of being" (*Nietzsche* 78). This attentiveness to the will-to-knowledge avoids the representational impulse to begin and end with "grand narratives" (Lyotard, *Postmodern Condition*) that reify particular, ideologically constructed versions of truth. Thus the genealogist proceeds with the critical assumption that there are "no fixed essences, no underlying laws, no metaphysical finalities. . . . [It] avoids the search for depth. Instead, it seeks the surfaces of events, small details, minor shifts, and subtle contours" (Dreyfus and Rabinow, *Michel Foucault* 106), seeking "strategies of domination" (109).

This text will attempt to explore the (im)possibilities for subjectivity in the wake of a postmodern critique of the subject who, complicit with the ultimate "strategy of domination," observes, objectifies, and negates the other in an act of violence, and of the Western metaphysical and humanist epistemologies which sustain that subject. It is my presupposition, informed by Lacan and the early work of Irigaray, that the logic and epistemology of the Western tradition necessitates very particular representations of Woman and female sexuality. Thus this text will address these questions: What do these representations of Woman tell us about male subjectivity and its complicity with the metaphysical tradition? Why does our inherited epistemology presuppose and take as *a priori* male subjectivity and female sexuality? What is the relationship between these two ontic givens? And is it possible to create beings and texts which are a function neither of a subjectivity based on a logic of identity nor of an epistemology based on a logic of representation?

According to Jean-François Lyotard, "[w]e have paid a high enough price for the nostalgia of the whole and the one, for the reconciliation of the concept and the sensible, of the transparent and the communicable experience" (*Postmodern Condition* 81–82). Indeed, as our reading of Gorgias of Leontini, Friedrich Nietzsche, and Jean Baudrillard will have demonstrated, the impulses of modernity and its will-to-represent have exacted from us the price of truth, of the violence committed against the "heterogeneity of language games" (Lyotard, *Postmodern Condition* xxv). We have paid too dearly for our subjectivity: the cost has been nothing less than our own subjection. Without attempting to "redeem" or "rescue" our subjectivity (which are, for example, Jürgen Habermas's and Susan Miller's projects), can Woman rebate our subjectivity? Woman, understood as the interstices between those forces, those positions, which constitute and sustain subjectivity as such, offers us an ethical alternative to the Western metaphysical tradition. By inhabiting these gaps, not by bridging them, we bear witness to that which is incommensurable, unrepresentable (*Postmodern Condition* 82).

This, then, is where we will begin and, again, end our discussion of Woman: with the rhetorical gestures of Gorgias, Nietzsche, and Baudrillard, who unlike Freud do not attempt to unveil Woman, to lay bare the truth of her genitalia, her sexuality. Gorgias's Helen (as *apatē*), Nietzsche's Ariadne (as the affirming, Third Woman), and Baudrillard's feminine (as seduction) acknowledge Woman's always already anatomical representation, while simultaneously deconstructing this figuration, in an attempt to confuse the boundaries between mind and body, male and female, being and not being, truth and deception, and thereby to attempt to thwart the violence upon which all identity rests.

But Why These Men? Can Man Speak for/as Woman?

To even pose these questions is to forestall the interrogation of truth. For they presuppose the truth of the categories Man and Woman and the truth of the speaking subject. To read Gorgias, Nietzsche, and Baudrillard philosophically is to (mis)interpret their projects as attempts to establish and to posit an essence, presence, or subjectivity of Woman. And, of course, to read them philosophically is to see them as engaging in the grossest and most blatant form of misogyny, that is, if they are read as defining Woman as a thing or a substance. However, we can read them rhetorically, in the terminology of Victor J. Vitanza, "as an 'art' of 'resisting and disrupting' the available means (that is, the cultural codes) that allow for persuasion and identification: the 'art' of not only refusing the available (capitalistic/socialist) codes but also of refusing altogether to recode, or to reterritorialize power relations" ("'Some More' Notes" 133). By "rhetoric," I do not mean the philosophical enterprises that have existed heretofore in the name of rhetoric: that is, Platonism, Aristotelianism, Habermasianism. To presume that Gorgias, Nietzsche, and Baudrillard are "masters of truth," are subjects supposed to know the truth (of Woman), is to conceive of their rhetorical agency as governed by a philosophic will, a philosophic subjectivity, and a philosophic control of language. That is, not only do we then presume that there is a truth of Woman, a foundational referent of such, but we also assume that language will accurately and faithfully represent that referent and, further, that the rhetor can accurately and faithfully convey or channel that truth. And it assumes that only so-called biological women can speak Woman, an assumption Cixous challenges ("Laugh of the Medusa").

These presumptions I am calling "philosophic" in order to distinguish them from "sophistic" assumptions. The philosophic will, I am arguing, is to codify, systematize, and control language, to reduce it to *logos,* defined as rational speech. Plato argues that philosophic rhetoric (dialectic) is a true rhetoric *(technē)* because it orders arguments rationally. Aristotle tells us that rhetoric is to serve dialectic and that "rational speech" or *logos* is man's greatest defense. Thus, philosophic rhetoric frames rhetoric as a logical appeal; people are persuaded (or should be persuaded) to believe that which is logically demonstrated to be true or probably true. Sophistic rhetoric, contrariwise, presumes that there is something about rhetoric that is seductive, even deceptive, and that language resists logic, that it desires to trope—to turn and to turn and to turn—until it gets dizzy and, in the words of Paul de Man, "radically suspends logic and opens up vertiginous possibilities of referential aberration" *(Allegories of Reading* 10). Therefore, again, to read Gorgias, Nietzsche, and Baudrillard rhetorically is to explore the referential aberrations of Woman.

Alice Jardine, in her influential work *Gynesis: Configurations of Woman and Modernity,* offers her neologism "gynesis": "the putting into discourse of 'woman' . . . as intrinsic to new and necessary modes of thinking, writing, speaking" (25). Jardine carefully follows the modes and methods of late-twentieth-century attempts to represent Woman discursively, including the works of Lacan, Derrida, and Deleuze and Guattari. My discussion of Gorgias, Nietzsche, and Baudrillard, then, may be seen as a supplement to Jardine's book, but additionally as a nonsupplement. Whereas Jardine is concerned with the production of Woman in continental thought, I am concerned finally with the seduction of Woman—that is, unthinking her, unrepresenting her. For although Jardine says gynesis is not a thing, but a woman-in-effect and in-process, gynesis is nevertheless a "putting into discourse" of woman. Such is the method, Martin Heidegger argues, of "thingification." Once spoken or written, a thing has been produced: it has been represented and, therefore, unavoidably subjected to the violence of such (recall Derrida's discussion of the "writing lesson" in *Of Grammatology*). Jardine's focus is, as a chapter title indicates, on "Thinking the Unrepresentable." My focus, in contrast, is on how Gorgias, Nietzsche, and Baudrillard are unthinking the representable, how they are attempting to un-represent Woman. The aim of this text, then, is to read these authors rhetorically in an attempt to resist rethinking Woman as merely the other that sustains the subjectivity of the selfsame. That is, the purpose is to examine in what ways Gorgias, Nietzsche, and Baudrillard are moving beyond, or at least resisting, the conventional dualisms of Western thought and to explore the implications that their Women have for the future (anterior) of rhetoric and composition theory.

Woman and the (Im)Possibilities for Subjectivity

The questioning of truth, representation, and subject production that this text explores is situated within and propelled by the greater postmodern movement characterized by an epistemological and legitimation crisis that has sustained critical theory for at least the past forty years. Writers and theorists such as Derrida, Deleuze and Guattari, Lyotard, Bataille, Irigaray, and Cixous, for example, have sought (1) to acknowledge the complicity of reason and the metaphysics of presence with systems of oppression, (2) to demonstrate the phallogocentric construction of subjectivity, and (3) to move beyond, or at least to resist, the Hegelian dialectic and the conventional dualisms of Western thought. The conceptual starting point is the political contestation of identity. This starting point, this by now well-rehearsed argument regarding "the problem of the subject," presupposes that the overlapping categories of "identity," "agency," and "subjectivity" are ideological constructions that serve particular power/knowledge matrices, as argued by such thinkers as Michel Foucault and Louis Althusser. The "subject" is thus constituted as a speaking-thinking-writing-voting being only insofar as it has been properly subjected by/through those matrices (that is, normalized). Because this subjectivity (which has been historically constructed in terms of a phallic logic of noncontradiction, presence, and selfsame identity) has effectively (and yet dubiously) privileged—economically, politically, and rhetorically—a particular few, while effectively marginalizing all others, postmodern theorists have sought to deconstruct the modern subject, to demonstrate how this stable, self-identical, self-representing subject is a powerful fantasy of the Enlightenment—a fantasy prefaced by Parmenides and Plato.

I risk, of course, a set of anachronisms here and throughout. I am aware that the Enlightenment is a historical moment, specifically an eighteenth-century epoch characterized by an attack on traditional forms of authority—an attack made in the name of Reason, as indicated by Immanuel Kant's slogan "Dare to know!" (quoted in Foucault, "What Is Enlightenment?" 35). Modernism, likewise, can be understood as a historical condition, specifically a twentieth-century aesthetic movement, answering to the "huge historical dislocations at the turn of the century" (Con Davis and Schleifer 22). For the modernist, the present moment—in its ruptured state—presents a novel response to tradition, a novelty to be sought, as evidenced by Ezra Pound's motto "Make it new!" (quoted in Con Davis and Schleifer 22). Humanism, or the belief in the primacy of Man, can be located as well in various historical moments, specifically the Renaissance when scholars speculated that Man had more determining power over destiny than an external force such as God, or much earlier as evidenced by Protagoras's dictum "Man is the measure of all things," which has often been taken to be a proto-humanist statement. Thus, although we can situate modernism, the Enlightenment, and humanism within specific historical moments, we can also speak of them, in the words of Foucault, as an "attitude," as "a mode of relating to contemporary reality" ("What Is Enlightenment?" 39). And it is with this attitude (of daring to know, of making it new, of fashioning a self-determined history, of promising progress and development) that modernism and the Enlightenment share with humanism a peculiar faith in the power and efficacy of Man. Although I acknowledge Foucault's warning of a "facile confusion" of humanism and Enlightenment thought, I want to stress how these three historical movements have worked in tandem with the rhetorical tradition to foster a subject-centered epistemology and to real-ise the sovereignty of Man. Whatever the question—the existence of God (humanism), the power of authority (Enlightenment), the efficacy of tradition (modernism)—the answer remains "Man." It is this attitude, characterized by Kate Soper as

> a profound confidence in our powers to come to know and thereby to control our environment and destiny lies at the heart of every humanism; in this sense, we must acknowledge a continuity of theme, however warped it may have become with the passage of time, between the Renaissance

> celebration of the freedom of humanity from any transcen-
> dental hierarchy or cosmic order [and] the Enlightenment
> faith in reason and its powers. (14–15)

And, according to Heidegger, what lies at this heart of hearts is a metaphysics ("Letter on Humanism" 225), specifically a metaphysics of
presence. Hence, however warped this trajectory may have become, we
can trace our contemporary mode of being to the metaphysical beliefs
in truth, in being able to know it, and in being able to communicate it.
In short, our contemporary mode of being has given epistemology the
status of ontology—has given Man the status of being by reasserting
the primacy and efficacy of a knowing/speaking subject.

Composition theorists as diverse as Susan Miller *(Rescuing the Subject)*, Lester Faigley *(Fragments of Rationality)*, David Bartholomae
("Inventing the University"), and Victor Vitanza ("Three Countertheses"), for example, have addressed the "problem of the subject," particularly as it informs or should/could inform writing studies and pedagogy. These theorists, excluding Vitanza, have sought ways to bracket
the complete deconstruction of the subject in order to posit a rhetorical and political agency without reaffirming the modernist subject, reestablishing individualism, or making essentialist claims. Despite their
deconstruction of the transcendental subject, these pedagogies reveal a
closer affinity with the modernist project (see Vitanza's "Three Countertheses"). Within the past several years, various pedagogical and theoretical movements have been conflated under the general nomenclature of postmodernism. Yet, most of what goes by this name has been
(mis)identified; postmodernism has been equated with "critical pedagogies" *à la* Berlin, Giroux, and Aronowitz. All these efforts, regardless of how nobly deployed, are implicated in the Enlightenment project
as they engage in the production of critical consciousness. "The irony
of this deployment," to appropriate Foucault, "is in having us believe
that our 'liberation' is in the balance" (*History of Sexuality* 159), that
our liberation hangs on the production of a self-reflexive writing subject.

Yet, insofar as our pedagogical goal remains within the realm of the
sovereignty of the subject (even if socially constructed)—with its rational and "human" capacities, with its emancipatory promises—we
remain modernists and subject to the program of modernism. Therefore, I will advocate postmodernism as an ethical alternative. By "postmodernism," I am referring specifically to the critical perspective developed by such theorists as Lyotard, de Man, and Derrida—theorists who
have attempted to deconstruct notions of truth and subjectivity and
who have simultaneously sought to avoid any new reconstruction of

truth or subjectivity (of Woman or otherwise). By "ethical," I am identifying a sophistic alternative to the rhetorical tradition, which has
figured rhetoric as political, civic discourse, as a service to the polis (and
ultimately as a service to metaphysics). An ethical rhetoric, in contrast,
is not co-opted by the polis or by its economy of symbolic exchange.
However, this ethical rhetoric is not reducible to Quintilian's good man
speaking well, nor the good woman speaking well, because this rhetorical subject is through and through a product of the metaphysical tradition. My use of "postmodernism" indicates a continuous process of the
decodification of, in Lyotard's terminology, the "grand narratives" that
sustain beliefs, communities, subjects, and systems of power and domination (*Postmodern Condition* 15, 37–38, 41, 60) My use also refers to
the accompanying movement of resisting and disrupting any subsequent attempts to recodify those or other narratives. This distinguishes
my efforts from those who attempt to recover or re-represent Woman
as a foundational referent and who produce her as subject (that is,
"speaking as a woman").

Rather than Woman-as-subject (and, of course, Woman-as-object),
postmodernism offers us the alternative move beyond modernism, a
move which Baudrillard terms "seduction." Yet, interestingly, tellingly,
we have been warned against this seduction: current rhetoric and composition scholars argue that subject production is our proper realm and
that we should not transgress it. John Trimbur, for example, writes: "I
suggest that we should not embrace postmodernism hastily. The purpose of this essay," he continues, "is to offer a cautionary tale—to argue that despite (or perhaps because of) its seductive appeal, we should
resist falling for postmodernism wholesale" ("Composition Studies"
118). The rhetoric of Trimbur's "cautionary tale" is telling: we should
not "fall" (as did Adam and Eve) nor "embrace" (as did Abelard and
Heloise) nor succumb to "seductive appeal[s]" (as did Helen). Insofar
as "seduction" remains the "limit" of our modernist discourse, truth
(and its representation) continues to circumscribe our subjectivity.

This is demonstrated through the work of contemporary scholars
in the field of rhetoric and composition. The continued emphasis is on
the production of Woman, the production of Woman-as-subject, and
the production of the subject-as-Woman. Let me acknowledge: This
work has positively affected the discipline—its pedagogical practices,
its historiography, and its research agendas—by giving a hearing to
heretofore excluded voices. Revisionary histories composed by Lunsford, Glenn, and Ratcliffe, for example, have sought to recover, reread,
re-present Woman in the rhetorical tradition. Some writers have specifically focused on locating female rhetors within the tradition and theo-
rizing what it means to speak/write as a woman. Others, such as those

collected in Susan Jarratt and Lynn Worsham's *Feminism and Composition Studies: In Other Words,* have sought ways to "forge a collective subject capable of making mass movement" while still attending to differences (329). Others still, such as those compiled in Louise Wetherbee Phelps and Janet Emig's *Feminine Principles and Women's Experiences in American Composition and Rhetoric,* have argued for a "feminization" of composition, that is, to produce writing subjects and writing styles that counter traditional male-gendered agonistic rhetorical models.[4] Again, let me acknowledge that this is warrantable work. But the concern of these theorists remains production. In contradistinction, I am interested in seduction. Although I am not the only one (other theorists such as Diane Davis and Victor Vitanza, for example, have been seduced by the possibilities of that which will have been beyond production), there are few rhetoric and composition scholars who have engaged the radical question posed by Baudrillard: We have all been produced, but can we be seduced?

The work of Baudrillard hinges on the distinction between production and seduction. According to Baudrillard, production means to "render visible, to cause to appear" and has as its project "to set everything up in clear view . . . this is . . . the project of our whole culture, whose natural condition is 'obscenity' " (*Forget* 21–22). The project of production is founded in the modernist's belief that at bedrock there is some referent, some principle of truth, and that one's purpose is to reflect it accurately, and to find one's self in that reflection—one's truth, one's cure, one's liberation. This belief, called the "reality principle" by Baudrillard, is the process of representation, of naming, of constituting identity, of positing truth, a process grounded in the dichotomy of presence/absence and its corollaries of active/passive and truth/deception, wherein one term is valued and the other is subjected—through a dialectical process—to a negation in order to establish an identity, to sustain the hierarchy. This, then, is the insidious violence of the subject's will-to-representation: to create identity, either of self or of truth, requires the negation and appropriation of the other. The philosophical drive to produce meaning, to create *vrai-semblances,* to establish truth, is a nihilistic enterprise. These sound like harsh words for the process of representation, a process so seemingly natural to us, Jardine remarks in *Gynesis,* as to be beyond question. Yet this process is "at the very roots of our Western drive to know all, and shown to be inseparable from the imperial speaking subject . . . [and] denounced as complicitous with a violence as old as Western history itself" (Jardine 118–19). In short, the mimetic impulse is symptomatic of the will-to-mastery which exhibits itself in the constant and desperate attempts made by systems of power and by subjected subjects to control, to dominate. Baudrillard characterizes this process of representation as requiring all things (all that is and, indeed, all that is not, but the naming makes it so) to be disclosed, brought into existence and categorized. This is the process of production, a process which has control as its goal: mastery of the world, of the word, and of the self. The will-to-mastery and its attendant violence ensures that all things are fixed with "true" representations, that all signifieds are fixed with "corresponding" signifiers, as a means of guaranteeing identity, truth, and presence.

Seduction, for Baudrillard, figures in contradistinction to production, and will be understood (that is, if one can speak of "understanding" seduction) in ways requiring no less than an epistemological shift—indeed a shift beyond epistemology. For our constructed subjectivity's first impulse is to examine seduction via the terministic grids or categorical *topoi* of the subject: active/passive, cause/effect, and the "sexual." That is, we still hold certain principles to be self-evident (such as one's biological sex) or referential (such as one's "experience"). Thus Jacqueline Jones Royster, speaking of her polyvocal subjectivity, says that "all my voices are authentic," acknowledging that her multiple voices make her subjectivity possible. Royster could have said "all my voices are false"—or rather "all my voices are neither authentic nor false." But that Royster said all her voices are "authentic," once again underscores how invested we are in the notion of "truth," and in the notion that rhetorical/speaking being has some essential relation to truth, or should have such a relation. Richard Lanham argues that the discipline of composition studies maintains, "a common-sense positivism that finds a real world out there, a sincere soul inside all of us, and a prose style that opens a transparent window between the two" ("Rhetorical Paideia" 136). We must question what our desire is as a discipline to retain these beliefs even as we vociferously argue contrariwise, even as we convince ourselves that we no longer posit a foundational self or truth.

Within the realm of production, "reality," "authenticity," and "communication" are the guarantors of subjectivity. But within seduction, there is no possibility of "real-ising" the subject. One's *cogito* is surrendered, Baudrillard suggests, to the "total illusion of signs, to immediate control by appearances, that is, going beyond the false into the absolute abyss of artifice" (*Fatal Strategies* 52). Production's impulse is to "real-ise"—to make something answerable to the principle of the real, to be an accurate representation of the real, to subject it to the demands of truth, and hence to give it being. Surrendering to the "absolute abyss of artifice," contrariwise, is to affirm that "nothing exists," that "artifice" or *apatē* (Gorgias) or art (Nietzsche) resists the imperative of the real. Within seduction, the real is unrepresented, and what is unrepresentable (nothingness—that is, what the metaphysics of presence has left for nothing) may come—but without being, without being subjected to truth. There is nothing nihilistic about this position, although our productive impulses warn us against this apparent and wanton will-less-ness. The will, as traditionally understood, or the causal ego, does not belong in the domain of the challenge. Indeed, it is this will itself which is nihilistic as it can only assert itself through the logic of the negative, can only identify or "real-ise" itself by establishing a "nothingness" against which it can claim its superiority and sovereignty. But within seduction, there is no victor nor is there vanquished; no player can be greater than the challenge. There is no seducer, no seductee, in seduction (unlike in Plato's sordid scenarios of the *Symposium* and *Phaedrus*).

To repeat Baudrillard's radical ethic: "We were all once produced, we must all be seduced. That is the only true 'liberation'" (*Fatal Strategies* 138). Thus, although radical pedagogical strategies may indeed produce subjects who may initiate some political and social change, they ultimately cannot make good on the promise for liberation for the subject. For, according to Baudrillard, it is precisely our identity (our subjectivity, our relationship to truth) to which we are held hostage: "called upon to assume it, to answer for it with our own lives (this is called security, occasionally social), called on to be ourselves, to talk, delight, realize ourselves . . . it calls on you to reveal yourself as you are [as a sign]. It is always blackmail by identity (and thus a symbolic murder, since you are never that, except precisely by being condemned to it)" (*Fatal Strategies* 40). Our world of overproduction guarantees that we will be subject to our identity and the categorical imperatives such as race, gender, and class that order our lives.

No More Hostages of/for Truth: Figuring Woman with/as *Différance* Beyond Sexual Difference

Rather than re-presenting Woman—that is holding her hostage to her identity as such—I am interested in the figure of Woman as that which resists the (phallic) logic of identity and exceeds the categorical imperatives of philosophic thought. In the parlance of the so-called French feminists, this potentiality is likened to the excesses of feminine sexuality, to the infinite possible erotic zones of woman, rather than the finite sexuality of Man and the phallus. Irigaray explains:

> woman . . . touches herself in and of herself without any
> need for mediation, and before there is any way to distin-
> guish activity from passivity. Woman 'touches herself' all

the time, and moreover no one can forbid her to do so, for her genitals are formed of two lips in continuous contact. Thus, within herself, she is already two—but not divisible into one(s)—that caress each other. (*This Sex* 24)

Thus, due to woman's always already duplicity and ambiguity, several French feminists have advocated women's writing—*l'écriture féminine,* "writing the body"—as a subversive enterprise, which disrupts metaphysical binary thinking and opens up new spaces for Woman and the feminine to be heard.[5] "Because," Sarah Kofman explains, "woman does not have the right to speak . . . , [she] creates an excess of mystery and obscurity. . . . Woman *lacks sincerity*: she dissimulates, transforms each word into an enigma, an indecipherable *riddle.* That is why [her] narrative is always full of gaps" (*Enigma of Woman* 43). These gaps or indecipherable spaces, Jardine explains, are spaces over which the grand narratives of phallogocentrism, finally, cannot exert control (25).

Thus woman is another stand-in for or trace of *différance,* Derrida's neologism for the radical indeterminacy of language (*Of Grammatology* 62–65, 167). And, as such, Woman renders the possibility of displacing the binary system. The concept of Woman, therefore, has been a tool for many postmodernists working against Man, truth, history, and meaning. Yet by figuring Woman as this revolutionary rhetorical gesture, we run the risk of essentialism. This is a risk I am willing to take. The accusation of essentialism is both valid and tiresome: valid insofar as the grand narrative of sexual difference consistently co-opts and appropriates all difference according to the prevailing, phallocentric logic of the selfsame, and yet tiresome insofar as this figuration of Woman as difference with a difference deconstructs sexual difference itself. Although Gayatri Spivak, as we shall note, specifically denounces this use of Woman, I adopt (perversely, I'm sure) her notion of "strategic essentialism," whereby one strategically figures Woman as a negotiation with masculinism and phallogocentrism ("In a Word" 126–27).[6] And yet, as Michel de Certeau argues, "tactic" is perhaps a more fitting term insofar as "strategy" assumes a "subject of will and power" (xix; 35–36), and "tactic" better describes the sophistic quality of *mētis* (or cunning) realized at the *kairotic* (or opportune) moment. My tactic, then, is to seduce us (or to lead us astray) from the truth of sexual difference that essentializes Woman as such.

Although a hyperactive hermeneut, Freud failed to question his question; that is, he failed to acknowledge his own presuppositions concerning women, desire, and subjectivity. Freud's question (What is it that Woman wants?) is off the mark because it ontically presupposes the woman; it takes as self-evident women's sexuality: it essentializes sexual difference. Thus Lacan finds psychoanalytic thinking guilty of replicating what is its very task to expose: how subjects are sexed. Juliet Mitchell phrases Lacan's critique as such: "Psychoanalysis should not subscribe to ideas about how men and women do or should live as sexually differentiated beings, but instead it should analyse how they come to be such beings in the first place" ("Introduction" 3).

One's sexual identification is not a biological given, but rather an ideological assignment, whose purpose is, in the words of Julia Epstein and Kristina Straub, to "delimit and contain the threatening absence of boundaries between human bodies and among bodily acts that would otherwise explode the organizational and institutional structures of social ideologies" ("Introduction" 2). This containment and boundary-marking (for example, via the incest taboo) is accomplished, in Lacanian psychoanalytic terms, via symbolic castration. This Lacanian concept explains how we are simultaneously sexed and made subject to the law. The price of both our sexuality and our subjectivity is no less than to live under the fear of castration. In the seminar published as "The Phallic Phase and the Subjective Import of the Castration Complex," we learn that "masculinity and femininity [have no] unmediated relationship to anatomical difference, a relationship of which they have no knowledge" (*Feminine Sexuality* 109). That is, the meaning of our gendered sexuality is not to be found via biology; rather, the meaning is realized within the symbolic register (109).

Ontic explanations of sexuality as genital, biological, instinctual, or socially "added" all presume being/subjectivity as self-evident and as distinguishable from sexuality. Lacan, however, as his "Guiding Remarks for a Congress on Feminine Sexuality" suggest, argues that it is impossible to posit "femininity" as outside of the very processes of the Symbolic which constitute femininity as such. He writes:

> [we must] remind ourselves that images and symbols *for* the woman cannot be isolated from images and symbols *of* the woman. . . . It is representation . . . , the representation of feminine sexuality, whether repressed or not, which conditions how it comes into play, and it is the displaced offshoots of this representation . . . which decide the outcome of its tendencies, however naturally roughed out one may take such tendencies to be. (*Feminine Sexuality* 90)

To be a woman is realizable, then, only within the realm of the symbolic, entangled with sexual difference and the Oedipal relation ("Function and Field of Speech and Language," *Écrits*). Kaja Silverman explains that sexual difference is "an organizing principle not only of the symbolic order and its 'contents' (signification, discourse, subjectivity), but of the semiotic account of those things" (*Subject of Semiotics* viii). To simplify, perhaps one could say that signification occurs through subjectivity through sexuality (as defined by sexual difference), and subjectivity occurs through signification through sexuality, and sexuality occurs through subjectivity through signification. Silverman's point is well taken: it is impossible either to separate or isolate the components of signification, subjectivity, and sexuality.

Lacan not only insists on this point (the impossibility of separating signification, subjectivity, and sexuality), but he also claims the impossibility of attaining, representing, or fulfilling signification, subjectivity, or sexuality.[7] For Lacan, the subject (and thus signification and sexuality) is defined by lack, as his narrative of a subject's formation (or, more appropriately, perhaps, de/formation) suggests:

> Two lacks overlap here. The first emerges from the central defect around which the dialectic of the advent of the subject to his own being in the relation to the Other turns—by the fact that the subject depends on the signifier and that the signifier is first of all in the field of the Other. This lack takes up the other lack, which is the real, earlier lack, to be situated at the advent of the living being, that is to say, at sexed reproduction. The real lack is what the living being loses, that part of himself *qua* living being, in reproducing himself through the way of sex. This lack is real because it relates something real, namely, that the living being, by being subject to sex, has fallen under the blow of individual death. (*Four Fundamental Concepts* 204–5)

Thus, according to Lacan, the subject experiences his[8] first loss by virtue of being sexually differentiated and thus suffers from the impossibility of being physiologically both male and female—a loss which echoes Aristophanes' myth as recounted in Plato's *Symposium* (*Four Fundamental Concepts* 205). The subject's second loss occurs as the body is territorialized, resulting in a channeled libido. The subject is no longer able to experience his oceanic self and unchanneled libido. Another loss occurs during the mirror stage as the self recognizes itself in and through a misrepresentation (Lacan, *Écrits* 1–7). The self is at that point defined via self-alienation. Alienated from self, the self is once again alienated from the Real as he enters the realm of the Symbolic. All this alienation and lack gives birth to the subject and simultaneously to desire. But the fulfillment of that desire remains impossible. Although the will to have, to possess, to experience presence, exists, its

fulfillment does not. There is only a *fort* to answer our *da*. And only a
da to respond to our *fort*.[9]

Further, for Lacan, Woman symbolizes the Real, and as such, is the
object of desiring (and castration-threatened) man. But as a simultaneous function of the Symbolic, she does not exist: she is impossible, Silverman explains, "consigned forever to a state of non-representation
and non-fulfillment" (176)—to, that is, a state of nonideal representation and nonideal fulfillment. Despite the impossibility of having
Woman-as-*objet-à*, desire is such that Man will continue to objectify
Woman, represent Woman, and thus appropriate her without ever fulfilling his desire.

Thus, although Man's subjectivity, sexuality, and signification is
impossible, Woman's is doubly so. Starting with a deprivileged relationship to the Symbolic, Woman's fading begins before she appears. She is
the impossible and absent subjectivity, the impossible and absent signification. Lacan tells us that *the* woman does not exist (*Feminine Sexuality* 137–61). That is, Woman has no essence and, thus, no presence.
She "is" only in absentia in the folds of the Real, as a symptom of Male
desire and subjectivity (*Feminine Sexuality* 170). Irigaray in *This Sex
Which Is Not One* hints that this absent place may disrupt all Man
knows of subjectivity, sexuality, and signification. She writes:

> by remaining absent as "subject," she lets them keep, even
> guarantees that they can keep, the position of mastery. How-
> ever, this is a somewhat risky business. . . . What if she were
> to discover there the cause of their cause? In the pleasure of
> "this *she* who does not exist and who signifies nothing"?
> This "she" that women might well understand, one day, as
> the projection onto that in-fant "being"—which they repre-
> sent for him—of his relation to nihilism. (95)

It is the metaphysical project (manifested in the enterprises of modernism, humanism, and production) that is nihilistic (*not* postmodernism). The symbolic register, according to Lacan, is governed by the law
of the father; its efficacy is sustained through the fear of the effects of
that law, namely castration. Judith Butler, in her *Bodies That Matter*,
explains:

> The symbolic marks the body by sex through threatening
> that body, through the deployment/production of an imagi-
> nary threat, a castration, a privation of some bodily part. . . .
> There must be a body trembling before the law, a body
> whose fear can be compelled by the law, a law that produces
> the trembling body prepared for its inscription, a law that

marks the body *first* with fear only then to mark it again with the symbolic stamp of sex. (101)

I am interested in a theory and praxis of rhetoric that is just insofar as it doesn't require trembling bodies that fear the horror of being mutilated or that project this fear onto others. This is the price that sexual difference exacts of us. This is the "pound of flesh" we owe under the symbolic contract (Lacan, *Feminine Sexuality* 120). To mete out a justness ("to dispel the fear"), I am arguing, we must challenge the sexual difference upon which our current rhetorical theories depend.[10] Julia Kristeva writes:

> Sexual difference—which is at once biological, physiological, and relative to reproduction—is translated by and translates a difference in the relation of subjects to the symbolic contract which is the social contract: a difference, then, in the relationship to power, language and meaning. The sharpest and most subtle point of feminist subversion brought about by the new generation will henceforth be situated on the terrain of the inseparable conjunction of the sexual and the symbolic, in order to discover, first, the specificity of the female, and then, in the end, that of each individual. ("Women's Time" 21)

And, indeed, attempting to "discover the specificity of the female" has been an important task for a generation of feminists. So-called women's ways of knowing/thinking/caring/speaking/mothering have been variously theorized and articulated as have more sophisticated theories of identity politics—of what it means to "be" a "woman." But the challenge for an even newer generation of feminists will be, in Baudrillard's idiom, to discover a "dual/duel" form of difference rather than to rediscover again and again the dialectical form of difference (*Transparency* 126). That is, whereas the specificity of the female has only been understood as the dialectical other of the male heretofore— that is, within the regulated terms of sexual dimorphism—and hence subject to the laws of negation and castration, it is necessary that our current agenda be to discover the radical otherness of the sexes—all of them, and there are more than two. So the work of "feminism(s)" will continue on the terrain "of the inseparable conjunction of the sexual and the symbolic," and its "sharpest and most subtle point of feminist subversion" will be to de-Oedipalize both the sexual and the symbolic.

This is no easy task, particularly since the metaphysical tradition has prescribed—indeed required as the basis of its existence—sexual difference (a specific instance of the negative). Although (as historians of sexuality including Dover, Halperin, Laqueur, and Foucault have demonstrated) sexual difference has been variously figured, all models of difference (whether one sex, two sex, hetero- or homo-) have had a necessary relation to another opposition: that between *erōs* (specifically physical desire) and cognition, as evidenced from early extant philosophic fragments of the pre-Socratics' thought about thought (Havelock, "The Linguistic Task"). Plato, for example, suggests that "we shall continue closest to knowledge if we avoid as much as we can all contact and association with the body" (*Phaedo* 67a). And, later, Augustine, in *The City of God*, argues that *erōs* suspends "all mental activity" (14.16.464). This opposition—as all other binary oppositions—presupposes a hierarchical relationship. In this case, cognition or thought is the valued term; *erōs* or desire is the term—which as the other— threatens the privileged position and so must be ideologically devalued (although, it ironically sustains and guarantees that very privileged position). Robin May Schott writes:

> The emphasis on distancing thought from sensuality grew out of an ascetic practice by which men sought to transcend the vicissitudes of the phenomenal world, to escape the mortal fate implicit in the natural life cycle of human beings [which, of course, women were associated with]. [Hence] the most threatening moments of birth and death were connected, through myth and ritual, with an interpretation of women's sexuality as polluting. (x)

To the purified philosophers, woman is the embodiment of *erōs*, of sensuality, of desire (and of death). Men who succumbed to inappropriate desire were compared with women (Dover, Plato). The Western metaphysical tradition, then, has demonstrated that the subject of Woman has been the subject of the body, of sexuality—that is, an object of male desire. This is how Woman's sexual difference has been essentialized. As Irigaray's *Speculum of the Other Woman*, Cixous's "Laugh of the Medusa," Elizabeth Spelman's "Woman as Body," Andrea Nye's *Words of Power*, and Schott's *Cognition and Eros* (among others) have argued, the rational/irrational, mind/body, and man/woman binaries are the very conditions of possibility for the existence of philosophy and of the philosophic/rhetorical tradition. Within this tradition, Woman exists as the dialectical other and thereby sustains the philosopher's identity as such. Although taken as "body" and "sexuality," by virtue of the process of representation, Woman has been figured as an abstract conception, as a representation, of sexuality and of body, just as the early goddesses Dikē and Sophia were reduced to representations of justice and wisdom, (dis)respectively. Thus, although corporeality in essence, Woman has always already existed only as a representation of incarnation.

I will explore the ways in which this representation of Woman has served particular interests and desires without attempting to posit or to reveal a "Woman" which exists prior to such representations, either biologically or materially. To do so would be an act of re-appropriation, of re-presentation, of re-essentialization, of the body and of sexuality. It is my presupposition that there is no "degree zero" of biological sex nor of sexuality, as Anne Fausto-Sterling's "The Five Sexes" and Thomas Laqueur's *Making Sex* have convincingly demonstrated.

For Gorgias, Nietzsche, and Baudrillard, Woman is a rhetorical process—not a place—explored in an effort to escape, elude, and displace the will to truth with its attendant violence, not to remain faithful to it. Woman is a play of appearances, a surface that absorbs truth, representation, and referentiality. How could this Woman influence current conceptions and goals of rhetoric and composition? Perhaps our discipline has not yet ears for these three sophists; perhaps we will continue to insist that they be excluded and dismissed as misogynists and as perpetuators of gender stereotypes. But in the face of this potential dismissal, I offer an alternative reading of Gorgias, Nietzsche, Baudrillard, and the figure(s) of Woman as a rhetorical gesture to question the philosophic concepts of being, truth, and subjectivity and to displace via a postmodern move the totalizing force of the metaphysics of presence. This Woman, again, is not a gendered construction nor is it representational of sex or sexuality. Whereas woman has figured only as the other negated term, used to sustain the identity and privilege of man, here Woman figures difference with a difference, as neither subject nor object, within seduction (contra to production): a rhetorical process that seeks to unthink the Western, phallogocentric tradition, a tradition founded on, in the words of Gayatri Spivak "epistemic violence" (*Post-Colonial Critic* 102). Thus I ask the questions: How does Woman figure in the works of each of these writers, and how does her figure seduce us in a way that disrupts and displaces truth and subjectivity?

Resisting Women

In response to the postmodern critique of the speaking subject, the complaint has been registered "How can women participate in the reading, writing, and making of the history of rhetoric? Just when the realm of rhetoric (and by extension, politics) begins to open up enough to allow woman to open her mouth as a speaking subject, the questioning of such begins." The issue for some, then, becomes "How can women achieve a subject position, now, after having been denied it for so long?" And by extension, "How can women gain political power and exercise agency in the face of the postmodern deconstruction of the subject?" The attempts to bestow women with the suspect status of a speaking subject remain questionable, although understandable. Due to the fact that the postmodern condition is characterized by a loss of faith in those grand narratives of truth and subjectivity, many have accused postmodernism of being the ultimate manifestation of nihilism. Postmodernism's refusal to assert a truth or to link in globalizing or totalizing ways is regarded by many as vulgar relativism and as politically and morally bankrupt. Paul Smith's *Discerning the Subject,* as just one example among many, critiques postmodernism by claiming that it is "compromised by its lack of a theory of subjectivity and agency" (xxxi). Jürgen Habermas takes a similar position by leveling the accusation against "anti-modernists" as betraying liberal politics by crushing the social hope guaranteed by the project of modernity: emancipation ("Modernity vs. Postmodernity" 12–14). As I have suggested, many theorists have likewise condemned postmodernism for its failure to attend to what they (and Smith and Habermas) envision the political, critical task at hand to be: to liberate the oppressed (students, women, minorities) by giving them a voice—that is, to constitute them as speaking/writing/doing subjects rather than as victims of authorial systems of power, that is, the educational institution, the patriarchal society, or the capitalistic economy.

In response to this charge, I would argue that such an endeavor invokes the very values that sustain the system of oppression from which we are supposedly emancipating ourselves: the values of the metaphysics of presence. Indeed, I am suggesting that the scene of subject constitution is the site of victimization not liberation. Although Baudrillard would never claim to offer a revolutionary program or agenda for liberation—for such claims are fraught with the totalizing impulses of modernism—he has, however, suggested that within the realm of seduction (vis-à-vis the realm of production), we may find ways to resist the dialectical violence of truth and subjectivity.

This particular rhetorical and deconstructive move certainly has its opponents. The major claims in opposition are that by deconstructing subjectivity, we deny agency and/or we deny the concerns of "real" people, specifically women. Patricia Bizzell, for example, as a keynote speaker for the 1996 Rhetoric Society of America conference, argued that she welcomes the postmodern conception of rhetorical subjectivity insofar as it deconstructs the traditional view of rhetoric as communication "taking place among internally unified, rational individuals who can more or less freely choose among available means of persuasion"

("Prospect of Rhetorical Agency" 37). Yet she admits that she is not "entirely happy" with the postmodern view because, she argues, it presents the subject as an "entity with little or no agency" unable to "determine the 'authenticity' or 'sincerity' of" discourses, claims, and evidence (38). Teresa Ebert's criticism of postmodernism is parallel, yet she further condemns what she calls "ludic" postmodernism for "trivializ[ing] the situation of women" (x), as "bracketing" the "reality" of material exploitation (5), and as "defer[ing] . . . the encounter with the social contradictions produced in the social relations of production" (273–74). I would argue that Bizzell's argument is a *non sequitur;* that is, it does not necessarily follow that a subject lacks agency because that subject is constituted by and through the symbolic. Foucault, for one, has argued that agency as a site of enunciation is, on the contrary, made possible through discursive means. Regarding Ebert's argument, I would argue that it begs the question of what it means to be "real"; Ebert's strong criticism of postmodernism for failing to address the "real" relies on circular reasoning regarding what the "real" of "material reality" is, precisely. Although it is not my intention to logically refute these arguments, I would like to respond to them in the course of this section.

To begin again, I am suggesting that it would behoove us, ethically, to allow ourselves to be seduced by postmodernism, understood as the (non)framework that (1) acknowledges the complicity of reason and the metaphysics of presence with systems of oppression, (2) demonstrates the phallogocentric construction of truth and subjectivity, and (3) attempts to move beyond, or at least to resist, the Hegelian dialectic and the conventional dualisms of Western thought. Throughout the course of this book, I will demonstrate that this phallogocentric thought has required a particular representation of woman: as the dialectical other to sustain the self-identity of the same (Man). Baudrillard has argued that it is necessary that any truly radical enterprise offer a challenge according to an economy other than the dialectic—because, as he has written, any system can "accommodate itself to its negative form, but understands the challenge of the *reversible* form as mortal" (*Seduction* 21). Therefore, the Woman offered here, by postmodernism, is no Iphigenia to be sacrificed for the purposes of sustaining the dialectical war that continues to battle in order to sustain Man. This Woman is no other. This Woman, according to the order of the challenge, is reversible, indeterminate, and unrepresentable, and remains more Woman than Woman—more than that which is the binary placeholder for Man.

Yet to take the name of Woman as the figuration of the instability of the sign and of being is heartily criticized by many, including Ebert;

Meaghan Morris, *The Pirate's Fiancée;* Rosi Braidotti, *Patterns of Dissonance;* and most prominently Gayatri Spivak. Spivak (who is otherwise an advocate of deconstruction) writes, "[W]omen can no longer be names for 'writing,' or the non-truth of *différance*. We cannot claim both the desire to identify with the oppression of woman in terms of an ontological deception, and the desire for the right to an impasse, to a deconstructive feminism which would take woman as a name for the graphematic structure and the non-truth of truth" ("Feminism and Deconstruction, Again" 217). Spivak's criticism has its justification in that the taking of the name of Woman to represent that which is not a specifically gendered or biological woman, runs the risk of slipping back into the very discourse that presupposes Woman's biology and sexuality. I acknowledge, with Spivak, the problem of calling upon Woman to, once again, represent what is "other"—here what is "other than the Other." This is, however, a calculated risk. Spivak herself has argued the necessity for assuming "strategic" essentialism and for negotiating "unacknowledged" masculinity. The strategic or tactical purpose for using the name Woman is to foreground the relationship that women, historically, have had with rhetoric or sophistry. "Rhetoric," defined by Spivak (echoing Paul de Man's description) as "the name for the residue of indeterminacy which escapes the system" (Sipiora and Atwill 293) is Woman, stereotypically defined as the name for indeterminable appearance. Thus taking the name of Woman is an act of negotiation with our "unacknowledged" masculinity, with the structures of violence that have constituted Woman as such. This act in no way, as Spivak suggests, excuses these theorists' nor our own masculinism (211).

But Braidotti refuses this act of negotiation, claiming that it is merely a "pretext for a new oppression" of women whereby men "divert and colonize women's speech and women's representations. Perhaps in order to preserve some vestiges of their former privileges and gains . . . [Woman] is a force which appropriates women's bodies, an exchange among the master thinkers of the feminine body. . . . It is still a misogynist mode of thought" (*Patterns of Dissonance* 123). Likewise, Naomi Schor asks: "What is it to say that the discourse of sexual indifference/pure difference is not the last or, (less triumphantly) the latest *ruse* of phallocentrism?" ("Dreaming Dissymmetry" 109; emphasis mine). These feminists are arguing that the act of taking the name of Woman as a deconstructive gesture is symptomatic of a legitimation crisis for patriarchy, instigated by the feminist movement and the gains made by women. Thus male theorists have attempted to thwart and to appropriate this new power through the patriarchal habit of representing women for their own purposes, specifically to ensure their power and subjectivity. Braidotti contends that only men can afford this privilege of indeterminacy because women "are still at the stage of trying to assert themselves as subjects of enunciation, sexed bodies" (121). Furthermore, it is Spivak's condemnation that "taking woman as a name" takes woman as an object being named, not as a subject capable of naming. It is my argument that Woman—by virtue of the logic of interpellation—has already been named. This fact of being named, however, as Judith Butler repeatedly asserts, in no way renders the possibilities of naming and assuming subject positions impossible but, rather, is the very condition for their possibility.

Critics of postmodernism and postfeminism argue that if subjects are constructed through the ideological processes of interpellation, cultural norms, power/knowledge matrices, and discourse, then subjects are merely the dupes of discourse, the victims of power, the will-less objects of culture. That is, if subjects are constructed, are constituted by forces other than their own will, then subjects lack will (as the unmoved mover), agency, and self-determining power. This power, this agency, this volition belongs to the constituting forces (that is, culture, power, and discourse). This argument presupposes the active/passive, will/will-less, subject/object dichotomies—the very set of binaries that sustain the humanist subject. The syntactical logic of subject/predicate remains intact. The deconstruction of subjectivity is, as Nietzsche has argued, the deconstruction of grammar's cause/effect foundation. Therefore, to claim that a subject's agency is necessarily and essentially denied due to the constitutive forces of culture and ideology is to claim that these forces occupy the grammatical position of subject (the agent), while the constituted human occupies the semantic equivalent of object (the one acted upon). This criticism further sanctifies the notion of humanist subjectivity, of pure will, of self-determining agency. Butler states that such a claim personifies discourse or the social, and "in the personification the metaphysics of the subject is reconsolidated" (*Bodies That Matter* 9). This reconsolidation of subjectivity as a unilateral force, therefore, misunderstands the postmodernist move which (whatever else it may be) is precisely the questioning of such a self-directed and insular notion of agency. Thus, the claim made by anti-postmodernists that postmodernism denies agency comes as misdirected criticism because postmodernists, with Foucault, acknowledge that language is simultaneously both disempowering and enabling (just as power is both prohibitive and generative). Indeed, as Butler argues, agency and subjectivity are made possible by and through the practices of signification:

> My position is mine to the extent that "I"—and I do not
> shirk from the pronoun—replay and resignify the theoreti-
> cal positions that have constituted me. . . . [T]he "I," this
> "I," is *constituted* by these positions, and these 'positions'
> are not merely theoretical products, but fully embedded or-
> ganizing principles of material practices and institutional
> arrangements, those matrices of power and discourse that
> produce me as a viable "subject." ("Contingent Founda-
> tions" 9)

Spivak further contends, "The name of woman cannot be the 'reality' of writing or of the necessary graphematic structure unless you
turn the theory into nonsense" ("Feminism and Deconstruction" 218).
It is my contention that when Gorgias, Nietzsche, and Baudrillard take
the name of Woman, they do so in vain—that is, they do so as a rhetorical gesture, which, unlike philosophy, has no desire to establish the
reality, identity, or subjectivity (or lack thereof) of Woman. Spivak
sounds strangely Parmenidean as she invokes the reality/nonsense binary. Of course, this is symptomatic of her Marxist predispositions,
which posit a fundamental materiality and which, therefore, of necessity must abhor that one should "turn . . . theory into nonsense." For
according to Karl Marx, Mas'ud Zavarzadeh and Donald Morton remind us, theory must operate as a "material force" ("Theory as Resistance" 54).

Yet we might ask, what would or could be taken as a specifically
"material" force, or as "material" per se? Again, critics of postmodernism argue that if "all is discourse/representation," how, then, does
one account for "material" sexuality or "material" bodies? Braidotti,
who is certainly not alone in her insistence, argues that "the valorization of woman as textual body, rather than female-sexed body, hides . . .
one of the most formidable types of discrimination exercised against
women in recent years. What is missing in these 'becomings' are women,
not only as a revolutionary political movement, but also as flesh-and-
blood human beings" (*Patterns of Dissonance* 134). This "flesh-and-
blood" representation of women is precisely the issue addressed by Butler in *Bodies That Matter*. It is Butler's argument that, like subjectivity
and sexuality, materiality is not a "site or [a] surface, but . . . *a process
of materialization that stabilizes over time to produce the effect of boundary, fixity, and surface we call matter*" (9). Thus, the "matter" of a
woman's body/sexuality has been historically/culturally delimited and,
thereby, made to materialize. This claim acknowledges that Woman and
Woman's "sexuality" has been signified (commonly as a lack). That is,
her sexuality has materialized through processes of representation and

signification. This claim is not to deny whatever "sex" would or could be extradiscursively or outside of representation and signifying practices, but rather to acknowledge that we could not (as constructs of our representations) refer to a "pure body" or "base sexuality" without simultaneously participating in, Butler argues, the "further formation of that body" (*Bodies That Matter* 10). Our act of reference, of signification, materializes our bodies, our sexualities, and, further, articulates what bodies will ultimately matter. Any effort to argue, Butler contends, that some aspects of "sex" are not constructed would necessitate a demarcation of "what is and is not constructed" and, by this very act of demarcation, would "once again through a signifying practice" construct the supposed materiality (11).

Furthermore, the act of signification via various forms of inscription produces or materializes "sexual difference," which is generally taken as ontologically prior to signification. As our discussion of Lacanian models of subjectivity has demonstrated, the symbolic inscription of sexual difference is the process by which subjects are materialized, by which they come into being. And this process is based on the logic of castration and negation, the very logic that sustains phallocentrism, the very logic Woman seeks to disrupt.

The demand that theory (as well as subjectivity and sexuality) be materially defined comes as a strange critique to theorists such as Gorgias, Nietzsche, and Baudrillard, who understand materiality (and subjectivity and sexuality) as a metaphor (as a moving army of such), and therefore as a fantasy, as a deception, as a construct. Woman is the name of such a fantasy. Within this fantasy, there exists the possibility for difference—again, not the difference which sustains the selfsame, but the *différance* which erupts at a kairotic moment. Simone de Beauvoir argued that "[o]ne is not born, but becomes a woman" (249). Although, admittedly, de Beauvoir intended another reading, I offer it as a pre/script to the subject of Woman. Our philosophic tradition has proffered a particular fantasy of Woman, thereby prescribing and circumscribing her being. Gorgias, Nietzsche, and Baudrillard are suggesting another fantasy of Woman, a fantasy that offers the condition of possibility for her (that is, our) becoming.

Situating Our Reading

The attention Gorgias's "Encomium of Helen" has received has, as John Poulakos argues in "Gorgias' *Encomium to Helen* and the Defense of Rhetoric," been too narrowly focused on "the historical dimension or the formalistic aspects of the preserved texts" (that is, the interpretations of Charles Segal, Laszlo Versényi, W. K. C. Guthrie, George A.

Kennedy, among others) (2). It is Poulakos's argument that an analogical reading of Gorgias's "Encomium" may prove to be a more insightful approach. Poulakos suggests that Gorgias chose Helen as a "personification of rhetoric" due to their marked similarities: "[B]oth are attractive, both are unfaithful, and both have a bad reputation" (4, 5). Poulakos examines Gorgias as he reads and represents Woman in an effort to defend rhetoric's disruptive power of "cultural iconoclasm" (6). That is, Gorgias uses Woman to disrupt the cultural hegemony in a subversive way. According to Susan Jarratt, in *Rereading the Sophists,* Gorgias accomplishes this by "reinterpreting elements of mythic history" (22). That is, by speculating about the possible causes of Helen's fate—without ever reaching a conclusion as to the one cause—Gorgias demonstrates the rhetoricity of history and "disrupts the continuity of the given historical narrative which uses Helen to take the blame for what could be re-seen as a disastrous adventure driven by the violent logic and *ethos* of a phallocentric culture" (17).

My reading differs from Jarratt's, however (in many ways, but specifically here), in that Jarratt further argues that rhetoric (Gorgias's or others') "must be able to move from critique to reconstruction" (27). That is, Jarratt insists that a distinction be made between Gorgias's vindication of a mythical Helen and his efforts to substantially emancipate "real" women (69). Jarratt's position, then, differs from mine in that her purposes are to establish a political agenda, a program of change— a move that, within the terms of this text, reinvokes notions of modernity. Likewise, my reading differs from Poulakos's in that Poulakos values and promotes the communicative function of language, the consensus—and political community—building purposes of public discourse. I, in contradistinction, will read Gorgias's use of Helen as a commentary on the irrationality of *logos,* which encourages dissensus not consensus. Thus my reading will more closely echo Victor Vitanza's reading of Gorgias ("A Feminist Sophistic?" and *Negation*) and Mihoko Suzuki's examination of Helen, in *Metamorphoses of Helen,* as a liminal entity who crosses borders and serves as an ambiguous sign. It is here, positing Helen as a chiasmic and disruptive—and thus ethical— figure, that my argument begins.

My argument will continue with a reading of Nietzsche, inquiring into the ethical subject and/as Woman. Derrida, in his reading of Nietzsche, argues that Woman figures as a chiasmic variable who displaces the rigid dualisms of Western metaphysics: "The question of the woman suspends the decidable opposition of true and non-true and inaugurates the epochal regime of quotation marks which is to be enforced for every concept belonging to the system of philosophical de-cidability" (*Spurs* 107). This suspension is accomplished through the distance, as Jean Graybeal's *Language and "The Feminine" in Nietzsche and Heidegger* suggests, "between one's language and one's discourse, between the sign and its meaning, between the subject's self-projection as transcendental ego and the disruptive disturbing effects of the unconscious" (38). This distance, she continues, is metaphorized by Nietzsche as Woman, "the image both of what the subject flees and of what it desires, both movements in distance, into distance, distance which is necessary, 'first of all and above all,' for the subject in process to take shape" (38). Although there are many similarities between Graybeal's reading and my own, our positions differ substantially in that Graybeal begins from a point which presupposes the existence of an unconscious. This psychoanalytic presupposition is at fundamental odds with the postmodern move, exemplified by Baudrillard, that regards all theories of depth as propelled by a search for the truth that only needs to be unveiled in order to be known.

David Farrell Krell's *Postponements: Woman, Sensuality, and Death in Nietzsche* also—as his title indicates—deals with Nietzsche's relationships with Woman. Krell specifically looks at Nietzsche's notebooks and the women he writes of therein, but of whom he postpones writing about in his published and public works. Krell argues, after a close analysis of Nietzsche's Ariadne, Corinna, Pana, and Calina, that these postponements were indicative of Nietzsche's relationship to death and sensuality. Although his argument is convincing and draws many of the same conclusions as my reading does, my argument differs in that its purpose is to examine how Woman functions rhetorically as the excesses and instabilities of language.

This examination is also undertaken by Kelly Oliver's *Womanizing Nietzsche: Philosophy's Relation to the "Feminine."* Although her text traverses some of the same terrain as mine, she begins with the claim that "even while opening philosophy onto other voices, [Nietzsche and Derrida] prevent the possibility of a feminine voice. Moreover, I argue that their strategies for opening philosophy onto its other(s) are often dependent on the preclusion of a feminine other . . . , especially the feminine mother" (x–xi). Therefore, Oliver's understanding of the "feminine" (what I am calling Woman) retains a relation to maternity and to the material, maternal body. (Oliver proffers the Mother as the ideal model for "an ontology of ethics" and for "an intersubjective theory of subjectivity" [xvii].) Although Nietzsche refers to the gestational philosopher, the figure of the Mother is not the Third Woman of whom I or Nietzsche speak (I will address the Mother in chapter 5).

The postmodernity of Baudrillard is generally read and regarded as a post-Marxist-inspired critique of capital and the American culture of simulated images and the "hyper-real" (e.g., Gary Genosko's *Baudrillard and Signs: Signification Ablaze,* Mike Gane's *Baudrillard's Bestiary: Baudrillard and Culture,* Doug Kellner's *Jean Baudrillard: From Marxism to Postmodernism and Beyond,* and André Frankovits's edited *Seduced and Abandoned: The Baudrillard Scene*). Of course, his work is primarily concerned with the fate of the "object" in a postproduction world. But what he has to say of women and of Woman is generally avoided or readily dismissed as blatant misogyny. Jane Gallop's "French Theory and the Seduction of Feminism," for example, critiques Baudrillard on the grounds of his "rabid attack" on feminism (113) and accuses Baudrillard of just feeding women "a line" (114). Suzanne Moore refers to Baudrillard as just one of the many "Pimps of Postmodernism" who are trying to get a piece of the other. Gane's *Baudrillard: Critical and Fatal Theory* offers a more positive reading of Baudrillard's views on femininity, women, and feminism. According to Gane's reading, it is Baudrillard's argument that the feminist movement—heretofore as it has been constructed and practiced—will not liberate women, but will further trap them "into a sexual order dominated by phallic values" (57). Gane further explains that since the 1960s, woman's body has become a phallic object "in which commercialism exploited and generalised the newly available resource," resulting in a "generalised pornographic culture" (58). Against this scenario, Baudrillard has sought to offer an alternative to feminism which shifts from an epistemology of the subject to an epistemology of the object within the realm of seduction. Although Gane stops short of espousing seduction, it is my argument that Baudrillard's alternative—although understandably subject to criticism—does indeed have something to offer "real" women—even feminists (and I consider myself one).

Becoming Woman: An Ethical *Différance*

"Man is only a recent invention, a *figure* not yet two centuries old, a new wrinkle in our knowledge, and . . . he will disappear again as soon as that knowledge has discovered a new form" (*Order of Things* xxiii; emphasis mine). So argues Foucault on return from an archaeological excavation of the sands of time. Foucault's dig, as we know, was prompted by the "exotic charm" of a Chinese encyclopedia's strange taxonomy of animals. Recognizing that he had encountered a foreign system of thought, Foucault asked the question, what makes it possible to think—not only this system—but anything at anytime? His proposed "answer" is that thinking, saying, or knowing occur only insofar as there already exist "certain codes[s] of knowledge" (ix), certain sets of conditions, certain epistemological fields, certain *epistemes* (xxii) that make thinking, saying, and knowing possible. These *epistemes* are the grammar of our being—the paradigms, the schemata of perception, the grids through which knowledge is acquired, created, and justified.

What *episteme*, then, allows for the conditions of possibility for the existence of Woman? That is, for the existence of Woman as other than Other. For characterized as she is in the epistemological grid of modernity via a lack, via negation, she is the other that is not truly other, but merely the underside of the one sex, of the one desire, of the one subjectivity. Woman is identified by the identical figures of mistress, wife, and mother. Such roles are defined by, according to Deleuze and Guattari,

> The law of the great Phallus that no one possesses, the despotic signifier prompting the most miserable struggle, a common absence for all the reciprocal exclusions where the flows dry up, drained by bad conscience and *ressentiment*, [quoting D. H. Lawrence] sticking a woman on a pedestal, or the reverse, sticking her beneath notice; or making a "model" housewife of her, or a "model" mother, or a "model" help-meet. All mere devices for avoiding any contact with her. (*Anti-Oedipus* 351)

These devices are means for avoiding any contact with what is truly other by constructing "model" representations and ideal forms.

Foucault prophesies the advent of a new *episteme* as he sees the "ground . . . once more stirring under our feet" (xxiv) as a new epistemological space, a rough beast, its hour come round at last, slouches towards Bethlehem to be born. Perhaps this rough beast to be born is none other than the other Other—the Other not of difference via the same, but the Other of difference via difference: the Other which is not one, which resists representation, which is—to borrow a phrase—*The Newly Born Woman* (Cixous and Clément). As Man is in the process of disappearing, perhaps Woman is in the process of becoming—of becoming Woman (Deleuze and Guattari), of becoming Helen (Gorgias), of becoming "Overwoman" (Nietzsche), of becoming feminine (Baudrillard). For this newly born Woman is only insofar as she is in process of becoming. She does not exist, as such (for example, Lacan). According to D. H. Lawrence, "A woman is not a 'model' anything. She is not even a distinct and definite personality. . . . A woman is a strange soft vibration on the air, going forth unknown and unconscious, and seeking a vibration of response" (quoted in Deleuze and Guattari, *Anti-Oedipus* 351). Perhaps this vibration (underfoot) will instigate the rupture that will signal the advent of the new *episteme* which is not one, announced by the "explosion of man's face in laughter" (385), an explosion that will accomplish the dispersion of Man's selfsame identity into so many molecular agglomerates (Deleuze and Guattari).

This text will thus "disperse" subjectivity and identity as follows: Chapter 1, "The Business of 'Isness': Philosophy Contra Sophistry, Woman, and Other Faithless Phenomena," offers a background of the metaphysical tradition, beginning with Parmenides' insistence on the existence of being as being whole, unchanging, and rational. Plato modifies but otherwise further articulates and extends the ideal of Parmenidean oneness and then posits philosophy as its handmaiden, a true and noble lover. In stark contrast, Plato presents sophistry as a wanton harlot with vulgar purposes (the creation of *doxa*) and deceitful ways. This distinction, this binary construction (along with its other attendant binaries: truth/falsehood, *technē/tuchē, physis/nomos*) serves as the foundation for Western subjectivity. This chapter serves to establish the relation that this dichotomy has to the constitution and representation of Woman.

Chapter 2, "Seduction and Sacrificial Gestures: Gorgias, Helen, and Nothing," begins with a discussion of Gorgias's "On Nature" as a sophistic response to Parmenidean and Platonic notions of existence and being in order to demonstrate how sophistry (as Woman) transgresses the metaphysical binary of being/not being. After an examination of the impossibility of positively establishing truth and being, pure epistemology and pure discourse, this chapter then addresses pure will, fidelity, and human agency by rereading Gorgias's "Encomium of Helen." This reading demonstrates agency's complicity with victimization; that is, this chapter posits that the logic of the polis demands a scapegoat, demands a sacrifice.

Chapter 3, "Nietzsche and the Other Woman: On Forgetting in an Extra-Moral Sense," begins with a discussion of Nietzsche's conception of subjectivity (as bad conscience) and its relationship to paranoia and nostalgia. Nietzsche's desire to transvalue Western subjectivity calls for the act of forgetting, a process personified by Woman, specifically the "Third Woman." This chapter will address three figurations of Woman that relate to his "Three Metamorphoses" of being, with the purpose of proposing that the Third Woman offers us the possibility of overcoming our metaphysical tradition, our traditional history of rhetoric, and our traditional politics.

Chapter 4, "*Après l'orgie:* Baudrillard and the Seduction of Truth," proceeds with three discussions on the tyranny of truth, the knowing subject, and communication. After demonstrating how each of these lieutenants serves a rapacious epistemology based on a logic of production and a particular stage of simulation, I explicate Baudrillard's alternative vision of seduction which, unlike production (which appeals to a referent, a principle of the real) challenges production through a strategy of appearance, a strategy which claims no referent. This chapter suggests the ways in which this tactic, the "feminine," can seduce truth, subjectivity, and discourse.

Chapter 5, "Seduction and the 'Third Sophistic': (Femme) Fatale Tactics Contra Fetal Pedagogies, Critical Practices, and Neopragmatic Politics" addresses various recent attempts within rhetoric and composition studies to come to terms with the postmodern condition, specifically those attempts that have been offered in the name of Woman and in the name of a Third Sophistic. It is this chapter's argument that none of these pedagogies can answer to the postmodern condition: that is, they are not Woman enough, not (Third) Sophistic enough to do so. The Woman offered by a school of feminist pedagogical theory is the figure of the Mother. I suggest that this is not the figure of the Third Woman, the affirming Woman, but rather is a figure complicit with the construction of patriarchy. The Third Sophistic praxis offered as neopragmatism, I further argue, is perhaps a sophistic praxis, but not a Third Sophistic praxis. After demonstrating how these rhetorical and political strategies have more in common with philosophic rhetoric than sophistic rhetoric, I counter with an alternate tactic, one evoked by sophistry itself: infidelity.

This infidelity may become the liberation of the mad woman from the attic, from her prison house of lack. With language's many-colored coats, Woman thus becomes beyond representation, beyond consciousness, beyond bad conscience. Woman, in Cixous's words, so "unthinks" the modern episteme of the selfsame through the laughter, the affirming "yes, I will, yes" laughter, the anticipatory resolute laughter of the Medusa, of Gorgias's Helen, Nietzsche's Affirming Woman, and Baudrillard's Femininity.[11]

1

The Business of "Isness": Philosophy Contra Sophistry, Woman, and Other Faithless Phenomena

> Philosophy is a battle against the bewitchment of our intelligence by means of language.
> —Wittgenstein, *Philosophical Investigations*

The centuries-old case against sophistry is a well-known one. Plato's infamous condemnation of the sophists in the dialogues *Phaedrus* and *Gorgias* articulates reservations about a group of traveling pedagogues, of teachers who are attacked as being merely, in the words of Theodor Gomperz, "intellectual acrobats, unscrupulous tormentors of language, or the authors of pernicious teachings" (422). Who were these sophists, and why were they burdened with the reputation for undermining Greek culture? It is not my intention to detail here the historical context or the biographical particulars of the sophists. There are many writers who have already effectively done this, including Werner Jaeger *(Paideia)*, George A. Kennedy *(Classical Rhetoric)*, Jean-Pierre Vernant *(Origins)*, and Mario Untersteiner *(Sophists)*, to name a few. My purpose here is not to deliver the definitive historical or philological text on the sophists, but rather to examine the suit against sophistry in order to suggest the ways in which this case has served as the primary precedent that has influenced subsequent judgments about thought, being, language, and subjectivity. I will investigate who the sophists were, why they were condemned so easily and so vociferously for so many years, and why they were universally despised for thousands of years and only recently "rehabilitated," beginning in the nineteenth century with E. M. Cope ("On the Sophistical Rhetoric"), G. W. F. Hegel *(History of*

Philosophy), and George Grote *(History of Greece)* and more recently by G. B. Kerferd *(Sophistic Movement)*, W. K. C. Guthrie *(Sophists)*, Susan Jarratt *(Rereading the Sophists)*, Jasper Neel *(Plato)*, John Poulakos *(Sophistical Rhetoric)*, and Victor J. Vitanza *(Negation)*.[1]

I will begin my analysis of the sophists with an acknowledgment of the inevitability of my anachronistic readings and interpretations. Perhaps this acknowledgment could serve as one of the most significant differences between my work and the work of others. Again, I am not trying to uncover any historical or philological truth about the sophists of yesteryear. Rather, it is my purpose to question the sophists and Plato's reading of them through the lens of today—of today's argument about subjectivity, agency, and voice in critical pedagogies and composition studies. Indeed, I do not think it is even possible to look to the past outside of the lens of today; hence, I do not think that nonanachronistic histories are possible (nor even desirable). But, more pointedly, I am reading the sophists in regards not to the past, but to the *future anterior—of what will have been* the relationships between thought, being, and language (Lyotard, *Postmodern Condition* 81). Thus, again, my reading of the sophists is not intended to reveal a historically grounded truth regarding sophistry nor a proper and legitimate representation of the sophists. This sub/versive historiography, to use a term coined by Vitanza, is contra traditional historiographical methods such as those advocated by Edward Schiappa, for example, which are characterized by an insistence on framing current interpretations of the sophists within strict philological and historical boundaries. Schiappa's methodology leads him to argue that what I and others call sophistic rhetoric is a "mirage," a useless fiction for contemporary rhetorical studies. Contra Schiappa, I take this "fiction" as an interesting point of departure, as a symptom of continuing prejudices and values insofar as the figure of the sophist has been consistently represented, not only in Plato's dialogues (as Poulakos points out [*Sophistical Rhetoric* 77]), but also in contemporary parlance. Thus my anachronistic (mis)readings are intended to reveal the fiction of the fiction and, in Nietzschean terms, to examine the marching army of metaphors that keep sophistry (and Woman) in check.

This examination attempts thus to rethink sophistry and Woman in terms, again, of the *future anterior,* or *what will have been,* the un/ presentation of these excessive figures. In this respect (but certainly not in all respects), my methodology resembles that of Poulakos. He writes:

> I treat past texts not as fixed monuments to be consumed cognitively but as elusive documents that can stimulate readers to rethink the constitution of their own lives and to

entertain possibilities for their reconstitution. . . . As I do so,
I assume that one studies the past . . . in order to make sense
out of and come to terms with some of the irresolutions of
the present. At the same time, I assume that one looks at the
past futuristically, so as to go beyond it, to forget it even
temporarily, to work against its burdens, and thus to become
able to express the hitherto unexpressed. (*Sophistical Rhetoric* 3)

In future chapters I will explore further the *future anterior* and "forgetting" (but without repression) as an ethical posture vis-à-vis the past and, in so doing, will align myself with Poulakos's methodology. But again, whereas Poulakos seeks to "express the hitherto unexpressed," I have no productive aims but only seductive ones: to lead us astray from the imperative to express (that is, communicate and/or represent) anything at all. In this way, my reading of the sophists more closely resembles/dissembles Vitanza's. He writes: "But to address them (How does one speak of, or even to, the Sophists?), to readdress them, we, or I, must re/address them not directly or in any referential-representational . . . [or] definitional mode" (*Negation* 27). Therefore, I readdress the sophists not to repress them, but also not to re-member nor to re-present them.

Whereas Schiappa, in Vitanza's estimation, attempts to "exTerminate" the sophists (and their current appropriation) (27), others have attempted to rehabilitate the sophists to serve current struggles. Jasper Neel, for example, has sought to "silence" Plato's condemnation of the sophists in order to "save" writing (*Plato* xi). Similarly, Susan Jarratt has found the sophists useful in her project to "save" feminism. Contrariwise, I have no interest in "rescuing" sophistry, of saving it from history or from Plato. My goals are not redemptive in nature. Rather, I am concerned with focusing on the relationships—conscious and/or unconscious (although we will later deal with the problematics of this distinction)—between sophistry and Woman (building on John Poulakos's insight) and on the relationship between how Woman has been figured heretofore and how Male desire or volition is constituted. It is my beginning assumption, informed by French theorists such as Jacques Lacan, Luce Irigaray, and Hélène Cixous, that philosophy or philosophical rhetoric (that is, Platonic, Aristotelian) can exist only if Woman exists. The questions I will address are why and how is it necessary for her to be represented in order to guarantee the being of philosophy or the being of philosophical rhetoric?

For centuries the names "sophist" and "woman" have provoked

the strongest of reactions; the sophist and Woman have shared the responsibility for representing that which is other—other than the good, the true, and the truly beautiful. This logic of polarity, of essential and determining otherness, is explained by Page duBois in *Centaurs and Amazons: Women and the Pre-History of the Great Chain of Being* as characteristic of early Greek thought. She writes, "In the fifth century, the earliest formulations about difference establish a series of polarities. . . . [T]he definition of the norm, the human subject, proceeds through a catalogue of difference. The human Greek male [and] . . . the culture of the polis, is defined in relation to a series of creatures defined as different. He is at first simply not-animal, not-barbarian, not-female" (4). Thus, Man is only insofar as he differs from what is represented as "other." Likewise, philosophy exists in opposition to sophistry as the "barbarian" (see also Jane Sutton's "The Taming of *Polos/Polis,*" which identifies the way Isocrates accomplishes this via the myth of the Amazon). This, then, is where we will begin: with Woman and sophistry as the scapegoats of metaphysics, with their condemnation as symptomatic of the perennial debate between being and becoming, philosophy and sophistry.

Although there was much pre-Socratic speculation concerning the nature of existence, Parmenides (writing approximately 475 BCE) was perhaps the first to offer a definitive, systematic articulation of "the way things are." It is his explanation and the sophist Gorgias's subsequent rebuttal that have generated and fueled a continuous debate between what George L. Kustas has called the "two psychic motors" of the Western world: rhetoric and philosophy (11).[2] I will begin here with Parmenides and Plato; in the next chapter, I will address the sophist Gorgias.

For the pre-Socratic philosophers speculating on the nature of being in fifth-century Greece, the oppositions between being and becoming, *technē* and *tuchē*, and between *physis* and *nomos*, nonsensible reality and appearance, were the crux of a very serious argument. What was at stake, and what continues to be at stake, is nothing less than the prescription of what exists, what has value, and what—by implication—has no value at all. We are the inheritors of this tradition, of this suspicion of changing phenomena, of this demand for stability, mastery, and fidelity that sustains notions of truth and subjectivity, but that has for centuries required that rhetoric (that is, the instability of language) and Woman (the instability of being) serve as negated other in order to sustain that tradition. Thus tracing the predisposition against sophistry exposes the roots of the metaphysical baggage that sustains us—you and me—as thinking, acting beings.

I am beginning from a position that argues that truth and subjectivity are never established positively but only negatively via the logic of the Hegelian master/slave dialectic. This dialectic constructs identity via the negation of the other. This is the phallocentric logic of being entrapped within a system of nonequal and nonopposing binaries. The subject/object, active/passive, Man/Woman dichotomies represent one as master, as possessor of control, and represent the other as—well, quite simply—as other (see the work of Cixous, Irigaray, and Wittig, for example). The other, as passive object, sustains relationships between subject and subject (that is, the community) and subject and his self. By positing an object (a barbarian, a monster, a freak, a Woman) as other than Man-as-knowing-subject, the binary opposition maintains, in the words of Teresa de Lauretis, the "politics of self-representation" (*Technologies of Gender* 7), which in turn maintains the hegemonic system. Thus the greater questions I will address are at what cost has establishing being, truth, and subjectivity been bought? And is there any way to rebate ourselves from this truth?

Introductory Contextualizations: Encomium to Man

Kerferd characterizes the time of the sophists as a period of "profound social and political changes, in which [b]eliefs and values of previous generations were under attack. The sophistic movement gave expression to all of this" (*Sophistic Movement* 1). Although his term "the sophistic movement" is unfortunate, since it implies a cohesive and shared sophistic program, Kerferd's characterization of the sophists points to Athens's shifting moral and epistemological ground. In addition to the great political changes of the time, fifth-century Greece found itself experiencing changes in discursive practices. Scholars such as Eric Havelock and Walter Ong have speculated that this period was a time submerged in the transition from oral discourse to literate discourse, or from, in Jacques Derrida's terms, mythomorphic discourse to phallogocentric discourse ("Structure, Sign, and Play").[3] This claim (or what has come to be called the "great leap" theory) is often challenged on the grounds that it denies agency to oral subjects (Jarratt, *Rereading the Sophists*, and Swearingen, "Literate Rhetors"). It is not my purpose to settle the orality/literacy debate but merely to acknowledge that what was at one point largely an oral society found itself in a time of transition to a literate culture, and I do so in order to foreground the instability of this particular cultural moment.

The demonization of sophistry (and Woman)—cast as unacceptable other—served to stabilize the ground in this intense moment of change. Of course, this demonization is most devastatingly articulated by Plato. His attack on the sophists hinged most successfully on controlling the use of the single word "sophist." As suggested, the sophists, although universally condemned as a group, shared very little in common save perhaps for the facts that they were foreigners, they accepted money for their services, and they shared the nomenclature "sophist" (although Gorgias refused this name [Cope, "II" 80]). Plato, nevertheless, succeeded in dismissing them in toto, and he did so by appropriating the name of "sophist" and by associating it with discreditable attributes—attributes which were not associated with its commonly recognized meaning (Versényi 6; Grote 156; Gomperz 416).

Plato's attack, fueled by personal and political interests, was symptomatic of a profound concern of fifth-century Athenians. Sophocles' tragically ironic "Ode to Man," beginning "Wonders are many on earth, and the greatest of these/Is Man" (*Antigone* 339–70), as a thematic presence in Greek drama, points to the concern of instability and shifting epistemological, ontological, and political foundations. Finding themselves in a rigorous time of war, social upheaval, and political change, the Greeks struggled with the issue of will, that is, the issue of what Man controls and what chance or ungovernable forces control (Nussbaum). *Tuchē* was the word that signified that element of human existence that humans do not control, that element of human existence which remained elusive and indifferent to human will and which was the realm of appearance and phenomena—of Nature. Nature in all its manifestations and the phenomenology of such was untrustworthy: always changing, always shifting, ungovernable by man. *Technē* (human art or science) was Man's best defense against contingency; in fact, *technē*, gift of the god Prometheus, was the guarantor of human progress and civilization. Thus *tuchē* and *technē* had a fundamental relationship with two other, opposing terms which served as the *topoi* for thought and debate in the second half of the fifth century BCE: *physis* (nature) and *nomos* (custom) (see Poulakos, *Sophistical Rhetoric* 111–30 and Guthrie 101–35). Bruce Thornton, in *Eros: The Myth of Ancient Greek Sexuality*, reminds us that "*Phusis* comes from the word *phuo*, 'grow,' 'spring up,' and refers to the organic world of material growth and decay, the givens of our bodies with their appetites and passions, and the earth and its forces, the ahistorical realm of necessity and chance, the raw material upon which custom and law [*nomos*] . . . act" (2). *Technē* in the service of *nomos* sought to control *tuchē* and *physis*; indeed, *technē* evidences the superiority of man's intelligence in the face of brute forces. The "mind and its projections—laws, customs, institutions—impose order on this welter of chaotic forces, carve out a niche for humans between the serene lives of the gods . . . and the brute necessity of the beasts" (Thornton 2). As evidenced by the fragments of

Protagoras, for example, discussions of *physis* and *nomos* generally centered on politics—that is, on the central issue of how to regulate or to control human nature—the desire of *physis*—in order to maintain the polis.

Interestingly, however, the characterizations of both *physis* (nature) and *nomos* (convention) all presuppose the existence of some ordered, accountable system of principles—whether it be the law of nature or the law of *nomos*. For example, Aristotle writes in the *Rhetoric*, "There are two kinds of law, one particular and one common. By particular laws I mean those determined by each people in relation to themselves . . . ; by laws that are common I mean those in accordance with nature" (1373b). Thus we see that these binaries *(technē/tuchē* and *physis/nomos)* are really false binaries, transgressive of their own logical principle of noncontradiction. My point, as I hope to demonstrate subsequently, is that the Western metaphysical tradition, which has constructed our truth and our subjectivity, is dependent on an imperative to master that which "is," to delimit its being, to demarcate within/by a set of prohibitive and illusory binaries used to prescribe, not describe, "reality" and to prescribe a certain set of social relations. As Kerferd argues, "The term nomos and the whole range of terms that are cognate with it in Greek are always prescriptive and normative and never merely descriptive" (111–12). And the prescription (and/as *pharmakon*) is specifically the exclusion of *erōs*, or desire. Yes, sexual desire, but not exclusively so; the term is used in reference to any excessive lust, whatever its object, which would seduce us and lead us astray. And hence my further point: the Western metaphysical tradition, which—again—has constructed our truth and our subjectivity, has required the mastery of desire, specifically female (that is, unrestrained) desire.

Not surprisingly, Kerferd's and Guthrie's discussions of *physis* delicately ignore a predominant and common usage of the term. John J. Winkler's study of sex and gender in ancient Greece, *The Constraints of Desire*, notes that in everyday, ordinary language, *physis* and *natura* meant genitals, most often female genitalia (217–20). Furthermore, female genitalia is a commonplace for her sexuality—and her sexuality is a commonplace for licentiousness, disorder, and bestiality. Thornton writes:

> Slang terms and imagery for female sexuality and genitalia . . .
> diminish women's humanity by presuming the animality of
> the indiscriminate sexual appetites. Pigs especially are extensively linked to women in Greek culture from comedy to
> ritual, partly because of their fecundity, but also because
> they are sexually wild—according to Aristotle, a sow in

heat will even attack humans. . . . "Sow" and "piggy" are comic favorites for denoting women's genitals, "piggy" usually denoting the hairless pudenda of younger girls, "sow" those of older women. (76–77)

With this understanding, we must reexamine the discussions regarding *physis* and *nomos*. Although admittedly, this common usage of *physis* cannot be conflated with philosophic usage, we can acknowledge that the philosophers were aware of its alternate levels of signification. We can, therefore, wonder to what degree these alternate connotations influenced philosophers' conceptions of *tuchē* and to what extent *tuchē*—the world of appearances, the world against which the world of being (of Man, of mind, of will) must be founded—was characterized by/as Woman, specifically female desire.

A note, lest I be misunderstood: This "female desire" is not to be taken as descriptive or representative of "real" female desire (if it could even be known or communicated). For barring the fragmented words of Sappho, what will we have known about female desire as such? Bruce Thornton argues that he knows female desire and that he can articulate it, which he does in *Eros: The Myth of Ancient Sexuality*. I must admit that I found a perverse pleasure in quoting from his text in previous paragraphs. He has made it clear that he thinks projects such as mine are "accompanied by the whine of ideological axes being ground" (xiii) and bury what the Greeks "actually" said with "polysyllabic sludge" (xiii). Although I would be curious how one could "know" what a Greek "actually" said thousands of years ago (and, furthermore, I would rather praise "polysyllabic sludge" than bury it), my ultimate disagreement with Thornton's argument is that he presents us with an essential and ahistorical female desire that has been articulated by men (is this what they "actually" said?).

Thornton argues that

> the modern reductive view of Greek woman as oppressed victim tells us very little about antiquity yet quite a lot about the late-twentieth-century politics of victimhood and . . . reflects as well the loss in our popular imaginations of the sexually powerful woman. . . . But the Greeks, and most humans before our smug twentieth century, knew that the power of woman was the power of eros, and the power of eros was the creative and destructive power of nature itself. (98)

Contra Thornton, I would argue that this fantasy of the "sexually powerful woman" has not diminished in force (nor in reductive power) for thousands of years. Indeed, it has been this fantasy that has constructed our very subjectivity—with its accompanying hermeneutic, interpretive grids and its epistemological hooks to hang the world on. It is a powerful fantasy: one that can characterize woman as a pig in order to pen her up as one, causing her to suffer all the violations wrought by a patriarchal order (for a catalogue of such violations, see Teresa Ebert, for example). That female desire is characterized as bestial is symptomatic of a fantasy—thousands of years old—that realizes itself in social and political constructs that empower men while simultaneously disempowering women. Thornton characterizes this reading as "reductive" (69). Perversely, I agree; although to agree is not to deny that Athens was a phallocracy (nor to deny that twentieth-century America is also), nor is it to deny that women were barred from the classical polis. And yet, lest we make the same mistake as Thornton, although the fantasy makes it so, it doesn't make it anything more (or less) than a fantasy. As Foucault has reminded us, power is simultaneously oppressive and generative. Hence, here I am interested in what ways this fantasy of Woman as *erōs* has produced our subjectivity and in what ways this fantasy can seduce that subjectivity. But we're getting ahead of ourselves.

A Fantasy of the Whole: Parmenides in Denial

Although Parmenides is certainly not the original author of the fantasy of untempered female desire (Hesiod, for one, prefigures him), he did pen a corollary fantasy: a fantasy of the whole. Parmenides takes his goddess in hand and runs from the world of *erōs,* of Woman—of deceitful appearances and uncontrollable, unlawful *physis*—to the realm of being. Parmenides, one of the three major Eleatics (Parmenides, Zeno, and Melissus), argued that only reason, not sense impressions, could lead to truth, and this is precisely what his poem attempts to articulate: how sense impressions lead to not isness or not truth, whereas, reason—*logos*—will lead to well-rounded being. Although the guide in Parmenides' poem is a goddess—a female—Andrea Nye writes, "it is not she whom Parmenides seeks; her role is only to instruct and aid him in a quest that she makes clear he is well on the way to finishing by himself" (19). That is, the presence of the goddess does not indicate an inclusion of Woman in the world of will and being, but rather demonstrates a highly successful appropriation of Woman in order to exclude Woman. Parmenides uses a goddess to help his project of establishing a realm of reality which refuses to acknowledge appearance—in fact, which annihilates the realm of appearances—by claiming that it simply is "not." Parmenides "quotes" his goddess beckoning, "Come, I will tell you—and you must accept my word when you have heard it—the ways of inquiry which alone are to be thought: the one that IT IS, and it is not possible for IT NOT TO BE, is the way of credibility, for it follows Truth; the other, that IT IS NOT, and that IT is bound NOT TO BE: this I tell you is a path that cannot be explored; for you could neither recognise that which IS NOT, nor express it" (Freeman 42; emphases in original). That is, according to Parmenides, that which merely appears has no being—thus it "is not."

Parmenides is not alone in his existential denial of appearances, of that which is apprehended by the senses. Other existing pre-Socratic fragments note a particular distrust of the senses. Anaxagoras, for example, informs us, "Through the weakness of the sense-perceptions, we cannot judge truth" (Freeman 86). And indeed, Plato tells us, the beautiful lies beyond the senses (*Republic* V.476b)—a destination that must be undertaken (as in *Phaedrus*). The good, the true, and the beautiful are objects of knowledge *(epistēmē)*, are objects which exist in themselves, objects which exist to be contemplated, recollected, observed, and above all, mastered. The truth, then, lies beyond the body, beyond the senses, beyond appearances as in Plato's *Republic,* which sets up the distinction between the lovers of beauty itself and the lovers of sights and sounds: "Those who love looking and listening are delighted by beautiful sounds and colours and shapes, and the works of art which make use of them, but their minds are incapable of seeing and delighting in the essential nature of beauty itself" (V.476b). In effect, Plato is positing that those who depend on a sensory epistemology, on sense perception, are chained to this illusory world of surfaces and are captives of the cave and *doxa* (opinion). They are deceived; they are seduced by the beguiling appearances of "beautiful sounds and colours and shapes"; and they are thus kept—indeed led astray—from the truth. For "real" essential truth does not reside in the world of "mere" appearances or sensual stimulus. And it is only ascertainable via the mind (via dialectic), the only sensible sense. Likewise, Parmenides offers the following imperative:

> For this *(view)* can never predominate, that That Which Is Not exists. You must debar your thought from this way of search, nor let ordinary experience in its variety force you along this way, *(namely, that of allowing)* the eye, sightless as it is, and the ear, full of sound, and the tongue, to rule; but *(you must)* judge by means of the Reason *(Logos)* the much-contested proof which is expounded by me. (Freeman 43)

According to the Eleatics, that which is real and true—That Which Is—is being. And being is characterized—as Parmenides' goddess points out—by the following: "Being has no coming-into-being and no destruction, for it is whole of limb, without motion, and without end. And it never Was, nor Will Be, because it Is now, a Whole all together, One, continuous" (Freeman 43).[4] In short, being is one. This fundamental Eleatic first principle influenced the majority of pre-Socratic and later philosophers in their formulations of cosmologies, geometries, and ontologies (Rankin 94). Of course, Plato takes Parmenides' logic to task in *The Sophist*. According to Andrea Nye, he argues that it provides sophists with a camouflage that "makes them difficult to track down in their hiding place, invulnerable to counterattack and to any charge of falsity or deception. If there is no nonbeing, there is no falsity and so no way to distinguish proper philosophical thought from improper, truthful statement from false, Sophist from true philosopher" (24). And, of course, Plato's desire to distinguish truth from deception, sophist from true philosopher is indicative of his "nostalgia for a divine order and a society that mirrors that order" (Nye 31). Plato's fantasy of the whole illuminated the uncompromising assumption that the universe was unified—ordered according to logical, rational principles, as Socrates so patronizingly reminds Callicles in *Gorgias*: "Wise men say, Callicles, that heaven and earth, gods and men, are held together by the principles of . . . order, by self-control and justice; that, my friend, is the reason they call the universe 'cosmos,' and not disorder or licentiousness" (507e–508a).

Disorder, licentiousness, and the deceitful veil of appearances (all appositives for sophistry and female desire) are *tuchē* embodied and must be resisted by the philosopher. For to live a life at the mercy of *tuchē* is to be at the mercy of sophistic deceit or womanly guile, of sophistic flattery or feminine desire. In *Gorgias,* for example, after identifying sophistry with the female artifices of make-up and fine garments, Socrates posits that sophistry is symptomatic of the desire for bodily gratification. The philosopher, in contrast, such as the Socrates depicted in the *Symposium,* has no erotic need because *technē* has "cured" him (Nussbaum 94). Rhetoric (sophistry) cannot provide this cure since, according to Plato, it is not a *technē* (art), but rather a *tribe* (knack), which scratches rather than soothes the erotic itch.[5]

Plato: (Philosophic) Rhetoric as *Technē*

In the *Phaedrus,* Socrates articulates the true "art" or *technē* of rhetoric as such:

> [A]nyone . . . who seriously offers a science of rhetoric must first with all possible accuracy describe the soul and make us perceive whether its nature is single and uniform, or like the

body, complex; for to do this, we declare, is to describe the nature of anything. . . . And in the second place he will state what object it is its nature to act upon, and what it does to this object; or what affect it is its nature to experience and under the influence of what agent. . . . And in the third place, when he has arranged in an ordered series the kinds of discourse and the types of soul together with their affections, he will proceed to give an account of causation that is complete for the entire series, linking each affection to its corresponding cause. That will show why, when a soul is of one sort and is acted upon by a certain sort of speech, it is necessarily moved to persuasion; and why, in another case, persuasion necessarily fails. (271a–271b)

Here, Plato has articulated rhetoric—his philosophic rhetoric (rhetoric with being, as being) as a *technē*: it is presented as being (1) universal: as applying to all men, (2) codifiable, and, therefore, teachable, (3) precise (match this soul type with this discourse), and (4) concerned with explanation (rhetoric is here described according to a cause/effect model) (Nussbaum 94–95). I use Martha Nussbaum's explication of *technē* because it most closely mirrors Plato's characterization of *technē*. Janet Atwill's *Rhetoric Reclaimed: Aristotle and the Liberal Arts Tradition* offers a more Aristotelian (and pre-Platonic) articulation of the term, which is more flexible and less *logos* (as reason) bound. Atwill's argument reminds us, once again, of Plato's power to reinscribe Greek terminology in order to serve his vision of what is. For Plato, philosophic rhetoric is, above all, logical and rational, like the mind. Conversely, sophistic rhetoric is presented as irrational, like the body.

Plato, grounded in this basic dichotomy of *tuchē* and *technē*, founded on the presupposition of the superiority of *technē*, attacks the sophists by claiming that what they teach is merely a *tribe* (knack) because it offers no rational account or *logos*, neither of the good, the true, and the beautiful, nor of its own machinations. Therefore, Plato's Socrates viewed sophistic rhetoric as misguided because it placed its attention on style, on matters of rhyme, meter, and presentation—all misplaced concerns, according to Socrates, because they were irrational and because their aim was to please the audience, an aim Socrates considered shameful because "it aims at the pleasant without the best" (Vickers, *In Defence* 112). In order to explicate and justify this criticism, Socrates, in the *Gorgias* (perhaps Plato's most pointed affront), offers the following analogy involving the significant dichotomy of mind and body. Socrates argues that sophists are "confused and do not know either what to make of themselves nor do others know what to make of them. In fact, if the soul were not in charge of the body . . . everything would be jumbled together" (465d). The mind, according to Nussbaum, has always been associated with *techne* and *logos*. She writes, "*Techne* is closely associated with practical judgment or wisdom (*sophia, gnome*) with forethought, planning, and prediction. To be at the mercy of *tuche* where *techne* is available is to be witless (e.g., Democritus B197)" (95). The body, alternately, has connoted *tuche* and the irrational. Similarly, to be witless is to be Woman, governed as she is by *eros*. Although Plato has Socrates claim in *Phaedrus* that *eros* is not a "bad" thing (as it originates from divinity), Socrates nevertheless argues that unmastered *eros* is. Again, to be governed by desire is to be a Woman or a sophist.

Plato, in his condemnation of sophistry, articulates his telling dichotomy, a "natural duality," as he calls it, between the mind/soul *(psuche)* and the body (*Gorgias* 464b). Regarding the mind and the body, there are four genuine arts *(technai)* and four spurious ones. The genuine arts regarding the body are gymnastics and medicine; regarding the mind are legislation and justice. The spurious arts regarding the body are cosmetics and cookery, regarding the mind are sophistry and rhetoric. The four spurious arts are spurious because, Socrates contends, they aim "at pleasure without consideration of what is best; and I say that it is not an art, but a knack, because it is unable to render any account of the nature of the methods it applies and so cannot tell the cause of each of them. I am unable to give the name of art to anything irrational" (465a). For Plato, sophistry, with its inexcusable irrationality, is further condemned because of its supposed aim of evoking pleasure, of merely flattering the crowd for vulgar and common Athenian political purposes. Plato condemns politics (whatever is not his conception of politics) and attacks rhetoric because it is politics' chief tool and medium. Again, rhetoric—equated here with sophistry and Diogenes-like practices—is seen as aiming merely at pleasure, at the satisfaction of bodily desires, among others, and therefore has no temperance *(sophrosyne)* and hence no virtue. Thus, notes Vickers, of "the three goals later given to rhetoric, to move, to instruct, and to please," Plato argues that sophistic rhetoric's goal is only and merely to please and to "gratify the baser appetites as he accuses Callicles of doing before the Assembly" (*In Defence* 107). This goal "to please," seen as a sophistic one, is historically—from Plato, Aristotle, Cicero, and Quintilian up through Locke and Kant—seen as a function of Woman, as well. Tzvetan Todorov in his *Theories of the Symbol* writes, "right up to Kant, pleasing, the rhetorical function par excellence . . . is women's business (the function of . . . moving, belongs to men . . .)" (74).

Thus, not only is sophistic rhetoric not even a true art or *technē*, she also prostitutes herself by servicing the populace, fueled by *doxa*, which according to Gronbeck, meant "generally received opinions" (29), rather than the truth. *Doxa* existed in that world of sensory experiences and shadowy perceptions. Those who allowed *doxa* to rule and to govern their lives were as those in Plato's allegory of the cave who mistook the appearance or belief of truth for the truth or for the real. In early Greek epistemology, as the etymology of the word *alētheia* (truth) suggests ("what is revealed," "what is brought out of concealment"), truth is what is behind our ordinary and human ways of thinking and believing, known as *doxa*. Nussbaum explains, "Revealing, uncovering, getting behind, getting beyond—these are some of early Greek philosophy's guiding images for the philosophical pursuit of truth" (241). This pursuit of the "motionless heart of well-rounded Truth," according to Parmenides, leads us far from the path trodden by Man, far from "the opinions of mortals, in which there is no true reliability" (Freeman 42). Therefore, Plato accuses Gorgias of being "unphilosophical"; that is, Richard Enos writes, for being a "pragmatically immoral opportunist who taught the appearance and not the reality of knowledge" (51).

In sum, under the guise of asking Gorgias what rhetoric is, Socrates usurps the occasion to answer, definitively, the question himself. According to Socrates, Dame Rhetoric is a "foul" and an "ugly thing" (*Gorgias* 463d)—not a virtuous woman. For Socrates, the infidel Rhetoric stands juxtaposed to the true love Philosophy (482a).[6] Rhetoric, like cookery, is capable of no more than of giving men pleasure, of producing gratification (462c). She is "shrewd" and "naturally clever at dealing with men" (463a). She is a flatterer and deceives men of the truth of her true appearance through the use of cosmetics (463b). She is "evil and deceitful" (465b), unlike Philosophy who is good and beautiful, and has a "natural loveliness" (465b). Philosophy's goodness and virtue, Socrates tells us, comes from her relationship to truth. She is faithful to men by leading them to truth, (echoes of Parmenides' goddess), to truth of justice and injustice, to truth of rightness and wrongness, never to mere appearances (That Which Is Not), nor to mere belief *(doxa)*, as Rhetoric does.

Herein lies Socrates' main contention with Rhetoric: that she is "merely a creator of beliefs" (*Gorgias* 455a), rather than a handmaiden of truth, that her persuasion produces "belief without certainty" and produces potentially false belief (454a). Reality or truth, then, is absolute certainty *(epistēmē)*; it is comprised of "facts" not "opinions"— of ideals not of experiences. Socrates underscores this conviction by repeatedly creating and emphasizing the distinction between what is "really" real and what is "merely" opinion. For Socrates, the search for knowledge is impeded by opinions, by beliefs—for knowledge is not comprised of opinion; rather, it is comprised of what is not opinion. This stance generates a desire for pure, unmediated, unadulterated truth. And Philosophy, not the harlot Rhetoric (flatterer that she is), fulfills that desire.

For Philosophy is the noble lover as characterized in the *Phaedrus* and as articulated in Diotima's speech in the *Symposium*. For philoso-phy, unlike sophistry, has as its purpose education not merely pleasure. Thus the relation between pedagogue and pupil is described as true love, the *tokos en kalo*, "the implanting of high thoughts and noble as-pirations in the mind," copulating in order to reproduce truth rather than pleasure. Cope writes, "[B]y the employment of dialectical art, a man plants and sows in a soul which he has formed fitted to receive them, words with knowledge, which are able to defend themselves and him who planted them; and are not fruitless, but have a seed, when propagated from one mind to another" ("I" 132).

But Who Is Adulterating Whom?

Of course the dark side of this supposedly noble and pure reproduction scenario is foreshadowed by the fact that the dialogue of the *Phaedrus* takes place near the spot where Boreas abducted Oreithyia (*Phaedrus* 229b). In the name of sowing seeds, Socrates wastes no time and soon violates Phaedrus. Seed by seed, step by step, question by question, Phaedrus is forced to submit to Socrates. For his questions have the answer as a foregone conclusion. This is not, contra Socrates, true love; but rather, it is discursive abduction. The way he conducts his "dialogues" makes it clear that he is leading—that it is he, not truth, not Parmenides' goddess, who grasps the interlocutee's hands. Socrates knows where he is going and where he wants everyone else to go, and that is to follow him. He assumes (at least in the later dialogues) that he has the truth, the true story, and that everyone else has mere belief or mere myth: "Then listen, as they say, to a very fine tale, which you may consider a myth [*muthos*], but I regard as a true story [*logos*]; for I want you to take everything I shall say as strict truth" (*Gorgias* 523a). Socrates leads, he is not led astray; incapable of being seduced himself *(Symposium)*, he abducts others. Yet wasn't Socrates being "ironic"? Perhaps, but he was not ironic enough to allow for seduction.

What Plato feared most was seduction—the power of *erōs* that is not mastered nor controlled, that knows no *technē*. This is suggested by his attack on writing. It is his argument in the *Phaedrus* that the written word is static, that it continues to say the same thing over and over again. Socrates argues:

> So it's not a recipe for memory, but for reminding, that you have discovered. And as for wisdom, you're equipping your pupils with only a semblance of it, not with truth. Thanks to you and your invention, your pupils will be widely read without benefit of a teacher's instruction; in consequence, they'll entertain the delusion that they have wide knowledge, while they are, in fact, for the most part incapable of real judgment. (275a)

Plato predictably accuses writing, like sophistry, of being a semblance, not a real truth. However, rather than addressing writing's static nature, Plato has revealed his fear that writing may perhaps not be so "static" after all. That is, writing (and, as Derrida has argued, all language is writing) has the capacity to seduce the reader, and the reader potentially can seduce the text, and most importantly, the text can "forget" Socrates' judgment, can resist his abduction.

The *Logos* of *Logos*

For the early Greek philosophers, because the "cosmos" was ordered and rational, the word was also, as it reflected the universe: "The statement *(logos)* like the system *(cosmos)* which it affirms," Havelock writes, is itself a "constant and a unitary construct, for it needs a 'comprehensive' intelligence . . . to understand it after coming into contact with it" ("The Linguistic Task of the Presocratics" 25). Therefore, the word was made rational, coherent, and noncontradictory. *Logos,* to Parmenides and subsequent philosophers, is as sound, valid, and true as the syllogism. And just as the syllogism's conclusion follows inevitably time after time, so should *logos* speak inevitably and inalterably time after time. Empedocles writes, "For what is right can well be uttered even twice" (Freeman 55). *Logos,* hereafter known as analytic and dialectic philosophy, is a faithful lover of the universe, of the truth: "It is she [philosophy] . . . who continues to say what you are hearing from me now; she is, in fact, far less capricious than any other love. For my Alcibiades says now one thing, now another; but Philosophy speaks always the same" (*Gorgias* 482a).

And philosophy—the king advocate of being—presupposes a corresponding relationship between *logos* and truth/reality. According to Kerferd, "Thought [at this time] was concerned . . . with the search for a one-one relationship between things and names, on the basis that the meaning of any name must always be the thing or things to which it refers" (*Sophistic Movement* 73). Hence, being/truth is speakable on the basis of the "correctness of names." Plato's Cratylus asserts, "Everything has a right name of its own which comes by nature, and a name is not whatever people call a thing by agreement, simply a piece of their own voice applied to the thing, but there is a kind of constituted correctness in names which is the same for all men, both Greeks and barbarians" (*Cratylus* 383).

Philosophers espousing this "correctness of names" dogma—this correspondence theory of *logos*—must have been distressed by the existence of verbs, words which "correspond" to movement, to change, to the past, and to the future. If being was unchanging, unmoving, and timelessly present, how was the philosopher to deal with conjugations of the verb—of the verb *einai* [to be], in particular? Havelock in "The Linguistic Task of the Presocratics" informs us that Parmenides resolves the problem by insisting on the use of the timeless present "is" *(esti)* to replace "the use of all other verbs and all other senses of the verb to be" (25). For being does not come into being or pass away; it always is: "The angles *are* equal to two right angles. They are not born that way or become or are made so" (Havelock 14).

Thus a name or a signifier is—it is "real" and "true"—and does not signify other than it is nor appear to be other than it is. It just simply is. That which merely appears, or merely signifies is not lacks being and therefore deceives. Parmenides writes:

> To think is the same as the thought It Is; for you will not find thinking without Being, in *(regard to)* which there is an expression. For nothing else either is or shall be except Being, since Fate has tied it down to be a whole and motionless; therefore all things that mortals have established, believing in their truth, are just a name: Becoming and Perishing, Being and Not-Being, and Change of position. (Freeman 44)

That is, there is no correspondent, no referent for what "is not"; therefore, not-being is impossible. Again, although Plato complicates Parmenides' dismissal of nonbeing, he does insist that language be "reflective of a higher reality" (Nye 31): "what we say can now be judged according to whether it mirrors the order of Forms, and whatever is not consistent with that mirroring can be condemned as false" (Nye 32).

Hence, because there existed some necessary, reflective relationship between being and *logos,* proponents of being also assumed that *logos* had a necessary, inherent responsibility and charge to speak truth, to uncover truth—"truth in its purity and clarity" (Untersteiner 138). Hence the good speaker speaks clearly, sincerely, plainly—as truth is clear, plain, and naked, as the etymology of truth *(alētheia)* suggests. Consequently, delivery, elocution, and style are sophistic tricks of deception, spurious uses of language. Philosophers, however, assume that *logos* speaks being, and that poets, playwrights, and sophists speak a false *logos*—a *logos* of imitation, of counterfeit, of falsity, of dressing up and covering. Heraclitus calls the bards "fabricators of lies," or artificers of falsehood, who speak a beguiling word (Freeman 26). In Plato's words, the mythmakers "proceed by approximating fiction to truth" *(Republic* 382D). Plato casts sophists, likewise, as poets, as falsifiers, for they spend "hours twisting phrases this way or that, pasting in this and pruning that," like a poet *(Phaedrus* 278e) concerned merely with appearances—with that which seems (mere probabilities) rather than with reality, that which is (certain truth) *(Phaedrus* 260a). Thus Plato's hostility toward the sophists: they practice "deceptive imitations of the genuine *technai*" (Kerferd, *Sophistic Movement* 4). Furthermore, Plato complains, the sophists pretend to know more than they do and pretend to be better men than they are. In short, Plato asserts that a sophist is the worst kind of seducer: a downright deceiver. Socrates quotes the Spartan as saying: "Without a grip on truth there can be no genuine art of speaking" *(Phaedrus* 260). By implication, there exists the genuine art of speaking "Truth" and the spurious "art" of speaking nothing—of offering nothing more than ornamentation. True speech (dialectic), then, may be compared with the mind, and sophistry (false *logos*) may be reduced to rhetorical wrappings such as a woman's dress, veil, and makeup.

According to Parmenides, this kind of dressing up is symptomatic of the world of *doxa* and is foreign to the world of being. In fact, Parmenides states there is only that which is. Parmenides uses the Greek verb *einai*—which means, Guthrie explains, "both 'to be' (which may refer to the relation of subject to predicate, individual to species, identity, etc.) and 'to exist'" (196)—and that which is "real" and "true." H. D. Rankin explains that no distinction is drawn between what "is," what is "real," and what is "true" before Aristotle (93; see also Loenen). The relationship between subject and predicate is one of identity. Therefore, a grammatical conclusion has been transformed into a logical conclusion, much as Nietzsche argues about the grammatical construction of the subject.[7]

Prometheus Bound

Historians such as Eric Havelock (in *Preface to Plato* and "Linguistic Task") argue that the period of the "Greek Enlightenment" is characterized by the philosophic attempt to produce thought about thought—

an enterprise made possible by the advent of literacy. According to Havelock, as language became increasingly literate, it began to be separated from the consciousness of the speaker as it became a "visible artifact," an object to be "seen and contemplated" (21).

Although Jarratt agrees that "the advent of writing initiates significant changes in the way humans think and act" (*Rereading the Sophists* 31), she wisely challenges the assumption that historians such as Havelock hold "that certain mental operations, specifically an elaborated syllogistic logic and the introspection or critical distance presumed necessary for such logic, are not possible within an 'oral' or 'mythic consciousness'" (*Rereading the Sophists* 31). Although I applaud Jarratt's argument, contra Jarratt, I am not trying to establish whether critical thought is or is not possible in oral cultures. My purposes, rather, are to investigate the ways in which the self—the thinking, acting subject— was represented and theorized. Therefore, although I will not reduce the change from, for example, the representation of Homeric subjectivity as fragmented to the Platonic prescription of subjectivity as unified and bounded to the "Great Leap" from orality to literacy (I have no desire to demonstrate definitively that Homeric man was or was not fragmented nor that subsequent, post-oral subjectivity was or was not unified), but, rather, I will point out how these theorized changes speak to the continued disparagement of Woman and sophistry.

That is, I am interested in the fact that, as A. W. H. Adkins's *From the Many to the One* argues, "a unitary self is little in evidence in Homeric poems" (44). Though the character indeed acts, his action may have been prompted by some part of him *(thumos, kradie)* or attributed to some force external to him (Apollo, Athena) (45–46). And though the character indeed may "decide" how to act, the decision is not rendered via "sheer thinking" (Havelock, *Preface to Plato* 200) or "dispassionate calculation" (Adkins 48). That is, there is a marked difference between the representation of the subject as Homeric actor and as Platonic/Aristotelian philosopher, between the fragmented, acting/performing self and the bounded, thinking self.

This bounded, thinking self, according to Anne Carson, has an affinity with the consciousness, afforded by literacy, of "edges," of boundaries. She notes that "from the way they wrote and the tools they used . . . ancient readers and writers conceived the Greek alphabet as a system of outlines or edges" (*Eros: The Bittersweet* 61). And hence the notion of the subject—of the self reflecting on thought about thought—of the thinker who establishes his edges (in contrast to Woman who has no boundaries)—of the thinker who stands above and apart from the object and Woman (the object *par excellence*) of the being who is delimited and demarcated from what is other. According to

Parmenides, speaking of being's boundaries: "And remaining the same in the same place, it rests by itself and thus remains there fixed: for powerful Necessity holds it in the bonds of a Limit, which constrains it round about, because it is decreed by divine law that *Being shall not be without boundary*" (Freeman 44; emphasis mine).

The creation of the "boundary" of "private consciousness" was one of the purposes of Greek tragedy, according to Derrick de Kerckhove's "Theory of Greek Tragedy." He posits that Greek theater was "one of the developments of the phonetic alphabet specifically" and "that its effect was to transform the sensory life of the Athenian community." He writes:

> While they were attending stage productions illiterates might be deemed to develop their attention span, their concentration, their critical faculties and their capacity for abstraction, their manipulation of language, and even train their visual skills from peripheral to centralized and directional vision. They might be encouraged for the first time to define and fragment experience in sequences and reorganize its patterns in a unified visual space. (23)

According to de Kerckhove, Aeschylus's *Prometheus Bound* serves as a model for the process of intellectualization and body control. Indeed, the character Prometheus himself is, de Kerckhove writes, the

> archetypal figure of Western man, repressed, long-winded, uptight, narcissistic and morbidly intellectual. He is the Woody Allen of Greek tragedy. He is the actor who does not move, let alone dance. The title of the play and the elaborate enactment of Prometheus' binding in the very first scene indicate that this immobilization of the central figure should be granted the utmost attention. As an emblem of muscular control, Prometheus can only respond by speech to environmental sensory stimulations. Thus divorced from action, this speech is the closest theatrical approximation of thought. (25–26)

This representation of the thinking subject who is limited, is bound, by his own morbid interiority (as opposed to what is exterior) necessitates not only the subject/object split, but also, the mind/body split, the intellectual/sensual split. Indeed, being is a function of thinking. Note Parmenides' version of Descartes' *cogito:* "For it is the same thing to think and to be" (Freeman 42). Pythagoras, according to Nicholas Lobkowicz, argued that the "spectator" (*theōrein*) is the "truly free man," freed from the exigencies of time and mortality (quoted in At-will 166). The emphasis on the "soul," which in Plato was certainly synonymous with the so-called mind or inner-cognitive functions, leads to a disparagement of the body, of its functions, of its desires, of its senses (see the *Phaedo*). A surviving fragment of Philolaus reads: "The ancient theologians and seers also bear witness that because of certain punishments the soul is yoked to the body and buries in it as in a tomb" (Freeman 76). Thus the body is seen as the prison house of the soul (just as *doxa* is Plato's prison house of language). The body, according to Pythagorean philosophers, becomes a mere garage to house the mind, just as the woman's womb becomes a mere garage to house the seed of Man (see duBois, *Sowing the Body: Psychoanalysis and Ancient Representations of Women*).

The intellect becomes associated with the good, the pure, the clean, the enlightened, and not incidentally, with man (Nye). And, in accordance with such dichotomous thinking, the body becomes associated with the evil, the impure, the dirty, the shrouded, and, again not incidentally, with woman (Spelman, "Woman as Body"). What is deemed becoming is *kosmos*—order and wholeness. What is unbecoming or disgraceful is *akosmos* (not cosmos). What is *kosmos* is the Parmenidean one. According to Empedocles, god "is equal in all directions to himself and altogether eternal, a rounded Sphere enjoying a circular solitude" (Freeman 56). The good and the pure exist in contradistinction to the somatic, the sensual, and the physical. For god [being], Empedocles asserts, "is not equipped with a human head on his body, nor from his back do two branches start; (*he has*) no feet, no swift knees; but he is Mind, holy and ineffable, and only Mind, which darts through the whole universe with its swift thoughts" (Freeman 67). And, like God, Man is mind (just as philosophy is the genuine art of the mind) and Woman is body (just as sophistry is the spurious "art" of the body). Therefore, the philosophic ideal is the rational, enlightened man, who is holy and whole, that is, free of bodily desires, which woman represents.

This fear of the body, of woman, is associated with the distrust of the sensual. Hence the world of the mind, coextensive with Parmenides' world of being and Plato's world of truth, becomes privileged as a world superior to the world of mere appearances, of sensual stimuli. Thus the mind, the only reliable organ, comes to be revered at the exclusion of bodily senses. In fact, the flesh and blood senses become appropriated by the mind, and we hear of the "inner Eye" that perceives truth. Hippon tells us: "The soul is very different from the body: it is active when the body is inert, it sees when the body is blind and lives when the body is dead" (Freeman 72). Thus the subject becomes not a participant in the sensual world around, but a spectator, an observer of reality, who remains rational and logical. Nietzsche's *Birth of Tragedy and the Case of Wagner* addresses this development of the spectator who stands apart from the chorus, the dancer who stands apart from the dance, who observes as a self-conscious individual. According to Havelock, Plato demands of people that they should "examine [their] experience and rearrange it, that they should think about what they say, instead of just saying it. And they should separate themselves from it instead of identifying with it; they themselves should become the 'subject' who stands apart from the 'object' and reconsiders it and analyses it and evaluates it" (*Preface to Plato* 46–47).

The birth of rationalism seems to have sprung full-grown from the mind. It was a clean birth—no blood, no bodily fluids—in fact, it would have nothing to do with the flesh.

Erōs and the *Technē* of Male Will

No wonder Plato exiled poets and sophists from his Republic; he recognized the relationship between poetry and Dionysian frenzy: too much delight, too much pleasure, and no restraint. In fact, as Gorgias argues, the power of language is equal to "abduction by force." It is irresistibly seductive, able to carry an audience away, magically (de Romilly, *Magic and Rhetoric in Ancient Greece*) and erotically (Gross, *Amatory Persuasion in Antiquity*). According to Havelock, the "metaphors applied to their speech dwell on its liquidity; it flows, it gushes" (*The Muse Learns to Write* 81). As Woman is characterized as boundless liquidity, so is sophistry: a perpetual motion ignorant of boundaries (of truth, of self). It is the advocate of the many, defender of no one.

But Parmenides, Plato, and the "Enlightened Ones" were concerned with regulating *erōs* and with imposing boundaries, edges, and limits, particularly of the self. The critical, reflexive, and autonomous self must stand in opposition to oral performance. The subsequent Cartesian, humanist, and scientific enlightenment only furthered this spectator mentality, based on interiority, identity, and self-reflexivity.[8] According to Slavoj Zizek, "I = I" is the fundamental equation of humanism, the absolute starting point for philosophy (*Enjoy Your Symptom* 87) and, subsequently, the death toll, which has been ringing for some time, for desire, Woman, and sophistry.

The original intention of this chapter—putting aside the problematics of both "original" and "intention"—was to assert rhetoric's desire as it has been suppressed by the desire, or the "pure" desire, of philosophy. That is, I had determined to demonstrate how the "heavenly" desires *philia* or *agapē* were appropriated by philosophy and then pitted against rhetoric's wanton, whorish, and sophistic desires. Furthermore, it was my intention to draw a comparison between the silenced desires of rhetoric and the suppression of female desire as accomplished by the Western, phallocentric, metaphysical tradition, and, by so doing, I had hoped to unveil rhetoric's and woman's unheard, unheeded, unfulfilled desires. But, as I made an audit of the historical accounts of *erōs,* I discovered that rhetoric and woman were not merely in "arrears" and lacking assets, but that they could not be accounted for except via the existence of philosophy and male desire. Female desire does not exist; it is an empty ledger.

According to Sigmund Freud's calculations, there are at least four people involved in every sex act; there are at least four desires operative in the bedroom, in the symposium. In the heat of the moment, there exists a great deal of confusion and anxiety concerning fathers and mothers. Upon his recommendation, I will take the number four as the common denominator, as the rule for my audit. The number four does seem significant in the consideration of *erōs.* For, by my calculations, there are at least two mythological creatures who go by the name of "Eros" and two who go by "Aphrodite." And again, I found a great deal of confusion and contradiction about who parented whom. In any case, since Eros and Aphrodite travel in tandem, their party appears to be four. First there is the Eros referred to in Hesiod's *Theogony* as a primitive deity whose birth long precedes that of Aphrodite or any of the other Olympians. According to Robert Flacelière, "He is said to have been born at the same time as the world itself, when only Chaos and Earth existed" (*Love in Ancient Greece* 46). This Eros, in Orphic cosmogony, was born from the cosmic egg and referred to in Aristophanes' *The Birds.* Flacelière continues, "Yet he was also represented by the Greeks, who do not seem to have troubled themselves about the strange contradiction involved, as a much younger boy, the son of Aphrodite" (47). She who goes by Aphrodite is likewise two: The first is the elder and the daughter of Uranus and who had no mother (36). She is referred to in Plato's *Symposium* as "Heavenly Aphrodite," coming as she did from Heaven's sperm. The second is called Common Aphrodite, the child of Zeus and Dione.

Working with these four representations, there exists the possibility of at least four kinds of relationships: Man with younger boy; Man with Man; Man with Wife; Man with Prostitute or Slave.[9] In all relationships and scenarios there existed delicate rules and often-elaborate protocols governing the development and exercise of desire—that is, there existed rules whereby Man ruled and governed himself in relation to his desire. But, within all possible relations, Man was the master of the object of desire and, it was hoped, master of desire. With Man as bearer of the phallus and therefore the subject of desire, erotic relationships were opportunities—in fact, ethical imperatives—to assert his will and his sovereignty. According to Plato's *Phaedrus*, "there are two ruling and guiding principles" in Man: "one of them is an innate desire for pleasure, the other, an acquired opinion which strives for the best" (238). Although these impulses are often at odds with each other, Man's potential for sovereignty enables him to be "stronger than himself" by exerting restraint. He demonstrates "self-control"—the Greek ideal of *sōphrosynē*—when he utilizes reason to master the baser drive named *hubris,* which as Plato reminds us goes by many names: wantonness, insolence, excess, gluttony. Thus we have the "myth of the charioteer" to illustrate man's inner battle. Recall that Socrates divides the soul into three parts, two horses and one charioteer. One horse is white, noble, temperate, and clean-limbed and "needs no whip, but is driven by word of command alone" (253e). The other horse is black, huge, insolent, a "jumble of a creature" that heeds no whip or spur (253e). The myth of the charioteer symbolizes the process whereby Man harnesses his desire and thereby constitutes himself as subject. Michel Foucault writes:

> Because [sex] was the most violent of all the pleasures, because it was more costly than most physical activities, and because it participated in the game of life and death, it constituted a privileged domain for the ethical formation of the subject: a subject who ought to be distinguished by his ability to subdue the tumultuous forces that were loosed within him. (*Use of Pleasure* 139)

For Plato, Foucault argues, virtue "was not conceived [of] as a state of integrity, but as a relationship of domination, a relation of mastery" (*Use of Pleasure* 70). Dominate desire and become a self—and a noble lover, at that—which by controlling itself is, therefore, capable of controlling others, commanding others, dominating others, mastering others. For those who, like the women, are enslaved to their "baser" drives are like the animals and slaves who must be ruled by their masters— their self-mastered masters, their self-delimiting, and, therefore, noble masters.

Evidently, subjectivity and self-mastery are the privilege of the phallus. For the soul of woman lacks the "true" *sōphrosynē* attained through reason. Although Aristotle allows that woman can attain some measure of *sōphrosynē* through dutifulness and obedience, she remains the black horse forced into submission by duty and phallocratic law. There is no self-motivated charioteer constitutive of her soul. As Anne Carson reminds us in her article "Putting Her in Her Place: Woman, Dirt, and Desire," woman's insatiable lust and wanton desire would run unchecked if it were not for man's greater capacity for temperance. So great is her licentiousness that she is often likened to a horse, to a filly in need of bridling and harnessing, as the horse is the beast (as Plato's myth demonstrates), thought to have been the most desire-driven animal.

By commandeering woman, Man proves his superiority by asserting his will, the pure will of *sōphrosynē*, the ethical and political ideal. To be subject to irrational desires is foolishness, is inappropriate for the ethical subject, the rational subject. Democritus writes, "To be ruled by a woman is the ultimate outrage for a man" (Freeman 103); and "The brave man is not only he who overcomes the enemy, but he who is stronger than pleasures. Some men are masters of cities, but are enslaved to women" (Freeman 111). The rational man is the master of passion, of bodily desires, of deceptive appearances, and is, thus, the master of woman (Aphrodite or otherwise).

The enemy is desire, is irrationality, is a black horse running loose in the polis or in the *psyche,* operating according to an economy of unbridled excess—an economy disruptive of the useful and ordered economy of scarcity and temperance. This baser desire is characterized in the *Symposium* as being "physical rather than spiritual," aiming only for the "satisfaction of its desires, and it tak[ing] no account of the manner in which this is achieved" (180e–182a). It is the dark horse run amok. But heavenly love—coming from the Heavenly Aphrodite born of Uranus alone—Plato reminds us, *"has no female strain in her"* and *therefore* is "free from wantonness" and directed only towards the male sex, "being naturally the stronger and more intelligent" (180e–182a; emphasis mine). Thus, conversely, Woman, as the embodiment of the baser desires, serves to sublimate Male desire as will. The Western metaphysical subject, newly enlightened, can maintain this mastery by setting Woman up to bear the weight of all nothingness and then by exercising mastery over her body and claiming it as a victory over death, not being, and mere appearance.

And the standard of this desire is the phallus. Eva Keuls in her *Reign of the Phallus* argues that artistic and comedic representations of women using dildos says nothing of woman's will, subjectivity, or desire, but rather functions as a projection of male fantasies. She writes, "Since Athens' society had promoted the male organ as the symbol of fertility, parenthood, creativity, and self-defense, it is only natural that

Athenian men could not conceive of women otherwise than as obsessed with insatiable lust to fill up their vaginal void with penises, real or artificial" (82). The significance of the frequency of such representations (painted by men for their use on flat drinking cups used by men and *hetairai* at symposia) is compounded by the striking infrequency of representations of nonphallic female masturbation or homosexuality. Even the "island of Lesbos, to the ancient Greeks," Keuls says, "was not associated with female homoeroticism, but with *fellatio*" (86). This is my point: However *erōs* has been constructed or represented, it has been exclusively and essentially phallic and male homoerotic. And furthermore, it has been sublimated as will and subjectivity.

I question Freud's accounting. What was four is now seen as three (Vernant, "One . . . Two . . . Three: *Eros*"). Apparently Male desire is really only able to count to three: a "three," however, that is reducible to one (via the dialectic: thesis, antithesis, synthesis). What is excluded from the equation, from the symposium, from the bedroom, from subjectivity, is female desire. The paradigm of Western consciousness remains the Oedipal triangle—a narrative told exclusively from the point of view of the omnipotent narrator: Male desire. Of tremendous note, but often passed over, is the origin of the Oedipal myth, an origin that bespeaks the homoeroticism of phallic desire. Oedipus's tragic existence is due to the actions of his father, Laius, King of Thebes, who abducted and raped the boy Chrysippus, son of Pelops. The tragedy was a result of Laius's homoerotic desire (Apollodorus, *Library* III.v.5). However, as we established before, it is not his desire per se that is condemned. His lust for the boy is natural and demonstrative of the superior, heavenly love. Rather, it is Laius's lack of restraint that is punished. Thus the paradigm of the construction of the ego is a tale grounded in the homoerotic desire of the father. Could we not reconstruct Freud's interpretation of the Oedipal myth and demonstrate the desire of the father, of Laius, who was referred to as the "inventor of pederasty" (Keuls 289)? The homosexual scenes depicted on Attic vase paintings from the sixth century, Keuls reminds us, show "an affectionate, almost tender, relationship between a mature man and a male child before puberty, which is sexual but has overtones of a father-son rapport" (277). The Oedipal triangle; two horses and one charioteer; one, two, three; Father, Son, and the Holy Ghost of *Erōs*. The Trinity that bespeaks the fantasy of the one. Where is woman? Where is woman's desire?

But I am not suggesting that if one looks into the labyrinth of desire one will find "female desire." I am not Camille Paglia, who has argued vehemently that attempts to "demystify" sex and gender go against the dictates of nature, nor am I attempting to re-essentialize Dionysus. Although some have argued that ancient rituals evidence the existence of a female desire, I would argue that these ritual practices say nothing of female desire per se, but rather are additional examples of institutionalized male desire and the projection of that desire onto women.

The first example is of the Adonia, the festival during which, Keuls explains, "Athenian women celebrated the love affair of Aphrodite and Adonis, and reenacted the death and burial of the young lover" (23). It could be argued that Adonis, the mortal lover of Aphrodite, represents the object of female desire: a gentle, timid lover in contradistinction to the aggressive, domineering Athenian male. It could be further argued that this is a case in which Woman occupies the position of subject of desire. After all, Adonis must be seduced by Aphrodite. It is my contention, however, that Aphrodite born of semen, without any "female strain in her," is a mythological embodiment of male, not female, desire. She is a creature, Hesiod's *Theogony* informs us, who has risen up out of the foam of her father's sperm. If she has sprung from the seed of male desire, how can her male desire for Adonis represent female desire? I propose that this is another case of homoeroticism. Adonis, as the barely bearded man, depicted as childish and innocent, represents the boy that never grows up. Although he is a man, he is still a legitimate object of desire. For homosexual desire was questioned and called "lawless love" and "against nature" only in cases of homosexual prostitution or homosexual relations among peers but specifically not in cases of pederasty (Keuls 287). Hence a homoerotic desire between peers is played out and celebrated insofar as Aphrodite's sex and Adonis's maturity are disguised.

The second example concerns the Thesmophoria, a festival during which women simultaneously lamented the sorrows of Demeter and celebrated her joy. Here again, it could be argued that during this three-day period of bacchic revelry, woman assumed the posture of a subject of desire and manifested her desire. Such an interpretation is questionable for several reasons. First of all, the Thesmophoria—associated with the god Dionysus, the god of ecstasy and rapture—merely reinscribes the male depiction of woman as essentially and exclusively ruled by hubris, wantonness, and excess. This is how Man has characterized female desire in order to deny her subjectivity, and to sublimate his own desire—characterized as more pure and more temperate. The Dionysian-Apollonian dichotomy—just as the Female/Male dichotomy—is a false binary, a convenient set of oppositions, used to ensure the sovereignty and superiority of male desire. Furthermore, Dionysus is fundamentally a phallic god, for "in the domain of religion, the phallus [belongs] primarily to the god Dionysus" (Keuls 76). The phallic emphasis of the festival is evidenced by the first day's activity; Keuls describes it this way:

On the first day of the festival, selected women descended into pits where pigs had previously been left to die. Their job was to bring up the decaying remains of the animals and place them on altars, together with seed corn. Some sources speak of snakes frequenting the pits, a likely phenomenon considering the free food, and others of facsimiles of male genitalia thrown in after the pigs. Since the pig is a consistent metaphor for the female reproductive parts, and the snake has phallic associations, a symbolic copulation took place in the pits. (352–53)

Not only is it once again assumed that the vagina—the pig—desires the penis, but evidently the pit—the earth—also voraciously hungers for the phallus. Can we not ask if displaced male desire is operative here? It is my argument that such a festival, again, reveals nothing of "female desire." Could we not question it on the sole basis that the men scheduled and paid for the festival? Ruth Padel concurs:

[I]t is men who create and use the myths depicting women "out of their mind," whose mental and physical displacement from the norm destroys society; and a male-ordered calendar contains the Thesmophoria. Male society controls, monitors, and also, one might say, exploits, the animal nature in women (as men perceive them), which requires emergence, but which is perceived as destructive to society if not controlled by it. (8)

Thus, female desire as such remains under the control and aegis of male phallic desire. The omnipresent male purse and the public depictions of proud herms underscores the supremacy of one desire. Thus in a world of phallic desire, the question "What does Woman want?" is ultimately irrelevant. Indeed, it is amusing that Freud thought to ask it at all. Perhaps, I would argue further, the concept of what woman desires *cannot even be thought.* Jean-Luc Nancy is correct when he claims that love is thinking ("Shattered Love" 84). Although he is perhaps blind to his own phallocentric desire, his point is well-taken: desire and consciousness are ineluctably tangled and, I would add, constitutive of each other, as evidenced by the interconnected themes of will, temperance, desire, anguish, guilt, and death.

In the *Timaeus,* Plato posits that lust is a sickness of the body. Desire represents the scare of disorder, the pathology of excess. The sperm overruns its limit and refuses to be enclosed and streams through the whole body. The individual is thus driven by "pleasures and pains in excess" (45). The disease, then, is excess, is desire, is *erōs*. Crates, along with Plato and many other Greek philosophers, "shared in the widespread and lasting conviction that *eros* was a disruptive disease best kept under strict control. Verses attributed to him suggest that hunger is a good cure for eros; if that fails, time will cure it; if that fails, hang yourself" (quoted in Rankin 236). Antisthenes, rather than curing himself of *erōs* by killing himself, argued for killing the source of the disease: Aphrodite. "He remarked that if he could catch Aphrodite, the goddess of sexual love, he would shoot her, presumably with her son's arrows" (quoted in Rankin 220).

Obviously Man has ambiguous feelings about *erōs* and what is. Despite the acknowledged pleasure of Plato's "sprouting wings" that accompanies desire and despite the existential denial by Parmenides, Plato, and subsequent philosophers of the sensory and sensual world, Man must continuously confront this nothingness, the dark horse often called *thanatos*, which rides alongside. Man fears this dark horse, this irrational desire toward nothingness. It represents chaos, *tuchē*, meaninglessness, and death because it challenges his power, it renders him terrified of his own impotence—to penetrate, to master, to be subject. This anguish, this recognition of possible loss, possible castration, constitutes male desire and male subjectivity. Desire is accompanied by the dread of exhausting into nothing. Objectifying woman—as other—as object and as death's representative is the easiest route to eroticism and to male subjectivity. Woman has long been associated with death. Her inner depth, her invisible and mysterious interior, reflected in the architecture of the women's quarters, called *muchos,* can refer both to Hades and to a hidden recess (Padel 10). Woman is the empty grave, the empty set, whose name is zero (Schneiderman 7). As such, her meaning, her desire, is symptomatic of male desire.

According to Georges Bataille, this objectification of woman, finding its logical conclusion in prostitution, has constructed our consciousness. He writes, "There will never be a lack of compassionate souls to protest the miseries of prostitution, but their cries conceal a general hypocrisy. It may be painful, humanly, to admit that the detour of prostitution played in the formation of our sensibility" (*Accursed Share* 2: 141). He goes on to argue that our subjectivity desires the shame that is connected to prostitution (taken as a model for sexual relations) and "that enters into the alchemy of eroticism from every slant" (141). The desire, often noted, to humiliate via penetration or to be humiliated during intimacy bespeaks the relation between *erōs* and shame, as does Stuart Schneiderman's Lacanian observation that the Oedipal "psychodrama" has as its chief spoil the pleasure of guilt (22). Guilt and shame, the spoils of male desire, are the conditions for male subjectivity. Nietzsche argues similarly when he speaks of *ressentiment* and bad conscience as the fundamentals of Western subjectivity. As I have said elsewhere, "Consciousness is always bad conscience" ("Extricating Ethics from the Ego" 105). But it—subjectivity—remains a fundamentally male possibility. For as Aristotle reminds us, man is the only creature capable of experiencing shame; "he denies to women a full measure of *aidos;* the female is ... 'shameless'" (HA 608b12; quoted in Carson, "Putting Her in Her Place" 142). "Exempt from shame as from all fear of drying up, woman goes at sex like a hippomaniac mare" (142), forever lacking the shame that evidences will and true *sōphrosynē.* Thus Woman remains the shameless cipher that nevertheless sustains the male's presumed sovereignty.

Just as Woman's sexuality has been experienced heretofore as a function of Male desire, so too has rhetoric been subject to prostitution at the will of philosophy. Thus I am suggesting the danger of positing rhetoric as the other, suppressed, desire. Such a move insidiously reinscribes the supremacy of philosophy's "pure" desire. For, it is my argument, rhetoric as the other has served heretofore as the catch-all basin for philosophy's displaced desire. The pitting of one against the other plays into the phallocentric logic of duality and noncontradiction, and thus serves merely to fuel its desire, to encourage its fantasies of master and servant, good and evil, truth and deception. With the rhetoric/philosophy duality, one finds not dueling desires but merely one master playing dueling banjos with *erōs.* I propose, then, that rather than identifying rhetoric's desire, one should acknowledge its absence and ask the Spivakian question: What is it that philosophy desires, what is it that it fears, that it would figure rhetoric's desire as such? For again, my purposes are not to rehabilitate Woman or sophistry (as the negated other) nor to reveal a truth or being of such. Rather, by using a Baudrillardian strategy of extremes (more Woman than Woman, more sophistic than sophistic), I hope to clear a space for the Third Woman, the Third Sophistic, for *what will have been* the other Other.

Ethics Without *Erōs*

Why would philosophy demand the philosopher to dissociate himself from the body and the world of *doxa* and appearances, and in fact demand the philosopher to live his life as if he were practicing for death (see Plato's *Timaeus*)? Herein lies the frigidity of truth and goodness. The good man is the dead man—the man who has gained dominion over his body and the bodies of others and has frozen them according to rigid, permanent, and static laws, ideas, principles. Nietzsche writes: "All that philosophers have handled for millennia has been con-

ceptual mummies; nothing actual has escaped from their hands alive"
(*Twilight* 35). Of the philosophic method he comments, "One error after another is coolly placed on ice; the ideal is not refuted—it *freezes* to
death. — . . . almost everywhere 'the thing in itself' freezes to death"
(*Ecce Homo* 284).

To freeze something is to control it. The "enlightened" self is the
one who is frozen into a harmonious whole, acting in accordance with
equally frozen principles of goodness. A "good" man, an ethical man—
Socrates has already told us—is a man who has mastered himself:
"every man is his own rule . . . temperate and self-controlled, having
mastery over his own pleasures and desires" (*Gorgias* 491d), mastery
over his irrational, inharmonious desires. The issue here is of control:
control of self. The "enlightened" self has mastered himself, has "bridled" passions, chaos, and chance. So admonishes Socrates, "If, then,
the better part of the intelligence wins the victory and guides them to
an *orderly* and *philosophic* way of life, their life on earth will be happy
and harmonious since they have attained discipline and self-control:
they have subdued the source of evil in the soul and set free the source
of goodness" (*Phaedrus* 256; emphasis mine). They have subdued the
disorderly and embraced *technē* in order to control, to predict, to master. In the *Protagoras,* Socrates asks:

> Haven't we seen that the power of appearance leads us
> astray and throws us into confusion, so that in our actions
> and our choices between things both great and small we are
> constantly accepting and rejecting the same things, whereas
> the techne of measurement would have canceled the effect
> of the appearance, and by revealing the truth would have
> caused the soul to live in peace and quiet abiding in the
> truth? (356d–e)

What man wants is not Woman, is not the other, but his self—
existing in peace, abiding in the truth. What he desires—despite, ironically, all his claims to "activity" as opposed to Woman's "passivity"—
is a static, immobile ethos that would reflect itself, according to Irigaray, "eternally self-identical" (*Speculum of the Other Woman* 308).
This is the final and ultimate good which, according to Cicero, "everything should be referred to, but which should itself be referred to nothing else" (*De Finibus* 1.29). This ethos finds its representation in the
phallus—as that which needs no other to signify—the prime mover
that causes all, but has no cause. And by extension, we can see the pa-
thetic frigidity of Western metaphysics: the good, the true, and the

beautiful—nothing but cold, marble obelisks raised to soothe Man's castration complex.

Unlike a Man (a philosopher), a sophist, like a Woman, can never be taken at face value. A sophist's use of tropes, rhythms, and figurative language is like a woman's use of cosmetics and veils; all are superficial and deceptive knacks used in order to obscure the truth, to flatter an audience without regard for consequences. They are bewitching, conniving, and faithless. Carson reminds us that the condemnation of women as infidels and as transgressors of boundaries can

> be traced to the earliest legends of the Greeks. In myth, women's boundaries are pliant, porous, mutable. Her power to control them is inadequate, her concern for them unreli-able. Deformation attends her. She swells, she shrinks, she leaks, . . . she suffers metamorphoses. The women of mythology regularly lose their form in monstrosity. Io turns into a heifer, Kallisto becomes a bear, Medusa sprouts snakes from her head and Skylla yelping dogs from her waist. ("Putting Her in Her Place" 154)

Thus, Carson explains, women are "as individuals, comparatively formless themselves, without firm control of personal boundaries. They are, as social entities, units of danger, moving across boundaries of family and *oikos,* in marriage, prostitution, or adultery. They are, as psychological entities, unstable compounds of deceit and desire, prone to leakage" ("Putting Her in Her Place" 159). And so, likewise, is rhetoric prone to flow. It could be argued that the history of Western metaphysics is the history of the attempt to stop this flow, to contain this leakage, and thus to demand an unyielding fidelity to the realm of nonsensory reality and a steadfastness to that which is, denying all phenomena.

Discourse Without *Erōs*

In the *Gorgias,* Socrates begins his discussion with the statement that, unlike politics, philosophy is not unstable, nor at the whim of its favorites (481d). Of course, Plato's political motivations justify his criticism. Plato was against Periclean reforms and democratic government in general, and advocated an elitist individualism. In response to Plato's condemnation of the sophists on these grounds, many modern-day interpreters of and apologists for the sophists have comforted themselves by offering a defense of rhetoric on political grounds. As Havelock states, "[D]iscourse is social or it is nothing; its topics and problems are by definition common ones, group notions; the words of men act on other men and vice versa. There is an exchange of opinion, alteration of opinion, discovery of common opinion, consensus and decision. It is not a discourse carried on in the private soul" (*Preface to Plato* 193). Here, rather than valuing, as Plato does, truth, the opposing term *doxa* is characterized as being ultimately of more worth—a case of inverting the hierarchy. What we have here is Protogorean rhetoric and proto-Habermasian rhetoric. Protagoras has defined his "discipline" as the study of the "formation of correct decision" in the family as in the state, that is, political *technai* (Gomperz 413). Protagoras writes, "this is prudence in affairs private as well as public; he will learn to order his own house in the best manner, and he will be best able to speak and act in affairs of state" (quoted in Gomperz 413). I will address this issue of consensual and socially constructed rhetoric in subsequent chapters. But for now, I only want to comment that this "apology" represents a false opposition to Platonic and Parmenidean positions, and is furthermore, complicitous with being and the attack on sophistry.

It is my argument that the recent attempts (beginning with Cope, Hegel, and Grote) to (as they say) "rehabilitate" sophistry are suspect. Without discounting or disparaging the careful research and the significant influence such scholars have had on me, I am suggesting that their rehabilitations have been attempts to make sophistry legitimate. Steven Mailloux suggests sophistry as a neopragmatic practice; Susan Jarratt offers sophistry as a model for the construction of a politics of *nomoi;* Takis Poulakos examines sophistry as a form of ideology critique; John Poulakos suggests a relationship between sophistry and Heideggerian philosophy. All these scholars have sought to codify sophistry—to make it something—to give it being and presence. The goal is to make sophistry into a true *technē* not a spurious art. My response to this is precisely my reaction to those who argue for the construction of a history of women rhetors.[10] It is an act of reappropriation, an attempt at "redemption"—of clearing Women from all charges of counterfeit in order to re-present her as respectable, legitimate, and proper. The (im)pertinent question then, is a Spivakian question: what is our desire that we desire to legitimate Woman? And what is our desire to legitimate the sophists, to appropriate them, to show their usefulness (and use-value) for the twentieth century and beyond?

2

Seduction and Sacrificial Gestures: Gorgias, Helen, and Nothing

> A giving which gives only its gift, but in the giving holds
> itself back and withdraws, such a giving we call *sending*.
> —Heidegger, *On Time and Being*

His fragments come to us like a message tucked in the space of a bottle—a bottle tossed in an open sea some two or more millennia ago. We unstop the bottle to stop the message from lapping to and fro upon the sands of time. We unfold the cryptic note and gaze at Gorgias's words with simultaneous wonder, amusement, and disbelief: "Nothing is; even if it did exist, we couldn't know it; and even if we could know it, we couldn't communicate it."[1] Many have speculated that Gorgias wasn't serious—that he couldn't possibly have meant to claim that nothing is.[2] But if he is taken "seriously," he is then, because of this abysmal insight, accused of espousing nihilism. It is my argument that to take Gorgias seriously is not, of necessity, to posit nihilism. This so-called tragedy of knowledge, rather, is a recognition, an affirmation, of all the possibilities of being through his affirmation of not being. This affirmation contrasts with the denial of not being as argued by the Eleatics, such as Parmenides and Melissus, who accomplished their denial by limiting being and by asserting this being only by way of the negative. That is, the Eleatics posited being's existence only by setting up its opposite, "Not Being," and by associating not being with phenomena, human opinion, and sense impressions. Whereas the Eleatics denied being to the world of "appearances" and the body, Gorgias— using Eleatic logic against itself—affirms not being. Situated within the perennial debate initiated by the early fourth- and fifth-century Greek thinkers between being and not being, this chapter considers the extant fragments of Gorgias, in particular his "On Nature" and "Encomium of Helen," in relation to the Parmenidean notion of oneness that has figured predominantly in our subsequent metaphysical tradition.

In his "Encomium of Helen," Gorgias refigures the case against Helen, exonerating her as neither subject nor object of desire. Reading this epideictic discourse in conjunction with his "On Nature," I will argue that Gorgias makes a proto-postmodern move to displace common assumptions of active/passive, subject/object, being/not being by recasting Helen as a woman with a seductive figure, which eludes capture and mastery. This argument takes for granted John Poulakos's analogical reading of Gorgias's defense of Helen. That is, Gorgias's defense of Helen is a defense of rhetoric. Both, Poulakos writes, "are attractive, both are unfaithful, and both have a bad reputation" ("Gorgias' *Encomium*" 5). Although I am expressly unconcerned with salvaging either's reputation, I am interested in Gorgias's sophistic insight into the deceptive and ambiguous nature of truth and subjectivity. For Helen and/as rhetoric, what I will here call Woman, is able, by virtue of infidelity and *kairos* to "break up the cycle of the antitheses [being and not being] and create something new" (Untersteiner 161).

I realize that this argument has its detractors, namely Edward Schiappa, who argues that such an interpretation is "underdetermined by the text" ("Gorgias's Helen Revisited" 314). Bruce McComiskey argues against "interpretations of Gorgianic rhetoric that locate its foundations in skeptical notions of opinion *(doxa)*, persuasion *(peitho)*, and deception *(apatē)*," claiming that Gorgias's rhetoric *is*—despite Plato's estimation—a *technē*, one with foundations in *alētheia* ("Gorgias and the Art of Rhetoric" 21). And Robert Gaines argues that our extrapolation of Gorgias's tragedy of knowledge ("If anything is comprehensible, it is incommunicable") is "at best obscure and at worst simply false" (1). Although I appreciate their careful scholarship and find many of their arguments convincing, I believe they are mis/taking the issue I am addressing here. For if we hear Gorgias's "On Nature," for example, as an attempt to prove the existence and/or "being" of something (whether it be being or not being), then we are reading him as a philosopher. But if we read him rhetorically, we see that Gorgias is demonstrating with his argument that he can prove that not being exists just as easily as Parmenides can demonstrate that being does. Both Parmenides and Gorgias have given us an argument, a text, a compilation of words, but neither Parmenides nor Gorgias can "guarantee" in any extralinguistic or extrasymbolic way the ultimate reference of those words. Likewise, Schiappa can prove that "Rhetoric" does not exist in pre-Platonic Athens, just as McComiskey can prove that Gorgias's rhetoric "is" (is a *technē*). Although Gaines concedes that "Gorgias does assert that words are not identical with existent things and, for that reason, cannot give rise to knowledge about such things," he suggests that this is a rather "obvious and elementary" statement and reductive of all of Gorgias's other claims (8). On the contrary, as I have argued in the previous chapter, this insight has not been taken by the rhetorical tradition as "obvious and elementary," and in fact the tradition has taken great pains to deny this in order to posit a truth. Hence, I am using Gorgias not in an attempt to prove any truth regarding the man or his texts, but as a pretext to discuss the instability of language and/as Woman.

It is important to repeat that Woman here is not to be taken as representational of sex or sexuality or as a gendered construction, despite the fact that heretofore, the chief advocates of being have slandered the instability of language by associating it with a very particular representation of the sexuality of women. This chapter will thus focus on the relationships amongst female sexuality, not being, and sophistry, and, conversely, the relationships amongst male sexuality, being, and philosophy. Although I have no intention of reessentializing Woman, or of reidealizing the "eternal feminine," or of calling forth the Goddess, I would like to suggest that by considering rhetoric as a Woman, as the Dame Rhetorica, we can reconsider subjectivity in a way that affirms life, that reclaims the sensual, and that values the moment (rather than mummifying the past or the future). To consider rhetoric as Woman is to acknowledge—without appropriating—that which exists exiled outside the city walls, so to speak. Just as the sophists were *metics*, women also were not endowed with full citizen rights within the city walls,[3] echoing Parmenides' insistence that nothingness is not within the limits of being. Exiled yet irrepressible, sophistry (that is, Woman as rhetoric) resists being and regenerates repeatedly: the first sophistic (fifth and fourth centuries BCE), the second sophistic (first century AD), and now the so-called Third Sophistic[4] and its afterbirth. It continually gives birth to a bastard child, born of Metis, sprung unnaturally (for we are not making that fateful essentialist argument) from Zeus's thigh as the illegitimate offspring of language.

Historical Contextualizations

Gorgias, born in Leontini around 500 BCE, first visited Athens in 427 BCE at the age of 73 and is reputed to have lived to the age of 108 (Enos 38).[5] Despite Plato's condemnation, Gorgias was actually highly regarded and respected by many prominent individuals such as Pericles, Thucydides, and Aspasia. Gorgias distinguished himself from the other sophists of the day, such as Protagoras, by never claiming to teach *aretē*, precisely because it was Gorgias's belief that *aretē* did not exist—that is, that it could not be attributed with a particular essence (Plato, *Meno* 95c; Guthrie 271). Whatever he did teach, he amassed significant wealth and attracted many prestigious students, the most famous of whom was Isocrates (Enos 39).

E. M. Cope, in his "On the Sophistical Rhetoric," identifies Gorgias as representing one of two general sophistic tendencies or schools of thought and taste. Cope names this particular style the Sicilian school. He writes: "The Sicilian school, of which Gorgias, Polus, and their follower Alcidamas may be taken as representatives, made εὐέπεια, 'ornate, fine speaking,' their object" (47). In contradistinction, the "Greek school," Cope continues, "of which Protagoras, Prodicus, and Hippias were the leading members, aimed at ὀρθοέπεια, correct speaking and composition. It is to be observed that the former style, popular as it was at its first appearance, never gained a permanent footing at Athens: it was of course eminently unsuitable for the law-courts, for which most of the extant speeches were written" (47–48). Thus, because the nature of Gorgias's sophistry was unsuitable for the machinations of the polis (just as Woman's nature was taken to be unsuitable for public life), rhetoric soon existed only insofar as it excluded sophistry (as seen in Platonic and Aristotelian rhetorics). Cope writes, "The 'Greek' rhetoricians are consequently those to whom the sciences of *grammar* and *philology* owe their origin; and Protagoras has the credit of being the first who attracted attention to the subject" (48; emphasis mine). It was Protagoras who began rhetoric's and philosophy's subsequent (and perhaps inherent) codependence with correctness. It was he who wrote a book entitled *Orthoepeia* (proper words, proper form of words) and another work called *Alētheia* (truth). It was also Protagoras whose etymological speculations first insisted on distinguishing the genders of the noun (Cope 48). And it was Protagoras who systematically made a division of *logos,* classifying its modes of expression under four heads (Cope 50). It was Protagoras, a rhetorician's sophist, certainly not a sophist's sophist, who fixed gender and genre.

. Whereas Protagoras, as representative of the Greek school, is seen as promoting a useful and prudent tool, Gorgias of the Sicilian school is dismissed as an audience pleaser and a man of style, not substance. Richard Enos, in "The Epistemology of Gorgias' Rhetoric," argues that the rhetorical tradition has acknowledged the role that Gorgias has played in part in rhetoric's birth and development and yet has undermined his contributions by "relegat[ing] Gorgias to the level of a glib nihilist who advanced no positive theories and was unconcerned with ethics" (37). George Kennedy reduces Gorgias's contributions to poetic devices (*The Art of Persuasion in Greece* 33). And W. Rhys

Roberts (a translator of Plato, I might point out), in Enos's assessment, "argues that Gorgias wrote no formal rhetorical treatise (techne) and that his oratory emphasized trivial matters with 'claptrap' strategies" (37). Those who read Gorgias, addressing his style specifically,[6] tend to either dismiss him because they see his style as "style-for-style's sake" or praise him because of his inventive and ingenious style. Either approach misses altogether the Nietzschean "Question of Style." That is, as Derrida writes in *Spurs,* the subject of style is the subject of Woman (37): a subject, a question (a subject-in-question) that I will address in this chapter.

Taking Gorgias (Seriously)

Are we to take Gorgias seriously? Gorgias, ineluctably identified with "style," shares the reputation of obfuscating the purity of language and thought, and thus suffers from "the" rhetorical tradition's condemnation.[7] Enos writes, "Rare are the occasions in which historical treatment of the sophists has varied from Plato's condemnation" (37). Gorgias's style, in particular, with its prominent use of antithesis, parallel expressions, and chiasmic constructions, has been accused of "exaggerating balance and antithesis to the point of absurdity: 'starting with the initial advantage of having nothing in particular to say, he was able to concentrate all his energies upon saying it'" (Denniston, quoted in MacDowell 18). Cope writes that critics have claimed Gorgianism was "affected," "ridiculous," and "pompous," using figures in "such nauseous superabundance" to convey "somewhat superficial ideas" (66, 68). To this charge, Bromley Smith responds, "While the criticisms in the main are just, they are made by those who had before them the written productions of Gorgias, by those who had never *heard* the man himself" (357). Without commenting on the "justness" of the criticisms, I would add that the Athenians had not ears to hear Gorgias, he who was a foreigner—who, Smith reminds us, "employed unusual words, far-fetched and poetic" (356). Further, the sophists, Gorgias in particular, are often dismissed on the grounds that they reveled in self-aggrandizement. Concerning this charge, Gomperz reminds us that "modesty was not a virtue of that age" (419). In addition, Gorgias was infamous for his epideictic oratory—the bulk of his extant fragments are epideictic, where, as Smith reminds us, the orator was expected to show off (356).

There was some scholarly contention, however, that several works credited to Gorgias are merely stylistic imitations, anonymously authored imitations.[8] At the time when Cope was writing, scholars argued that "[t]he two orations which pass under his name, the Apologia

Palamedis and Encomium Helenes, are now regarded as imitations of his manner by some later Sophist" (67). (Although current scholars now accept their authenticity, that there existed, at some point, some question as to the authenticity of the works I will examine is, within the terms of my discussion, irrelevant. Gorgias is used here as a *topos*— as a conceptual starting place. While it may be of great interest to some scholars, and in fact, the primordial issue, it simply is not an issue here. For it is not our purpose to look for the Man behind the style.) Therefore, the effort to take Gorgias "seriously" is complicated by the historical controversy surrounding the authorship of Gorgias's attributed works and further compounded by his dismissal as a "mere" stylist. But on this point, we will heed Gorgias's advice and take him neither seriously nor lightheartedly, but rather we will "spoil the opponents' seriousness with laughter and their laughter with seriousness" (Aristotle, *On Rhetoric* 1419b).

(Im)Possibilisms

Gorgias's treatise "On the Non-Existent, or On Nature" is predicated on his own advice. The object of his criticism is the Parmenidean notion of being as the only existent possibility, and Parmenides' assertion that not-being is impossible. That which is "impossible" nevertheless finds its possibility in Gorgias's so-called tragedy of knowledge (Nothing is. If anything exists, it is unknowable. Even if anything exists and is knowable, it cannot be communicated to others)[9] which—rather than an espousal of nihilism—is a recognition of the tragic element of existence due to the tragic element of signification. That is, a recognition, according to Thomas G. Rosenmeyer, of the "frequent discrepancy between words and things [known as *apatē*]. . . . *Apate* signals the supersession of the world of the *logos*"—of the irrational, incorrectness, noncorresponding *logos* (232). According to Rosenmeyer, tragedy is comprised of ambiguous material: "It presents itself as a complex pattern, as a *two-faced* proposition. It is likely to say one thing, and to mean another, and to give perfect expression to neither" (226; emphasis mine). The tragic is ambiguous, paradoxical, contradictory—deceptive—there is no one-to-one correspondence. And, Rosenmeyer states, "Mental befuddlement seems to be the principal notion associated with this use of the word 'tragic.' . . . And always, there lurks behind it the suspicion of downright deceit" (227).

Gorgias's assertion that "nothing is" is an assertion that dividedness is, that incoherency is, that contradiction is, that change is, that irrationality is, that chaos is (all without "being," however), and that *tuchē* laughs at *technē*. Of course, all of this not isness is in direct contradiction to the Eleatic dogma of isness. It is most commonly argued that Gorgias is parodying Parmenides' and Melissus's notions of being (Loenen 177). But this parody is not merely flippant. Gorgias is criticizing the Eleatic's denial of the many-sidedness of reality and of the multiplicity of possibilities—in short, of the irrationality of "Reality," and their overarching faith in *technē* and *logos* to reflect being. Rather than being or order, Gorgias is positing not being as the "order" of the day. We experience not a rational universe, but a polyverse of phenomena. We impose order on it via *logos* via *technē*. We are deceiving ourselves to think that order exists, that unity exists, that rationality exists *a priori*—as the fundamental foundation of reality.

Gorgias's claim that "nothing is" should not be taken (as it is generally and perhaps inevitably taken) as an espousal of nihilism, as an essentially negative worldview. What Gorgias espouses, to the contrary, is an affirmative (non)position. In order to understand Gorgias's apparent negation of Parmenidean ways as an affirmation (rather than as a simple inversion of the binaries being/not being or as a de-negation of Parmenides' primary negation of not being), one must understand the concept of the negative. Perhaps the most famous discussion of the negative is to be found in Theodor Adorno's *Negative Dialectics*. Adorno states that the philosophic enterprise of establishing presence *(esti)*—being and existence—has always been accomplished by way of a negation. Elucidating Adorno's claim, Victor Vitanza writes:

> Both Plato and Aristotle—though with different ends— never defined what a thing *is,* but always by mutual exclusion defined what a thing *is not.* Hence, definition by negation. . . . All is done by difference/exclusion, however, with the sole purpose (quite paradoxically) of groping for ultimate identification/affirmation. Adorno, in his "Meditations On Metaphysics" . . . has made evident just how morally and politically dangerous such strategies can be. Dialectics by negation led, he says, quite logically to Auschwitz: "Genocide is the absolute integration [totality]. It is on its way wherever men [sic] are leveled off . . . until one exterminates them literally, as deviations from the concept of *their total nullity.* Auschwitz confirmed the philosopheme of pure identity as death" (362; emphasis mine). Presence literally discloses itself *to be* death (Metaphysics = death instinct, *thanatos.* Or the will to knowledge = the will to death). ("On Negation" 4)

This will to death is evidenced in all modernist discourses by their absolute dependence on the binary system through which identity is sustained. That is, two opposing terms exist in relation to each other:

good/evil, being/not being, man/woman, philosophy/sophistry. The one exists by way of negating the other, according to the Aristotelian law of noncontradiction: I am this *because* I am not that. Further, this negation of the other denigrates, excludes, and potentially annihilates the other. The modernist enterprise succeeds in establishing its identity and presence by insisting on the absence of the other (not being does not exist), by insisting that the other is defined by a lack. Freud's infamous discussion of the sexes turned on the *a priori* principle that Woman existed insofar as she lacked the male sex organ. The concept of desire as explored in psychoanalytic models (Freudian, Lacanian) also presupposes a lack—desire exists only insofar as it lacks its object of desire. Subjectivity, as constituted by modernist and humanist traditions, is also based on a lack as demonstrated by Hegel's discussion of the master/slave dialectic. Writers such as Nietzsche, Deleuze, Guattari, and Vitanza have focused on the affirmative—not the negative, not a lack—in order to reveal the insidious will to death of the negative (and of all modernist projects). Those who acknowledge the insidious dependence of truth, being, and subjectivity on the negative and who embrace a Gorgianic perspective are often attacked on the grounds that claiming "nothing is" is "just another truth claim." The attack is a reactive one and misses the mark altogether. Gorgias's claim that "nothing is" confuses the binaries *physis/nomos* and being/not being. Untersteiner explains, "Things are, but to predicate true or false of their corresponding manifestations is impossible, because they have no absolute reality as their foundation" (163). Hence, Gorgias is not claiming either that nothing exists "in itself" or that being exists "in itself."

Further, Gorgias argues that even if anything did exist, it would be impossible to know it. Things are, but it is impossible to know them. Knowledge, in the Platonic schema, was reserved for that which was known via the rational deliberations of the mind. Gorgias responds that we never know things "in themselves," truth "in itself," being "in itself." All we know—if knowledge is possible—is *logos*. And this *logos* does not—regardless of the Eleatic insistence—correspond (really or truly or directly) to things in themselves. Gorgias writes, "The one who speaks does not speak [a sound] or a colour, but a word" (quoted in Untersteiner 157). Hence, according to Kerferd, "*logos* . . . is always other than the things themselves" (*Sophistic Movement* 80). *Logos* is thus one among the many faithless phenomena which constitute our world. Kerferd writes:

> Gorgias is introducing a radical gulf between logos and the things to which it refers. Once such a gulf is appreciated we can understand quite easily the sense in which every

logos involves a falsification of the thing to which it has reference—it can never, according to Gorgias, succeed in reproducing as it were *in* itself that reality which is irretrievably *outside* itself. To the extent that it claims faithfully to reproduce reality is no more than deception or *apatē*. Yet this is a claim which all logos appears to make. So all logos is to that extent Deception. (81)

H. D. Rankin explains: "In formulating and uttering a logos we do not express the existent or reality about which the logos intends to communicate. All we express is *logos*" (42).

I would stress at this point that Gorgias's insight is radically different from that of the phenomenologist who would argue that epistemology is human experience. Thus my reading of Gorgias is fundamentally different from, say, that of Bruce Gronbeck, who according to his own "rehabilitation" of Gorgias, claims that Gorgias was a proto-phenomenologist and compares him to the phenomenologist Georges Gusdorf. Gronbeck argues, in "Gorgias on Rhetoric and Poetic: A Rehabilitation," that these men both see language as a miserably illusive and subjective medium in which to order one's own world and to communicate that world to others. And, Gronbeck continues, "both see self-affirmation in spite of the tragedy of the human condition [as] the essential mark of *manhood*" (37; emphasis mine). Gronbeck reveals his humanistic and phenomenology's fundamental belief in the self (and an "affirmation" of the self, again based on the negative), whether it exists *a priori* and is thus "remembered" or created via "life's experiences." The value system remains Platonic with its disparagement of language and its conception of tragedy as being an unfortunate by-product of human existence, rather than, as Gorgias suggests, the very dimension of our (not) being—and it has nothing to do with proving one's manhood or establishing virility, or with controlling *tuchē* or language or Woman. Hence, Gorgias's "playful exercises," Versényi writes, "prove not that rhetoric is untrustworthy and misleading but that, since all human inquiry moves within the realm of opinion where deception is easy, all persuasion [and hence "knowledge"] is a result of the force of eloquence rather than of rational insight" (47).

This brings us to the third part of Gorgias's trilemma: Even if it could be known, it couldn't be communicated. Knowledge is always already rhetorical, an effect of rhetoric. Just as Gorgias has argued that what is could never be known (unmediated) in itself, so too does he argue that what is cannot be communicated (made known) to another. That is: *logos* does not convey what is to another. *Logos* doesn't properly convey or communicate anything but itself. *Logos* refers to itself, or, to state the case in semiotic terms, *logos* is unlimited semiosis. Signs point to other signs, not to reality. Hence, what is is incommunicable. Further, *logos* is incommunicable to itself—as its referential instability precludes stable meaning. Plato accounts for this instability by suggesting this is the result of willfully deceitful and manipulative rhetors who use language to lead audiences away from the truth. Plato theorizes that sophistic uses of language have the purposes of flattering and deceiving hearers and obfuscating the truth, whereas his system of dialectics will produce truth, based on the belief that *logos* (rational, deliberative *logos*) has the function of communicating and revealing being. Gorgias argues that there is no way to get a "grip" on truth [Plato, as we have previously mentioned, argued that without a "grip on truth there can be no genuine art of speaking" (*Phaedrus* 260)]. For "truth" or "what is," according to Gorgias, is not stable, still, or whole. It is not possible to get a grip on flux, on Heraclitus's river. Furthermore, there is no way to get a grip on truth with *logos*. For *logos* only grips (tentatively and loosely) *logos*, not truth in itself. Hence there is no genuine art of speaking.

Nor is there a genuine (real and true) speaker. The speaking subject, rather than speaking truth, is speaking deception. All speakers, Gorgias argues, are fabricators, all are poets and mythmakers, all are sophists and counterfeiters (hence the "Paradox of the Liar").[10] There is no genuine speaker who has mastered truth, who speaks being (unified, coherent, corresponding to truth), nor is there an authentic self who has mastered self, who is being (unified, coherent, and real). Gorgias would argue that rather than human beings, we are human not beings—that is to say, human becomings: selves in flux, in process, in motion, in *kinesis* (see Havelock, *Muse* 41): we are false selves, always already in self-contradiction. This subject in flux is the necessary complement to a fluctuating reality. Gorgias's notion of *kairos* is based on the notion of occasion—of vacillating moments, time, and opportunity—and of the relativity (hence the irrationality) of argument and truth. In short, different rhetorical moments occasion different subjects. This discourse situationality is not to be mistaken for the Platonic notion of matching discourses and souls (as argued in *Phaedrus*), nor for the Aristotelian requirement of assuming a different ethos to match the audience (*Rhetoric* bk. 2), for both these methods assume the control and mastery of the discourse situation lies in the speaker—governed only by exigency and purpose.

On the contrary, Gorgias is suggesting something other than a *technē*. He is not suggesting that one be "true" to the rhetorical situation by adopting the appropriate posture. Rather, he is arguing that the situation, the kairotic moment creates a new subject—a hypocritical subject, from the Greek word *hypokrites*, which was the name of the first actor whose function was to interpret the action of the play to the audience. Of note, originally, the word "hypocrite" had no dissembling connotation. The hypocritical subject interprets what appears to be happening, and is engrossed (indeed, his existence is made possible by the acting) in the events of the stage. The hypocritical subject is what one appears to be. We are nothing in essence, but rather, as Guthrie explains, a "shifting panorama of 'becoming' or appearances" (194). We have no being, no self, to be "true" to, only a "theater" of enacted, performed selves. This theater of selves stands in opposition, in *dissoi logoi*, to the tyranny of being, the slavery to self. For the unified self wears and is enslaved by only one mask—the mask of one, of being, coherent and rational. The unified self is caught in a double bind (not to mention the restricting binds and bondage of rationality). First, the self is enslaved by its requirement to control and to master itself. And second, it is enslaved by its very unity—its fixed, immobile state. The self is enslaved, Richard Lanham writes, in "the nightmarish prison of unchanging essence" (*The Motives of Eloquence* 8). This theater of selves liberates selves from the bondage of self, of the transcendental ego, of phallogocentric discourse, which speaks only by silencing all other voices, all others. Julia Kristeva's version of this theater is the "polyphonic" subject—a heterogeneous subject—a "questionable *subject-in-process*" (*Desire in Language* 135). Michel Foucault's version is the "discursive subject" (as identified in *Order of Things* and *History of Sexuality*).

This polyphonic subject, as it speaks many voices, as it wears many masks, will experience, as does a poet, a "multitude of visions" (Pindar quoted in Untersteiner 111). Lanham prophesies: "If he [man] relinquishes the luxury of a central self, a soul, he gains the tolerance, and usually the sense of humor, that comes from knowing he—and others—not only may *think* differently, but may *be* differently" (*Motives of Eloquence* 5). Thus denying the central self is not an act of cynicism, of annihilation. On the contrary, Lanham continues, "he can resist such centermentalism because he knows that his own capacity to make up comforting illusions is as infinite as the universe he is flung into. Naked into the world he may come, but not without resource" (*Motives of Eloquence* 8).

Deception and *Apatē* in an Extra-Moral Sense

And this very resourceful resource is deception. Untersteiner notes that the word "*apatē*" (deception) represents the creative activity of *logos*. Gorgias argues, "Speech 'has the power to put an end to fear, to remove grief, to instill joy and increase pity'" (quoted in Untersteiner 114). Thus, Untersteiner writes, the function of *logos* is to create "a new situation in the human mind" (114)—the function of *logos* is thus not to communicate truth but to create illusions, to deceive. Untersteiner writes, "Deception [is] the constructive action of . . . a thought-process which creates" (126ff).

Deception stands in contradistinction to the notion that *logos* is truth, transparent and speakable. Gorgias objects to the Platonic and Parmenidean preference for the so-called plain style on the grounds that (1) truth is not—that it "certainly" is not pure and clear; (2) truth cannot be known—that it "certainly" is not self-evident; and (3) truth cannot be communicated—that it "certainly" is not transparent. The speakable is not plain—it is (always already) deception. Hence, within the Gorgianic, rhetorical world, all is deception, all who speak are deceivers; all is illusion—an illusion imposed via *logos*. As Gorgias argues, we can never know things "in themselves." Thus to know is to be deceived. According to Plutarch, Gorgias claimed that whoever has allowed himself to be deceived is wise, for anyone not lacking in sensibility allows himself to be won by the pleasure of the words (Plutarch in Sprague 65). Hence, Gorgias's tragedy of knowledge. Knowledge is possible only through deception, although Socrates (among others) would have us believe otherwise. Socrates would argue that knowledge—true and certain—is apprehended via dialectic. Once apprehended, it would be "seen" to be logical; it would be seen, recognized, and remembered. There is, thus, no need to talk about it, no need to be persuaded of its truth and certainty. Socrates—or at least Plato's Socrates—argues in favor of a real correspondence between a thing in itself and *logos*. Hence knowledge is unproblematic: it speaks for itself. Probable knowledge, or opinion *(doxa)*, on the other hand, does require persuasion. Rhetoric, utilizing the enthymeme, pathos, and (shifting and shifty) *ethos,* has as its *raison d'être* to compel people to believe, and to make a judgment—of past fact, future fact, or present fact—seductive and irresistible. The rhetor, then, often beguiles his audiences, captivates them with the magical and forceful drug of deception. Gorgias would respond that this characterization of the rhetor's performance is also an "accurate" description/prescription of the philosopher's performance. Everybody deceives and everybody is deceived due to the unavoidable ambiguity and irrationality of *logos*. The deception is a function of *logos* not of the rhetor's will.

It is necessary to assuage the modernist's fear that to claim all is deception is to advocate a vulgar immoralism. It appears to do so to the modernist, for the modernist suffers from his epistemology based on the binary system. According to this epistemology, if one claims Deception, one perverts truth; if one claims Deception, one perverts the morality of the polis. However, this reactive position exists only insofar as the binaries truth/falsehood and good/evil exist. In Gorgias's universe, truth and falsehood do not stand in opposition to each other. The etymology of the Greek words "truth" and "falsehood" suggest that this opposition does not exist. Heidegger's *Parmenides* closely examines the Greek word *alētheia* (truth), as does Nicholas Denyer's *Language, Thought, and Falsehood in Ancient Greek Philosophy,* although they employ radically different agendas. In brief, *alētheia* is ordinarily translated as "truth"; however, if we were to translate the word "literally," we would read "unconcealedness." Heidegger extrapolates:

> On the one hand, the word "un-concealedness" directs us to something like "concealedness." What, as regards "un-concealedness," is previously concealed, who does the concealing and how it takes place, when and where and for whom concealment exists, all that remains undetermined. . . . Second, the word "unconcealedness" indicates that something like a suspension or cancellation of concealedness belongs to the Greek experience of the essence of truth. The prefix "un-" corresponds to the Greek ἀ, which grammar calls "α privativum." What kind of *privatio*, deprivation, and taking away is at stake in a privative word-formation depends in each case on what it is that is exposed to the deprivation and impairment. (13–14)

Although this relationship between concealedness and unconcealedness suggests a struggle or dialectical opposition, it nevertheless cohabits the same word for truth. Further, there is no opposing word for "Untruth." Those words which for the Greeks indicated the "False" in no way represented an opposition to *alētheia*. Heidegger continues:

> The opposite of the "unconcealed," the concealed, can easily be found, in name at least, if we simply revoke the α-privativum, annul the cancellation of the concealed, and let it, "the concealed," remain. Terminologically, the crossing out of the α leads to ληϑές. But nowhere do we actually find this word as the name for the false. Instead, the Greeks call the false τὸ ψεῦδος. This word has another stem entirely and another root and accordingly another basic meaning, not directly ascertainable. (20–21)

Neither does *apatē*, or deception, stand in opposition to truth. Untersteiner argues that this is demonstrated by the Muses of which Hesiod writes in the *Theogony* (vv. 27–28). Untersteiner suggests that the affinity between truth and falsehood can be traced to "the twofold genealogy of the Muses who according to one tradition are the daughters of Uranus and Earth, according to another, of Zeus and Mnemosyne. To them, therefore, belongs a position intermediate between the world of the chthonic gods and those of Olympus: they oscillate between the world of irrational mystery . . . *(apate)* and the logical world of the Olympian gods" (109–10). Versényi finds the connection between these two worlds as constitutive of *apatē*. He writes, "when human blindness *(ate)* and *logos* meet, deception *(apate)* results" (46). (Versényi also points out that *peitho, apatē,* and *ate* "are already associated in Aeschylus as the means the gods use—means for good rather than evil" [fn. 41, 46].) Gorgias writes,

> For if all men on all subjects had [both] memory of things past and [awareness] of things present and foreknowledge of the future, speech would not be similarly similar, since as things are now it is not easy for them to recall the past nor to consider the present nor to predict the future. So that on most subjects most men take opinion as counselor to their soul, but since opinion is slippery and insecure it casts those employing it into slippery and insecure successes. ("Encomium of Helen" 11)

This is precisely why Plato condemns deception: not because it is contrary to truth, as its binary opposite, but because it is operative in the realm of *doxa,* not a realm contrary to truth, but a shadowy realm that has no being—no essence, no fixedness, no certainty. For Plato, truth and falsehood don't even exist in the same dimension of being.

Nevertheless, despite the etymological and mythological facts which suggest otherwise, Gorgias's acknowledgment of the role played by *apatē* in the constitution of *doxa* is the reason why Plato—and even Aristotle—condemned Gorgias as "immoral" and as a "corrupting" influence on the youth of Athens. The Sophists were accused of trickery, false persuasion, artifice, and deception for making the worse case seem the better. Grote writes that the philosophical tradition has elaborated on Plato's charge and has asserted that the Sophists "poisoned and demoralised, by corrupt teaching, the Athenian moral character, so that it became degenerate at the end of the Peloponnesian war, compared with what it had been in the time of [Miltiades] and Aristeides" (174). To this charge, Grote responds with two arguments: first, as has been noted previously, the sophists were "not a sect or school with common doctrines or method: they were a profession with strong individual peculiarities" (174); and, secondly, Grote states outright, "Athens, at the close of the Peloponnesian war, was not more corrupt than Athens in the days of Miltiades and Aristeides" (175), providing for the reader several representative incidences of previous corruption. Grote also furthers his argument by suggesting that it was in the Sophists' best interest to send forth "accomplished and virtuous" students; if not, why would fathers continue to send their sons to the Sophists, and why would the Sophists continue to amass great fortunes (202)?

Seduction and the (Im)Possibility of Will

Regarding Gorgias's epistemology, Enos stresses that Gorgias was greatly influenced by the Pythagorean philosophy of opposites, which defines the universe as constitutive of and functioning as a "synthetic and harmonious proportion of opposites" as well as by the sophistic notion of *dissoi logoi,* or dissociation of concepts (44).[11] This viewpoint is in contrast to Plato's conception of the universe as an ideal world of "immutable nature, which when discovered, would reveal certain knowledge" (Enos 44). Now this notion of Pythagorean opposites is to be distinguished from the philosophic binaries which sustain Platonic thought. As we have discussed, Plato's "essences" are dependent on negation of one pole of the binary; on reducing the conflict between the two by annihilating the other. This other, this that which is not, is an opposition in denial. The Pythagorean doctrine suggests that, in contradistinction, "opposites" cohabit and exist simultaneously, in conflict and in harmony. Untersteiner explains:

> This Pythagorean line of thought taught that "nothing is simple and pure, but earth has a portion of fire, and fire of water and wind . . . and thus also the beautiful a portion of the ugly, and the just of the unjust, and other things likewise" [*Iambl. Vit. Pyth.,* 130]. The last examples, beautiful and ugly, just and unjust, correspond to the categories used by sophistic philosophy when it was necessary to illustrate the properties of καιρός, in order "to make the same thing, *according to circumstances,* appear either beautiful or ugly, just or unjust"; this was explicitly said in that Pythagorean teaching which explained the rhetorical method of creating either meaning by a use of the theory of opposites, which justifies καιρός. (120)

The rhetorical concept of *kairos* (the opportune moment), then, suggests that what is (just, right, true, for example) does not precede the rhetorical moment, but rather is a function of a particular moment, a particular rhetorical occasion. Although one could speculate as to how a rhetor could respond kairotically to the kairotic moment or, indeed, how he could teach his students to do so (see, for example, John Poulakos' "*Kairos* in Gorgias' Rhetorical Compositions" and Phillip Sipiora's "The Ancient Concept of *Kairos*"), here I am less interested in mastering the kairotic moment (subjecting it to *technē*) than in understanding how the kairotic moment seduces us, renders itself unmasterable, and challenges our conceptions of will and agency—rhetorical and otherwise. To begin, we must reconfigure our understanding of temporality as a trajectory of causes and effects. Kairotic moments entail, according to Eric Charles White, "a conception of temporality according to which the flow of time is understood as a succession of discontinuous occasions rather than as duration or historical continuity. That is, instead of viewing the present occasion as continuous with a causally related sequence of events, *kairos* regards the present as unprecedented, as a moment of decision, a moment of crisis" (14). Likewise, to "act" (rhetorically or otherwise) in a kairotic moment, presumes that the rhetor/subject is not a causal agent. Rather, one "acts" as the kairotic moment makes possible.

Kairos, the opportune moment, when something happens despite the ambiguity and irresolvable conflicts: here, then, lies the possibility for action, the condition for choice, which was—prior to the kairotic moment—unavailable. This view problematizes the post-Enlightenment notions of will and agency that presuppose a unified, rational self who first deliberates and then acts from knowledge. Additionally this challenges our contemporary belief that moral and ethical behavior is a function of choosing (after rational deliberation) some action in the face of being free to do otherwise. These notions are not ahistorical although we presume that they are (see Susanne Bobzien). Our humanist tradition predisposes us to assume that this conception of will is what, in fact, makes us human as opposed to animal. But a pre-Enlightenment, pre-humanist Gorgianic perspective presumes that action (and ethical action) is not an effect of the rational deliberation of knowledge. Hamlet, as I will discuss in the next chapter, epitomizes the humanist subject who, enmeshed in tragic conflict, is rendered impotent to act because of his endless deliberations, and who, by and through his deliberations, allows the kairotic moment to escape unnoticed. Untersteiner writes:

> "I know the irreconcilable conflicts and yet I act": this is tragic action. And in every action—which cannot be defined as other than tragic, given the nature of Being and Knowledge—it must nevertheless be thought that a decision is carried out, even if not always consciously, because the power

of one of the two alternatives may have been such as—
provisionally—to cancel out the other, as in the case of
Helen. . . . Epistemology, when it is transferred from its own
proper theoretical plane to the realm of the practical, becomes will, decision, which was realised in a καιρός endowed with the property of breaking up the cycle of the
antithesis and creating something new, irrational: that epistemological process defined as "deception," "persuasion,"
the power of which lies in the imposition of one of the two
alternatives. (161)

Note, though, that the rhetorical process at work here is not an orator
who deceives an audience. The kairotic moment here is characterized as
a seduction which "imposes itself equally on the seducer and the seduced," explains Charles Eric White. "That is," he continues, "in order
to achieve success, the orator as seducer must be 'seduced' in turn by
the occasion of speech. Persuasion depends on self-effacement, on ac-
ceding to the terms laid down by the circumstances confronting the
speaker" (38–39).

Seduction and/as Helen, therefore, must be seen as a third term—
beyond the active/passive binary by which philosophic will is praised
and by which seductive strategies are condemned. Wayne Brockriede,
for example, in "Arguers as Lovers," identifies three rhetorical stances:
"rape," "seduction," and "love." He distinguishes between the first
two stances by arguing that whereas "the rapist conquers by force of
argument, the seducer operates through charm or deceit" (4). And,
finally, he distinguishes the first two stances from the third, "love":
"Whereas the rapist and seducer see a unilateral relationship toward
the victim, the lover sees a bilateral relationship with a lover" (5), echoing Socrates' pronouncements of the intersubjective quality of the dialectic. Once again, Brockriede's characterization of the various rhetorical possibilities emanate from the rhetor as the causal agent of the
rhetorical moment. And the outcomes of the rhetorical intercourse are
dependent on the rhetor's intentions and postures vis-à-vis the audience—even if it is a bilateral relationship.

Seduction, as all other metaphysical constructs, has been constituted heretofore across the passive/active binary. That which is active
is the will; the passive is the will-less. To seduce, then, is to impose one's
will on others by means of artifice and deceit—to unload a sham, a
pretense, or an illusion—that is, to merely appear, rather than to be.
Seduction, thus defined, is synonymous with abduction—although not,
perhaps, abduction by brute force. The dichotomy subject/object is
clear, as are its attendant binaries: man/woman, victor/victim. In fact,

the act of seduction-as-abduction secures the sovereignty of the subject as it negates the object; maintains the masculinity of the Man as it ensures the passivity of Woman; proclaims the victory of the victor as it dominates the victim; asserts the presence of the phallus as it penetrates the lack. Subjectivity is thus defined in an arena of violence, within an economy of domination, as a virile stance (see Dover on subordinate and dominant positions).

Socrates presents dialectic as an erotic discourse situation (in *Phaedrus,* for example). But his notion of dialectic—even if characterized as a bilateral scenario—disregards the will and desire of the other, the interlocutee. Using Brockriede's categories, this troublesome state of affairs suggests that the philosophic search for knowledge requires the rape of the other. The Socratic method of *elenchos,* or cross-examination and refutation, is meant to expose the inadequacies of the other's argument until "the other speaker *concedes* the point"—Socrates' point (Vickers 91). Vickers continues, "Socrates never allows his opponents to go back over his arguments critically, but forces them to accept Socrates' terms and Socrates' tempo—as Socrates puts it, 'in order that the argument may be carried forward consecutively' (*Gorgias* 454c)" (94). Socrates' dialectic is a game played to win, until the other admits defeat. The syllogism propels one, with its sheer, brute, and logical force, unwillingly forward from minor premise to major premise to conclusion. The outcome of the dialectical act is not negotiable; but rather, it is predetermined and necessarily foregone. The conclusion is forced upon us. We cannot refuse its violent power. We are bound by the "violence of the logical sequence" of the syllogism to submit (Untersteiner 118). As we have previously noted, the dialogue *Phaedrus* takes place near the spot where Boreas abducted Oreithyia (228), just as Socrates, likewise, will abduct Phaedrus. Step by step, question by question, Phaedrus is forced to submit to Socrates. Thus Socrates, despite his talk of the noble love of the philosopher, is not demonstrating the process of seduction; he's demonstrating the methodology of a ravisher.

Is the speech act—as an act of the will—then, "abduction by force"? Does virility demand a victim? Apparently—in an economy of domination—just as the woman (the other) is relevant to the sex act only insofar as she is victimized, the audience (the other) is likewise relevant to the rhetorical act only insofar as it is passive. Thus the other is defined by its passivity, its femininity, its lack of will. Heraclitus spoke of his audiences as "well-fed cows" and "sleep walkers" with no "power of understanding" (Freeman 30). Plato's dialogues typically feature Socrates' audiences as stupid "yes men," who are led against their will by Socrates' condescending line of questioning. They are, like the Greek slave boy in the *Meno, idiots savants*—more idiot than savant, however. Aristotle is downright patronizing about his audiences' abilities. He assumes (as does Plato) an audience of "untrained thinkers" who "cannot take in at a glance a complicated argument, or follow a long chain of reasoning" (*Rhetoric* 1357a). They are unable to do so, Aristotle tells us more than once, because they are uneducated. Not only do they have a want of education but, also, a "want of intelligence" (1395b). Elsewhere he refers to the "weak-minded tendency" of the hearer (1415b). Rather than reasoning truth, Aristotle snidely argues, man is blindly, helplessly led to accept the orator's truth.

Thus if a man wants to abduct a woman—like Helen, for example— he can count on her "*willing* submission" (Guthrie 192; emphasis mine) due, paradoxically, to her lack of will. To the philosopher king, they are all, indeed, slaves. This is the dialectical economy of the master/ slave, which sustains the truth, the subject—the master of the world of appearances—who enslaves the other. This is the violence of the subject—to cast all others as ideal objects of manipulation, of desire, of knowledge. And, Baudrillard reminds us, "we know that the only ideal object is a dead one" (*Fatal Strategies* 105). In place of this abduction, Baudrillard suggests a new sense of seduction: "Seduction against terror: these are the stakes" (*Fatal Strategies* 51).

If we presume that rhetoric is a theory and praxis of the good man speaking well and that seduction is a theory and praxis of the evil man speaking deceitfully—that is, that the rhetorical act is preceded by and defined in terms of the subject—then we are subject to the active/passive binary that sustains the will to truth. If, on the contrary, we attempt to bracket this binary, we will have read Gorgias's "Encomium of Helen" in the middle voice, thereby confusing rhetorical will.

Tracing the probable causes for Helen's journey to Troy, Gorgias's "Encomium" offers four possibilities: "For either by will of Fate and decision of the gods and vote of Necessity did she do what she did, or by force reduced or by words seduced [or by love possessed]" (6). Gorgias's text itself is kairotic as it asks us to participate in the choice of the causes, but we cannot will a choice. Gorgias's "Encomium" defends Helen's actions on all counts, but this defense, Versényi argues, is a pretext for his argument concerning "the nature and power of *logos*" (44). Although Gorgias states that *logos* is a "powerful lord" ("Encomium" 8) comparable in force to "necessity" (12) or divine fate, violence, and *erōs,* we are never certain where or what *logos* is. Further, although Gorgias's text pretends to offer us four neatly packaged and delineated causes or reasons for Helen's seduction, they keep slipping into each other. The categories cannot hold. Therefore, even though via *logos* Gorgias can defend Helen, his *logos* continually dissembles itself. Hence, to claim that the text is a pretext to argue the power of *logos* is

not to—once again—reassert the will/will-less, active/passive binaries. *Logos* is not the *causal* agent of Helen's seduction any more than
Paris—as rhetorical agent—is. This is not to say that *logos* is not seductive nor is it to say that Helen is not seduced in and through *logos*. On
the contrary, *logos* is seductive because *it* is—as is Helen—the nonbeing of being and the being of nonbeing. James L. Porter argues that this
points to the "*limitations* of language, not to its powers" (285), challenging those such as Charles Segal who suggest that Gorgias is positing
an autonomous *logos* as an "independent external power which forces
the hearer to do its will" (quoted in Porter 269). But such a characterization—*logos* as lacking—makes sense only within an either/or
framework: either *logos* is "incapacitated" or it is all-powerful. It is neither will-full nor will-less. And this is what makes it seductive.

Porter argues convincingly that Gorgias's "Encomium" reveals an
unpersuasive *logos*. If, as Porter writes, Gorgias was positing a *logos*
that was powerful precisely because of its persuasive capacity, then why
did Gorgias create such a "glaringly unpersuasive" text? "Gorgias's individual arguments in his best-preserved writings, including even those
that concern persuasion, tend to unravel one another" (Porter 270),
producing "exasperation and bafflement more than any other response
in his audience" (269). Specifically, Gorgias organizes his *logos* or his
speech in terms of four possible defenses for Helen. Although he states
them as separate reasons, his *logos* continually confuses them. That is,
the more clearly he states his *logos,* the more obfuscated his *logos* becomes. Porter's careful reading suggests that

> Gorgias manages, through a never-spoken logic of entail-
> ments and verbal repetitions, to equate without quite con-
> flating necessity, violence, persuasion, and *eros,* by "show-
> ing" in effect that each of the terms may be viewed as an
> aspect of the remaining terms: (divine) necessity is a kind of
> violence; persuasion is a form of seduction; but *eros* can be
> violent and "necessary," like divinity and persuasion; etc. . . .
> His four alternatives dissolve into a series of approximations
> and analogies. (274)

His *logos* is slippery.

Indeed, we are never sure what *logos* is or where it is. Gorgias's use
of *logos* resonates with polyvalence, echoing, of course, the multiple
significations of the word in circulation at the time (Liddell and Scott's
dictionary entry runs three columns). But, in Gorgias's brief text, we
experience this slippage repeatedly. He begins the "Encomium" using *logos* as "speech" with the virtue of "truth" *(alētheia)* (1). He soon

introduces "reasoning" *(logismon)* into his *logos* (2). He defines poetry as *logos* with meter (9). "Sacred incantations" can be sung with words *(logon)* (10), just as in paragraph 12, *hymnos*, or "song," is rendered as *logos*. Persuasion can be "added" *(prosiousa*—go near, approach) to *logos* (13). Yet in paragraph 12, persuasion is conflated with *logos*—or at least not identified as an "additive" to logos, but rather *logos* itself. These are just a few examples, and a cursory view of the text gives credence to the claim that Helen is a pretext for a discussion of *logos*. As John Poulakos argues, Helen is an analog for rhetoric, but as Gorgias's characterization of Helen and/as *logos* demonstrates, neither are precisely what we take them to be. They are slippery and multiple and have no single or proper identity. Just as Helen has her phantom and just as Gorgias's defense of Helen is the defense of her phantom (according to some ancient poets, it was the phantom who left, not Helen herself; it was the phantom for whom men fought), Gorgias's defense of *logos* is the defense (or, rather, the praise) of the phantom quality of *logos*. "*Logos*," then, writes Porter, "is situated somewhere in their midst, a troubling, nagging *question* mark, like Helen" (291).

Why then, we might ask (if *logos* is the perpetually unanswerable question, the mark of impossibility), does Gorgias speak of "false" *logos* and why does he claim that the virtue of *logos* is truth? The beginning sentence of the "Encomium" states the particular virtues of a city, of a body, of a soul, of an action, and of a speech *(logos)*, stating that what is "becoming" to each. He uses the word *kosmos* (good order, decency) here, and the word *akosmos* (disorder, indecency) for its opposite. Though as his very text demonstrates, *logos* exceeds good order and thereby goes beyond the order of decency. Likewise, in his "defense" of Helen, Gorgias's *logos* disassembles and disorders itself. Gorgias cannot be decent and tell the "Truth," although he claims that this is his goal: "It is the duty of one and the same man both to speak the needful rightly and to refute [the unrightfully spoken]. . . . For my part, by introducing some reasoning into my speech, I wish to free the accused of blame and, having reproved her detractors as prevaricators and proved the truth, to free her from their ignorance" (2). His defense cannot grant her decency; his *logos* "plays" with her reputation (21). *Logos* is the prevaricator. Once again we have the paradox of the liar.

Logos then—by way of a Gorgianic perspective—is a "powerful lord" because of its seductive ability to lead us and Helen astray—not because it is a will-full agent and Helen a will-less woman, but because *logos* and/as Helen is neither active nor passive. Our relationship to rhetoric then must be refigured in the middle voice. According to Eric Charles White, "The middle voice in fact disappeared as an identifiable linguistic form during antiquity when, as it were, a 'hardening' of grammatical categories led to its replacement by the fixed opposition of the active/passive dichotomy" (53). Jean-Pierre Vernant, White notes, "has remarked that the disappearance of the middle voice coincides with the gradual emergence during the Classical period 'of a vocabulary of the will . . . precisely the idea of the human subject as agent, source of actions,' the idea, in other words, that the subject authors rather than participates in its experience" (53). This is the challenge for rhetorical theory and praxis: to refigure itself as seduction, beyond the active/passive binary, which has delimited rhetors and audiences, and beyond the truth/deception binary, which has held rhetoric hostage to metaphysical demands (see also Vitanza, *Negation* 284).

Seduction for Baudrillard is reminiscent of Gorgias's *apatē*. For Baudrillard does not oppose seductive appearances to reality. To do so would be to engage in the dialectical impulse, which does not figure in the play of seduction. For as Gorgias plays deception against deception, he dissolves the binary of truth and deception.[12] Likewise, as Baudrillard plays appearance against appearance, he renders the age-old dichotomy of appearance and reality obsolete. Both Gorgias and Baudrillard suggest that all is surface, that there is no essential nor latent truth. According to Baudrillard:

> Illusion is not false, for it doesn't use false signs; it uses senseless signs, signs that point nowhere. This is why it deceives and disappoints our demand for meaning, but it does so enchantingly. This is what the image does in general, more subtly than the real, since it has only two dimensions and is therefore always more seductive. . . . Seduction is also falser than the false, since it uses signs, which are already semblances, to make them lose their meaning. . . . Someone who has never lost the meaning of a word or a look cannot know what this loss is, that of abandoning oneself to the total illusion of signs, to immediate control by appearances, that is, going beyond the false into the absolute abyss of artifice. (*Fatal Strategies* 52)

The notion of "false signs" or deceptive signs only exists insofar as one presupposes "correct signs"—as did a number of early philosophers. We may as post-Saussureans have lost our belief in the correctness of names, but we have not, according to Nietzsche, lost our faith in grammar. That is, we have not lost our faith in that which is—which is: the Enlightenment's fundamental assertion of the subject, of the "I who speaks," who acts from a position of authority over the predicate. It is this faith that Baudrillard's notion of seduction absolves us of. For "[t]here is no active or passive mode in seduction, no subject or object, no interior or exterior: seduction plays on both sides, and there is no frontier separating them" (*Seduction* 81).

Seduction confuses the boundaries between to seduce and to be seduced. There is no master position from which one seduces; thus there are no victors nor victims. Because there are no subjects, there is not the accompanying terror and violence that sustains subjectivity in the realm of seduction. But, in contradistinction, in the realm of being, it is precisely this terror—the terrorization of the subject—that must be denied in order to protect us from the truth: that is, from the non-truth of the truth. Gorgias prefaces Nietzsche's well-worn words: "What is truth? a mobile army of metaphors, metonyms, anthropomorphisms, in short, a sum of human relations which were poetically and rhetorically heightened, transferred, and adorned. . . . Truths are illusions about which it has been forgotten that they are illusions, worn-out metaphors without sensory impact . . . " ("On Truth and Lying in an Extra-Moral Sense" 250). This is seduction—not the will-to-annihilate that goes by the name of seduction—but seduction in the Baudrillardian sense: it is a forgetting of the forgottenness of truth's illusions, truth's metaphors. It is a "liquidation of the metaphor" (*Fatal Strategies* 121), letting flow what has been represented and thus repressed (but which has no truth nor depth of its own): *apatē*. This illusoriness of what is is what is unbearable, and thus—to those who refuse to seduce and to be seduced—remains un/bare-able.

On Subjects, Objects, and Victimization

The case against Helen has been tried, retried, disputed, reputed, contested, and retested. Helen has been the subject of deliberation and debate. But she has rarely been represented as a subject of desire.[13] More often than not the arguments are as follows: If she was abducted, she was the object first of Theseus's desire and then of Paris's. If she was seduced, she was compelled by *erōs*, by Aphrodite, or by desire in language. Thus represented, Helen is Woman *par excellence*. For regardless of the charge, and regardless of the jury's verdict—whether she is found guilty due to seduction or guilty due to abduction—Helen is still charged with passivity. Whether accused as object or defended as object, she remains sentenced to bear the weight of the representation.

My purposes here are not to resolve the judicial dispute: Did Helen will or was she merely willing? Was she a subject or merely an object? Was she given in seduction or taken by abduction? For the case is already determined. She is both. Flip a coin to decide: heads you lose, tails you lose. For subject and object are merely two sides of the same philosophical coin. Thus the case against Helen is hardly an agonistic struggle. Hardly a game, really. For the toss is too predictable, too probable. It makes for a very heavy toss indeed. Helen is so overdetermined, so saturated with meaning, that she can hardly move. I would prefer to cast Helen's fate with a throw of the die. That is, to challenge Helen, the Woman with the rhetorical figure, to flow beyond the false dichotomy of subject/object.

The subject/object, active/passive, Man/Woman dichotomy, as I have previously argued, represents one as master, as possessor of the will, wielder of the phallus, and represents the other as Other. Woman as other, as passive object, sustains relationships between Man and Man, and Man and his self. Figured as other, as Non-Man, Woman endows Man with identity. Woman as the overdetermined—yet empty—sign, refers man to himself, refers the subject to its I, and thereby evokes the pleasure of the narcissistic gaze. According to Teresa de Lauretis, woman is posited "as at once the object and the foundation of representation, at once telos and origin of man's desire and of his drive to represent it. . . . In this context subjectivity . . . [is] inevitably defined in relation to a male subject, that is to say, with man as the sole term of reference" (*Alice Doesn't* 8).

Opposed to Woman's passive role, Man in the subject position possesses an authochthonic power as origin and source of production, of reproduction. Luce Irigaray writes: "The point being that man is *the* procreator, that sexual *production-reproduction* is referable to his 'activity' alone, to his 'pro-ject' alone. Woman is nothing but the receptacle that passively receives his *product*" (*Speculum* 18). As the proper one, Man's "activity," his (re)production, authorizes him to designate himself as "master-proprietor" to claim author/ity and property rights. He will signify via his signature and, Irigaray writes, "will mark the product of copulation with *his own name*" (23). His act of naming ensures boundaries by defining, delimiting, and fixing the other. He must "fix" the other, in order to assure himself that he will not suffer castration, that he will not suffer from a lack of proper identity. By stabilizing the other, he attempts to stop the infinite regress of the mirror's empty reflection.

Agency and free will—the will to produce, the will to represent—are thus revealed as the fetishes of man. Eric White in his *Kaironomia* writes, "the desire to master one's self as a controllable object by mastering the Other as a subservient complement" is "equivalent to the desire to finalize the meaning of a text" (83). And, I would add, the desire to finalize the meaning of a text is equivalent to the desire to produce a meaning for all texts, for all things. The master's will ensures that all signified are fixed/fixed up with a signifier in an attempt to stabilize his world, his word, his self.

Roland Barthes writes "*Everything signifies:* by this proposition, I entrap myself, I bind myself in calculations" (*A Lover's Discourse* 63). Thus, the will to power as the will to signify is equivalent to the master/slave mentality which signifies a will to death. According to Gilles Deleuze, the "mania for representing, for being represented, for getting oneself represented; for having representatives and representeds: this is the mania that is common to all slaves" (*Nietzsche* 81). The will to mastery, the will to represent, constantly attempts to master, to dominate, and to appropriate the real by "materializing [it] by force" (Baudrillard, *Seduction* 34). According to Baudrillard, "Everything is to be produced, everything is to be legible, everything is to become real, visible, accountable; everything is to be transcribed in relations of force, systems of concepts or measurable energy; everything is to be said, accumulated, indexed and recorded" (34–35). To produce is to count, to codify, to systematize, to homogenize, to regulate via *technē.* Unable to be a man of action (rather than merely of dialectical reaction), he produced a plan of action. He (Plato) mis/took *aretē* for *technē.*

Will, according to de Lauretis, like "Desire, like symbolization, is a property of men, property in both senses of the word: something men own, possess, and something that inheres in men, like a quality" (*Alice Doesn't* 20). So writes Irigaray: "Property, ownership, and self-definition are the attributes of the father's production. They define the work of the father 'as such.' To be. To own. To be one's own. Properties." (*Speculum* 300). Thus the desire of Man is based on an economy of the selfsame,[14] the proper, property, and profitability. It is a limited economy of appropriation in which all things figure in terms of exchange or use value. Within this economy, Woman—figured as a lack—has value in that she ensures the function of the negative. That is, in a dialectical move, she as other sustains Man's positive identity. The subject, posited by way of an appropriation, a violation, a negation, is the master enslaved by his other. Thus subjectivity and objectivity are both entrapped in the master/slave dialectic that is bound and weighted with the gravity of *ressentiment* and bad conscience: saturated by negation, guilt, responsibility, and betrayal; overdetermined, overproduced, oversignifed, overconstituted. This is subjectivity: to be kept in a state of permanent guilt (Clément 46). Can Helen then ever be exonerated? No, for there is no innocence in the master/slave dialectic. Guilt figures as the constitutive factor for both master and slave; guilt produces both subject and object.

Rhetoric, Guilt, and Sacrifice

From Protagoras and Aristotle to neo-Aristotelian Habermas, rhetoric has been "fixed" as a *genre;* that is, it has been understood (and thus appropriated) as political discourse. Aristotle writes that rhetoric "come[s] under politics, which is the *architechne* or master art of the good for man" (*Ethics* 1.1.1094b3–4). Likewise, rhetoric has been defined and delimited as a particular kind of epistemic speech act with persuasion as its end, manifesting itself as judicial, deliberative, or epideictic oratory. The speech act, then, is the sacrificial ritual which maintains the polis and secures the community. Analogously, the orator—the speaking subject—has been ordered with gendered identity. It is my argument that by being subjected to gender, the self is sacrificed upon the altar of the polis, offered in the name of solidarity, order, harmony, peace. The gendered self, then, becomes the burnt offering: overcooked, overdetermined, overcoded.[15]

The ritual act of sacrifice—as studied by anthropologists and ethnographers such as Marcel Mauss and Claude Lévi-Strauss, and as explored by René Girard and Georges Bataille—has as its purpose, in the words of Girard, "to restore harmony to the community, to reinforce the social fabric" (8). Sacrifice is an act of violence committed in the guise of the sacred—thus legitimated and justified—as the fundamental gesture to create community. The so-called sacrificial crisis which precedes the sacrifice is characterized by a general state of parataxis—that is, by a general state of anarchy—or at least by the threat of it. The sacrificial crisis manifests itself as a loss of hierarchy, as the ordering system has become unclear, and thus initiates the ritual sacrifice in order to restore the order of the Great Chain of Being (Lovejoy)—those hierarchical ties that bind being into specific *topoi* and terministic grids required for community and communication. Some other must be excluded—symbolically or literally killed—as the prerequisite for harmony.

This is the sick logic of the polis, which manifests itself microcosmically in the logic of the subject. That is, the sacrificial gesture required to create community—the identification of the many—is the same gesture required to constitute self-identity. I am referring, of course, to the master/slave dialectic in which identity is sustained only via the negation of—the sacrifice of—the other. In this way, the political subject and the speaking subject (are these not substitute terms, for citizens of the polis are granted both the vote and the voice?) gain identity—recognition by the polis as legitimate—that is to say, as a proper subject, a profitable subject. The economy of identity is a limited economy of appropriation in which all things figure in terms of exchange or use value. Within this economy, gender serves as the mark, as the inscription of the other, and thus her truth value, her exchange value, is as the negative. That is, in a dialectical move, she as other is sacrificed in order to sustain the subject's positive, proper, and present identity. The subject requires a constant scapegoat to temporarily assuage and redeem. Sending the scapegoat out into the wilderness, spending "the accursed share" (Bataille) is not a sending without a return, not an expenditure without investment. The return is presence and identity; the investment is order and control. The sacrifice is the gift that keeps on giving back.

The currency of the polis is the name—the proper name. The sacrifice is done in the name of and for the name of the name. Thus the polis is maintained by creating subjects who are self-identical and, most importantly, who answer to their name. A "proper" name is one which returns to itself, to its origins, and to its debts. This answerability serves the consumptive appetite of the polis. Valuable subjects are those who prove worthy of the name—the name of the father—just as products are identified with their brand name, indeed are substituted for the name itself as in Frigidaire or Xerox (Baudrillard, "The System of Objects" 17). The individual is the goat banned from the city limits never to return; but it is the name which comes back—predictably, accountably (Derrida, *Post Card* 98). Indeed, the subject is spent, as Iphigenia, so that once dead, she—or rather, her name—can be remembered, each time with no less violence and with no more justification than for the glory of the state. Derrida writes, "The name is made to do without the life of the bearer, and is therefore always somewhat the name of someone dead" (*Post Card* 39). That is, identity is always somewhat a state of death—or in Nietzsche's terminology a "will-to-death." Identity—conflated with the name—is a determinable, terminal state of being: a commodification, an objectification, a thingification that can be counted on, signed, sealed, and delivered. Jean-Luc Nancy writes, "I am constituted in absolute self-possession, in unlimited self-presence. What is thus required is sacrifice, the production of the object as reject, even if this object were its own subject" ("The Unsacrificeable" 35).

It is this economy of the sacrifice that I would like to address—but with an illegible address, and certainly with no return address. The polis and, by extension, identity operate according to the postal principle—a logic, called into question by Derrida, of sending and returning, a sacrifice made according to, in Bataille's words, a "restricted economy." This economy is played out in the *fort/da* game that Freud's grandson plays with the spool—or rather, in Freud's interpretation of that game—a game of presence and absence, a game of sending in which presence and absence is controlled. Derrida writes:

> What the grand(father-)speculator [Freud] calls the complete game, thus, would be the game in its two phases, in the duality, the re-doubled duality of its phases: disappearance/re-turn, absence/re-presentation. And what binds the game

> to itself is the *re-*of the return, the additional turn of repeti-
> tion and re-appearance. He insists upon the fact that the
> greatest quantity of pleasure is in the second phase, in the
> *re-*turn which orients the whole, and without which nothing
> would come. *Revenance,* that is, returning, orders the entire
> teleology. Which permits one to anticipate that this opera-
> tion, in its so-called complete unity, will be entirely handed
> over to the authority of the PP [the Postal Principle]. Far
> from being checked by repetition, the PP also seeks to recall
> itself in the repetition of appearing, of presence, of represen-
> tation, and, as we shall see, via a repetition that is mastered,
> that verifies and confirms the mastery in which it consists
> (which is also that of the PP). The mastery of the PP would
> be none other than mastery in general. (*Post Card* 317)

The postal principle controls what gets sent, and guarantees that
everything has a price. It requires a destination, an address, an addres-
sor, and an addressee. It controls, orders, and situates the sender and
the receiver in findable places: for example, with zip codes, first with
five-digit codes and then with nine, and now with e-mail, to economize,
to make the sending more efficient, to help it reach its destination more
promptly. What would the post office do with a letter that was not
coded? What would the post office do with a letter that had no stamp?
No address? It would be impossible to "send" it. The logic of the post
office requires an address, a destination. The letter would either be re-
turned to the sender or discarded, sentenced to the dead-letter office
with some Bartleby character, whose job it is to try to make meaning of
the letter—that is, to try to endow the letter with some exchange value.
For the letter without destination has no exchange value, just as the
subject without teleology has no exchange value. This is the sacrifice,
the gift, given according to a restricted economy, and one that demands
a return, a profit. If you are not going anywhere—if you are not up-
wardly mobile—you have failed the American Dream, the fantasy constructed by the polis, to protect us from the real.

But what of a "general economy"—one without reserve? This is
not what is being sent/said here. Such notions of total expenditure, or
of "potlatch," fail to escape the profit margin. The potlatch is a mecha-
nism to reinstate the hierarchy, to once again establish the power relations, just as ostentatious displays of luxury are gestures of the ruling
class. Furthermore, the potlatch is used to instill obligation and to impose a debt—to forge a memory. This "general economy" is not without destination or return.

What remains unnameable is not the sacrifice of the subject, or the
sacrifice of gender, but the sacrifice of sacrifice, that is, the gift that is

beyond the postal principle, and thus beyond the identity principle.[16] Such a gift, Derrida writes, "begins with a destination without address, the direction cannot be situated in the end" (*Post Card* 29).[17] Such a gift is beyond the payment principle—it is a "duty-free" (281) agency, genre, or gender. Such a gift is not an investment, but a risk (Baudrillard, "On Seduction" 162). It is the "gift as throw of the dice" (*Post Card* 130), as a chance sending of one's self, of one's message, as a calling beyond all names (130), a tossing beyond all genders.

What rhetoric would send without destination—would not find its *telos* in a sacrificial speech act; what rhetoric would "forget" its address, its addressee? Such a rhetoric has no debt to communication or community or to the violence that is constitutive of identity—specifically gendered identity. Such a rhetoric we call "sending." Heidegger writes "A giving which gives only its gift, but in the giving holds itself back and withdraws, such a giving we call sending" (*On Time and Being* 8).

Sending Gorgias: The Rhetorical Figure of Woman

In order to send Gorgias, one must "forget" one's self as a modern subject. The modern subject, bolstered by Platonic insistence that reason and *logos* exist as the *a priori* foundation and referent point for truth, has constructed a will (based on the negative) that assumes it is to master knowledge, rather than to be seduced by it. Early Greek thinkers (often including Plato, despite himself) sustained a different relation to knowledge (Nietzsche, *Philosophy in the Tragic Age of the Greeks;* Heidegger, *Early Greek Thinking*). Richard Palmer writes, "the ancient Greeks, saw their thinking as a part of being itself. . . . Knowledge was not something that they acquired as a possession but something in which they participated, allowing themselves to be directed and even possessed by their knowledge" (64–65). This conception of knowledge confuses the binary of will and will-less, of seduction and abduction. It is this conception of subjectivity, this proto-postmodernist notion of subjectivity, of which Gorgias speaks through and by Helen.

The rhetoric of Gorgias seeks to challenge the comfortable straw woman argument that grounds Parmenidean, Platonic, and subsequent Western thought and subjectivity. Following Poulakos's lead, it is my argument that an *analogical* reading of Gorgias's "Encomium of Helen" provides insight into Gorgias's rhetorical purposes. Gorgias's argument, however, exonerates neither Helen nor rhetoric as neither subject nor as object of will, for to do so would be to merely reestablish philosophy's terms. That is, in the "Encomium of Helen," Gorgias characterizes *logos* as he does Helen: neither are exactly what we presume them to be. Gorgias begins his "Encomium" by calling attention to Helen's "univocal and unanimous" bad reputation (2). Because not all poets condemned Helen, as Gorgias has stated, we are immediately confronted with Helen's doubleness and with Gorgias's duplicity in representing her. She has been condemned, and yet she has also already been defended (in the *Iliad* and by the poet Stesichorus, for example). Likewise, Gorgias claims that "it is not unclear, not even to a few" that Helen was from divine parentage (Leda and Zeus). Yet, in the very next sentence, he points to an alternate myth regarding Helen's paternity (Tyndareus—a mere mortal [3]). Gorgias further notes that Helen's name figures a bad omen (*pheme*, "significant sound") owing to the fact that her name is a homonym for destroy *(helein)* (2). Yet this cause of destruction (Helen), this "one body" was also the figure which was the "cause of bringing together many bodies of men thinking great thoughts for great goals. . . . And all came because of a passion which loved to conquer and a love of honor which was unconquered" (4). The text follows this pattern: first it gives, then it takes away. It "clarifies" Helen, and then it "obscures" her. Who is Helen? Where is Helen? The text refuses to answer. Indeed, every "answer" dissembles itself. Gorgias's "Encomium of Helen" offers us the mythological Helen of the poet Stesichorus who "claims that the Helen who went to Troy was a phantom (εἴδωλον), a being that is not (a pure semblance)" (Porter 278), a phantom (image) who is so "real" that even Menelaus is unsure of her being (Loraux 194–210; Bergren; Austin). Helen thus has "all the being of a nonbeing" (Porter 277). It is this personification of Helen that is the analog for *logos*. As our previous discussion of *logos* suggests, *logos,* too, has "all the being of a nonbeing." To echo Jacques Lacan's famous rewriting of Descartes' *cogito* ("I think where I am not, therefore I am where I do not think" [*Écrits* 166]), *logos* as/and Helen is what we do not think—Helen and *logos* seduce us, lead us astray, but the capacity to do so does not emanate from their will, but rather from their impossible figurations. The question then, is *not* does Helen will—that is, does Helen (or rhetoric) possess a will? But rather, does Helen (as the personification of rhetoric) figure in the disruption of the cultural codes which have sustained philosophy's hegemonic dualisms? I would contend that Helen figures rhetorically as chiasmus. As such, she is the figure that is not one, that has no Parmenidean relation to being.

But the shadow of the figure of the father lies across Helen's surface. It is the shadow of unbearable weight and signification. It is a shadow manifesting itself in three forms—all of which are ultimately reducible to one. The father most often represents himself in the figure of the triangle, the three triangular foundations of Western thought: dialectical, Trinitarian, and Oedipal (Derrida, *Disseminations* xxxii,

25). It is the figure of the delta (Δ), Derrida writes, and "according to Plato [is] the first and most perfect of all letters in the alphabet, the one out of which all the others are born" (*Disseminations* 333). It is the figure out of which all the same are born via the negation of the other. The triangle produces a geometrically aligned self and an even-angled truth. By fixing the truth and opposing himself to error, the self avoids being swept away and therefore negates the possibility of seduction.

The father also figures as a circle. The circle is the whole one, the healthy and holy one. Irigaray writes, "the *circles, rings, spheres, envelopes, enclosures,* in which being has (been) kept since its conception. Ideas, but also Universe, but equally All, and One . . . Privilege of the Father's logos" (*Speculum* 340). The father's *logos,* thus represented as an abundant whole, as a filled hole, claims to suffer from no gaps, no fissures, no breaks in the signifying chain.

The father's figure also represents itself in the form of the Y, a figure of binary and exclusive opposition. Vickers writes, "This use of binary categories to privilege one pole and exclude the other is Plato's favourite weapon throughout the *Gorgias,* and reference to Dodds's notes will show the extent to which Plato either invented new antitheses or pushed them farther than any Greek had done before" (110). This upsilon is the arborescent figure *par excellence*—the tree upon which all identity hangs. It links the name of the son to the name of the father. It establishes origins and plots them on a family tree. It asks the philosophical question "why?"—and produces a cause to explain the effect—an unmoved cause which will stop the infinite regress of the effect. The Y is, in French, called a "Greek I" (Derrida, *Disseminations* 362). The Y and the why, like the triangle, like the circle, establish an I. A unified I, an I of unity. These are the figures of Man—the forms of production and appropriation, the shapes that give rise to the master/slave.

Chiasmus, represented by the Greek letter χ is the figure of ambiguity, uncertainty. Unlike the Y, the chromosome which determines sex, fixes gender and genre, the X figures indeterminately. X is the "principle of uncertainty" (Baudrillard, *Seduction* 12) and reversibility in gender and genre. This reversibility is not, however, to be taken as the dialectical negative. As we have seen, the negative sustains the positive. The reversible form is what according to Baudrillard "abolishes the differential opposition" (12). He writes, "every *positive* form can accommodate itself to its negative form, but understands the challenge of the *reversible* form as mortal. Every structure can adapt to its subversion or inversion, but not to the reversion of its terms" (21).

The reversible form is the form of Thoth (Derrida, *Dissemination* 93) and of Helen—those forms which do not cut a "respectable figure" (74), forms without a proper (thus irreversible) identity. According to

Irigaray, "The woman does not obey the principle of self-identity, however the variable x for self is defined. She is identified with every x variable, not in any specific way" (230). The reversible and thus variable figure of woman is "double-faced" with, in Derrida's words, a "double that doubles no simple, a double that nothing anticipates, nothing at least that is not itself already double. There is no simple reference" (*Dissemination* 206). And there is certainly not any *faithful* reference. She is not faithful to a proper form. She will not wait; she continually moves from referent to referent to referent and establishes no appropriate relationship.

One cannot count on the rhetorical and seductive figure by "virtue" of its reversibility and double doubleness (Bergren, "Language and the Female" 80, 83; Austin 137). She is not predictable, nor prescribed in a logic of probability. She is constantly "going astray," "leading astray," as the verb *se-duire* suggests. Her discourse is discursive, as the etymology suggests. According to Barthes: "*Dis-cursus*—originally the action of running here and there, comings and goings" (*Lover's Discourse* 3). Derrida occasionally uses the word *errance,* as this is "the accepted French translation of Heidegger's *die Irre,* a term which appears frequently throughout his work . . . [the word] incorporates not only the sense of 'error' but also that of 'aberrance,' i.e., of being off course, wandering away from the truth."

It is thus impossible to "figure" her out. She is the *pharmakon* that seduces "a play of appearances" (*Dissemination* 103). "She plays at dissumulation, at ornamentation, deceit, artifice" (Derrida, *Spurs* 67). She is a surface that absorbs truth, representation, and referentiality. Helen is thus a sign without reference. After all, the Greeks had not seen Helen for twenty years (Suzuki 35). Her presence is elusive and indeterminable, as is her identity. For "As wife of both Menelaus and Paris, is she Greek or is she Trojan?" (Suzuki 18). She certainly caused the Greeks to wonder and to wander. As woman, she *crosses* and transgresses boundaries as a "liminal entity that is neither here nor there; [she is] betwixt and between" positions (Turner, quoted in Suzuki 18). Thus X never marks the spot.

Helen runs away with empty signs—not with Paris. She breaks her bond to syntax—not to Menelaus. This is what carries Helen away, what Helen carries away: She ventures language, accepts the challenge offered by the kairotic moment, and thereby seduces meaning.

Gorgias's Seductive Gesture

Gorgias makes a proto-postmodern move to displace common assumptions of active/passive, subject/object, being/not being, by recasting

Helen as rhetoric—that is, as the instability of language with the seductive gesture which eludes capture and mastery. Gorgias, as we have established, believed that *logos* could not faithfully represent or signify the truth, and certainly not a single and whole truth. For, Untersteiner explains, "If man, as happened for Helen, comes into immediate contact with logos—that is, with the divine transformed into logical power—*logos* in its working *splits into two opposite directions* which with their antithetical existence destroy the ideal of a rationality to be recognized in all nature" (140–41; emphasis mine). The Parmenidean one is now—at least—two. Thus, by virtue of infidelity, *kairos* "break[s] up the cycle of the antitheses [being and not being] and create[s] something new" (Untersteiner 161).[18] This "something new" offers the possibility to break up the tyranny of truth and being which has held us hostage. Gorgias is offering, in effect, a paratheory of the invention of the self—a "tragic" self who maintains a distance from truth and all other totalizing theories of unity and community.

The so-called tragedy of knowledge is a recognition, an affirmation of the indeterminacy of the world, language, and truth. Gorgias is not propounding inaction or fatalism. Ethical action or subjectivity for Gorgias, constituted by *kairos,* aims at the "right thing at the right moment" and, therefore, cannot appeal to any preexisting foundation for its justification or rationalization; as the author of *Dissoi Logoi* writes, "To sum up, everything done at the right time is seemly and everything done at the wrong time is disgraceful" (2.20). This, in the words of Steven Mailloux, rhetoricizes the "assumption of an absolute opposition between unprincipled preference and universal principle" (*Reception* 37), thereby deflating the common criticism of antifoundationalism as nihilistic: either we have preexistent, knowable, and universal foundations, or we have nothing but vulgar relativism and a veritable "free for all." This is not the case at all: to assume antifoundationalism is to argue that those presumed given foundations are already rhetorically constructed as "principled preferences"; that is, "it is only through contextualized suasive force that this or some other preferred principle or principled preference carries the rhetorical day" (Mailloux 38). Platonic and Parmenidean preferred principles are so because we have been persuaded to prefer them as principles.

Mailloux then extrapolates that—in the face of antifoundationalism—it is "the task of sophistic rhetoric to investigate and theorize how this rhetorical process takes place, to establish what rhetorical 'devices,'" quoting F. C. S. Schiller, "'make concordant [one man's] measures with those of his fellow-men'" (28). Mailloux is echoing here the sophist Protagoras's unprincipled preferences: "About gods I cannot say either that they are or that they are not" and "Man is the measure of all things, of the things that are that they are, and of the things that are not that they are not" (Plato, *Theaetetus* 152a). That is, without sure knowledge of the gods nor of their will, Man constructs what is according to his own preferences—preferences, however, that must be "negotiated" with other men.

Although sophistic rhetorical practices are interested in how subjects "negotiate" their preferences, they don't presume that the individual precedes the preferences, but rather that the individual itself is a function of already existing rhetorical preferences, rhetorically constructed. Hence to be an individual is already to have been subjected to the unprincipled preferences that have "rhetorically carried the day." This rhetorical coup, however, has been accomplished philosophically (not [Third] sophistically) and hence has abducted us via the logic of the negative. And this is a point at which neopragmatism's Protagoras and postmodernism's Gorgias part company.

The foundations which have been laid—rhetorically—have reproduced the metaphysical preference for presence. As we have seen, beginning with at least Parmenides, the philosophic project of establishing presence, or what is, is accomplished by the logic of the negative. To assert what exists is to assert what is not. Hence, to make Man the measure (to endow him with being), man must negate Woman (deny her being). This is the insidious violence of the will to know: to create identity, either of self or of truth, requires the negation and appropriation of the other, and further requires that the subject subject himself to this process in order even to be a subject of knowledge.

Gorgias's rhetoric challenges this logic of identity by confusing rhetorical subjectivity with *logos*, kairotically constituted. In this way, Gorgias's rhetoric overcomes the binary logic of the negative. Further, because *logos* is seductive (not persuasive—or rather it is persuasive only insofar as it is seductive), the rhetorical subject is no longer a "proper" or decent rhetorical subject situated within the realm of epistemology. As a sophist he does not know, but this does not make him subject to Platonic criticisms. Within the realm of seduction rather than epistemic rhetoric, Woman and/as sophistry recognizes that foundations will be laid, have been laid rhetorically, but she participates in the resistance of laying new foundations, the resistance of establishing new "knowledges." That is, as performed by Gorgias's "Encomium of Helen," *logos* resists itself, dissembles itself, renders itself disconcordant and incommensurable with a final "cause" or narrative to sustain Helen.

As *logos* and/as seduction is ambiguous, paradoxical, and contradictory, so is the rhetorical self and/as Helen, who maintains a distance from the other and from the self, remaining (at the least) two-faced, twofold—stretching the distance of distance. Thus the tragic self becomes distance itself—and thereby becomes Woman, living moment by moment by moment, kairotically anew. Perhaps in this space of Woman, in the space of Helen's paradoxical position—in the space of her boudoir, draped as it is with shimmering veils, mask after mask, and all the costumes of history, here will be found, as writes Nietzsche: "Perhaps this is where we shall still discover the realm of our *Invention*" (*Beyond Good and Evil* 150): in the company of Woman.

3

Nietzsche and the Other Woman:
On Forgetting in an Extra-Moral Sense

A labyrinthian human being never seeks the truth, but . . .
always and only his Ariadne.
— Nietzsche, *Kritische Studienausgabe*

Supposing truth is a woman—what then?
— Nietzsche, *Beyond Good and Evil*

Could I have meant to be a woman?
— Nietzsche, *My Sister and I*

Friedrich Nietzsche was very much a "posthumous" man. While he wrote, there were few (and certainly no Ariadnes) who had ears for him. He continues to be a misjudged figure today. Fueled by his sister's lust for fame, Nietzsche's reputation has been tainted by the infamous Nazi appropriation of his concept of the Overman. He has been deftly dismissed by many feminists due to his historically misogynistic statements. And his damning critique of morality and religion, underscored by his proclamation that "God is Dead," has earned him the unearned labels of "immoralist" and "nihilist."[1] In short, although virtually every aspect of current thought is indebted to Nietzsche's influence, Nietzsche remains an unpopular and, yes, tragically misunderstood figure. If Nietzsche, however, is listened to sophistically, his words (and his questions) clear a space for a revolutionary, ethical critique of truth, representation, and subjectivity.

Regarding Women

Nietzsche's supposed blatant misogyny is usually traced to a particular line from *Thus Spoke Zarathustra:* "Are you visiting women? Do not forget your whip!" (93). An intriguing comment, no doubt. However, it reads more as a signifier than signified and reverberates with a number of possible interpretations. There are many to quickly label Nietzsche a misogynist and hence no ally in the struggle of women, and certainly (as a Man, in addition to being a "misogynist") he is incapable of "speaking *of*" women and—most certainly—of "speaking *for*" women (Schutte, "Nietzsche on Gender Difference"). There are those, however, who challenge this predictable interpretation, including Armstrong (quoted in Patton xii), Graybeal (52–54), Ackerman (123–24), and myself, for wouldn't it be unwise, if not hermeneutically careless, to read this infamous line without reference to the equally infamous photograph in which Lou Salomé wields a whip as Nietzsche and Paul Rée are yoked to a small wagon? It is Woman who wields the whip. It is Nietzsche and Rée who are, as they say, "pussy whipped."

Beyond the "whip" comment there is, I argue, no *one* "woman" to whom Nietzsche makes reference. Although Jean Graybeal's *Language and "the Feminine" in Nietzsche and Heidegger* and Kelly Oliver's *Womanizing Nietzsche* both address Nietzsche's relationship to Woman, they both represent the "feminine" as the maternal. The maternal is only one manifestation of Nietzsche's women, and not particularly his finest. "The Mother," Gilles Deleuze writes, is "the infernal feminine power," which is "negative and moralising, the terrible mother, the mother of good and evil, she who depreciates and denies life" (*Nietzsche* 20). Although there are mothers and gestating philosophers in Nietzsche's works, the mother is not the affirming Third Woman. When Nietzsche does positively characterize the mother, he typically does so with an emphasis on her pregnancy and on her delivery—not on her "maternal" or "mothering" activities (see *Gay Science* 35, for example). Indeed, there are many women in Nietzsche's works, and he espouses no one opinion regarding them, nor does he offer one characterization of women but at least three. I argue that two of his characterizations serve to demonstrate how Woman has been produced, constituted, and represented heretofore, and that his Third Woman attempts to unrepresent these women via the excesses and instabilities of language. It is my purpose to examine these three figurations of Woman, to show what will sustains them, and to tease out the implications that the Third Woman (which is not one) has for an ethical (Third Sophistic) rhetoric.

The Will to Truth

But before we regard the Third Woman, we must understand the will to truth that produces the other two women. This will to truth of the

Western metaphysical tradition manifests itself in the so-called first principles of that tradition, including cause/effect logic, the law of non-contradiction, and the dialectic. Nietzsche's project was to demonstrate the illusory foundations of these principles, to further demonstrate that this illusion is used to guarantee subjectivity, and to finally demonstrate that this truth and this subjectivity is indicative of a will to death.

The early philosophers—including the pre-Socratics, the atomists, the Stoics, Plato, and certainly Aristotle with his "four causes"—began a tradition of, an obsession with, really, the *topos* cause and effect. The motivating force in Western metaphysics is to establish a *causa sui*, a prime mover, an unmoved mover, a first cause that is its own motivating force, as does Plato, for example, in the *Phaedrus:*

> Only that which moves itself, since its motion does not derive from any source outside itself, never ceases to move. Moreover this is the source and beginning of motion for all other things which are in motion. Now a first principle cannot be derived. For everything that is derived must come from a first principle, but the principle itself cannot be derived from anything at all. (245e)

The fact that Plato's first cause here is the soul is symptomatic of philosophy's imperative to construct truth as a mirror of the soul. Again, I repeat Nietzsche's oft-quoted definition of truth as "a mobile army of metaphors, metonyms, anthropomorphisms . . . illusions about which it has been forgotten that they *are* illusions" ("On Truth and Lying" 250). Hence the so-called truth of causal logic is an *anthropomorphism;* thus, Nietzsche argues, "nobody has ever 'explained' a push. . . . How should explanations be at all possible when we first turn everything into an *image,* our image!" (*Gay Science* 172). Nietzsche's critique of first principles is a damning critique of the methodologies and assumptions of science and philosophy with their claims to truth. He writes:

> If someone hides an object behind a bush, then seeks and finds it there, that seeking and finding is not very laudable: but that is the way it is with the seeking and finding of "truth" within the rational sphere. If I define the mammal and then after examining a camel declare, "See, a mammal," a truth is brought to light, but it is of limited value. . . . it is anthropomorphic through and through and contains not a single point that would be "true in itself," real, and universally valid, apart from man. ("On Truth and Lying" 251)

Thus if Plato, for example, hides "Truth" in the dialectic, then finds that the dialectic brings that truth to light, he hasn't demonstrated, as he would have liked, that the so-called philosopher (lover of knowledge) seeks some truth beyond the shadowy realm of human opinion *(doxa)*, simulacra, and phenomena. This is precisely why Nietzsche criticized the Kantian notion of immanent critique (Deleuze, *Nietzsche* 73–110). Reason, according to Kant, should critique itself. Nietzsche's question to Kant is "what is the will which hides and expresses itself in reason?" Nietzsche engaged a critique of reason itself, the fuel of the Hegelian dialectic—but not by reason itself, for that would take reason's will for granted. For Nietzsche, reason is a smokescreen erected to dissuade anyone from looking behind it; it is a dogmatic value that asserts that the thinker (who thinks rationally) seeks and loves truth, that the thinker is diverted from the truth by "forces foreign to reason" (the body, the passions), that the thinker only needs a method to think correctly. Nietzsche calls "reason" in language a "deceitful old woman" (*Twilight* 38). This "deceitful old woman" is definitively not the Third Woman, contra to Plato's representation of her as the faithful, beautiful, truthful handmaiden. For Nietzsche, thinking should be valuing, revaluing, and, more significantly, creating. This is thinking that affirms life (by placing life in the realm of sense and value), that discovers and invents new possibilities of life. This creation is not a real-ising; it is not the production of some thing vis-à-vis the real. This would be a creation prompted by "the desire for *being*": "to fix, to immortalize" (*Gay Science* 329) and would be in service of being and what is. Nietzsche is espousing a creation, motivated by the desire for "change, and becoming . . . an expression of an overflowing energy that is pregnant with future" (*Gay Science* 329). Such a creation has no belief in universal, abstract truth and therefore opposes the Socratic, "what is?" question by answering in the particular, "which one?" and "what is it for me?" Thus Nietzsche's critique of critique reveals his perspectivism, which emphasizes that there are no truths, only anthropomorphic interpretations of phenomena or becoming.

(Re)Evaluating Subjectivity: The Psychopathology of Consciousness

Nietzsche is interested particularly in a transvaluation of human subjectivity as a corollary of the metaphysical belief in truth and causality. Nietzsche, employing a metaleptic strategy, reveals the subject as merely an effect of an effect, rather than (as historically characterized) as the cause of an effect. The subject—alternately referred to as the "soul" and the "ego"—is an effect of our belief in the cause/effect *topos,* an effect of our grammatical habits. Since our language posits a cause—a subject position—for every action/verb, we assume that we are the (self-propelling) agents of our actions. Nietzsche would argue that subjects/selves/egos are effects of language, grammar, the unconscious, social *mores*—in short, of forces or of relations of forces. For example, for Nietzsche, "thinking" is a force that has no cause and certainly has no master such as a subject. In *Beyond Good and Evil,* he asserts that a thought comes when "it" wishes, not when "he" wishes (24; 67). For Nietzsche, it is a falsification to say that the subject "I" is the condition of the predicate "think." Indeed, the indeterminate pronoun expressed in the sentence "it rained" is what the ego is, that is, an "it" that doesn't cause the raining. In *Twilight of the Idols,* Nietzsche claims that it is our belief in grammar (our revered God) that leads us to assert a subject, to believe in an ego-substance, and then to project that substance on to all things, thereby creating the concept "thing" (38).

This belief in the subject not only serves the concept truth but also the political machinations of that truth. The political demand is for total integration, for totally integratable subjects according to the totalizing logic of the selfsame: the proper, property, and profitability. All that cannot be appropriated by the system, all that fails to function within and for the state, must be excluded or exterminated. Thus the totally integrated state functions with totally integrated and functional subjects—paradoxically referred to as individuals. Those proponents of the transcendental ego and the transcendental state would present man as the being possessing individual rights and individual consciousnesses and individual agencies. However, Michel Foucault has argued that the very notion of the "individual" is a "product of power" ("Preface" xiv)—a product produced in order to sustain and maintain that very power.

In his *Discipline and Punish,* Foucault elaborates on the construction of the individual by presenting us with the Enlightenment's innovative disciplinary method: the panopticon. As Foucault reminds us, the panopticon is a tower erected in the center of a prison compound. The prisoners' cells circle the watchtower, and each isolated prisoner is subject to the constant gaze originating from the panopticon (although, and herein lies Bentham's brilliance, no one needs to be present to do the gazing—the threat of the gaze is enough). Indeed, the gaze constructs the individual, disciplines the individual, normalizes the individual, individualizes the individual, for the sake of the polis.

The aim of the gaze is to create a consciousness of self that is single and self-identical, that is subject to self and to authority, and, thus, that is legally accountable and socially useful. Nietzsche argues that "consciousness does not really belong to man's individual existence but rather to his social or herd nature" (*Gay Science* 299). "Consciousness" is a construct that serves the demands of the herd, making subjects answerable to the herd. According to Foucault, the "practical" aim of individualization, of normalization, is to ensure control and utility. He writes: "Its aim is to strengthen the social forces—to increase production, to develop the economy, spread education, raise the level of public morality; to increase and multiply" (*Discipline and Punish* 208). The subject thus constituted becomes a panopticon in relation to himself. He is a subject only insofar as he is the object of the normative gaze— that gaze that commands agency, lucidity, transparency, and presence— in short, that requires self-mastery and self-knowledge in the composition of the self.

The gaze, Foucault continues, "assign[s] to each individual his 'true' name, his 'true' place, his 'true' body, his 'true' disease" (*Discipline and Punish* 198). According to the logic of the panopticon, "diseased" individuals are those who are dysfunctional and the cure is normalization and integration: an ego. It is this belief in the ego as *causa sui* (*Twilight* 37) that maintains the ego, *normalizes* the ego, and that sustains, according to Foucault, "the fascism in us all . . . the fascism that causes us to love power, to desire the very thing that dominates and exploits us" ("Preface" xiii). The ego and its attendant desire for mastery is the deliberative faculty gone mad. This counters the wisdom of ego psychology, which argues that insanity is caused by an unstable ego and that the cure is to construct a functioning ego. Surely, the cure is worse than the disease. For has not the "cure"—the totally integrated ego—been responsible for Buchenwald, Dachau, Treblinka, Auschwitz? Has not, Stuart Schneiderman asks—as Theodor Adorno and Jean-François Lyotard have before him—the "refinement of the human spirit" associated itself with the "wanton destruction of human life?" (160). The ideal of total identity has manifested itself in total annihilation. Thus Gilles Deleuze and Félix Guattari maintain that "true sanity [—and, let's add, true ethical being—] entails in one way or another the dissolution of the normal ego" (*Anti-Oedipus* 132).

From a Lacanian perspective, "normality is the apotheosis of psychopathology," and for Jacques Lacan, "beyond psychopathology lay ethics" (Schneiderman 16). In other words, the ethical is beyond normality, beyond the ego. The ethical has no place in the Oedipally territorialized ego, characterized by narcissism, intellectualization, rationalization, paranoia, procrastination, and paralysis: none of which are a basis for action, and specifically not for ethical action.

The ego is narcissistic by virtue of the fact that the ego discovers itself through a visual system of representation, generally through the mirror stage. According to Jacques Lacan, it is in "the field of primary narcissistic identification, that is to be found the essential mainspring of the effects of the ego ideal" rendered by the sight of "that being that he first saw appearing in the form of the parent holding him up before the mirror" (*Four Fundamental Concepts* 256–57). The "ego reflects and observes, imparts an order to spatial representation" (Schneiderman 147). The ego becomes the totalizing gaze that fixes everything in relation to him, to his self. The ego seeks to control, to fix his relationship to the other, and to the discourse of the other. The ego, according to Schneiderman, accomplishes this through the twin processes of intellectualization and rationalization:

> Intellectualization, if it means anything, is a perversion of the mind in the service of the ego. More commonly it is called rationalization—for a failure to act or for a mistaken act. . . . Intellectualization is intimately related to procrastination. It implies a will to explain away things, to interpret them to death, to concoct an endless series of reasons telling why and wherefore and leaving the deed undone. Or else, if the deed has been done, the rationalizations declare that the ego wishes to undo it, wishes that it never happened. (171)

A related symptom evidenced by sufferers of the ego is extreme paranoia: the ego operates as if everything is overdetermined, oversaturated with meaning and significance. This paranoia surfaces as the will to represent and the will to knowledge. The ego's fundamental paranoia exhibits itself also as the insistence on establishing "the cause" of everything. In *Twilight of the Idols,* Nietzsche refers to this belief as the "error of false causality." He writes:

> We had *created* the world on the basis of it as a world of causes, as a world of will, as a world of spirit . . . every event was to it [the paranoid ego] an action, every action the effect of a will, the world became for it a multiplicity of agents, an agent ("subject") foisted itself upon every event. Man projected his three "inner facts," that in which he believed more firmly than in anything else, will, spirit, ego, outside himself—he derived the concept "being" only from the concept "ego" [Descartes's *cogito:* I think therefore I am], he posited "things" as possessing being according to his own image, according to his concept of the ego as cause. (49)

Schneiderman presents a Lacanian reading of Shakespeare's *Hamlet* as the epitome of the ego—as the subject "procrastinating, doubting, tortured by narcissism and guilt" (17). The ego will always suffer from guilt.[2] Nietzsche writes, "Everywhere accountability is sought, it is usually the instinct for *punishing and judging* which seeks it. One has deprived becoming of its innocence if being in this or that state is traced back to will, to intentions, to accountable acts: the doctrine of will has been invented essentially for the purpose of punishment, that is, of *finding guilty*" (*Twilight* 53). The ego, characterized by paranoia and guilt, is the supposedly "sane" character who sustains a so-called ethical system. But, as exemplified by the character of Hamlet, it is possible to see how the ego prevents the truly ethical. Faced with an ethical dilemma, Hamlet reduces it to a deliberative problem of binary proportions: to kill or not to kill, to be or not to be. The result is a state of paralysis and inaction; he is unable to do the "right" thing at the "right" time. He is unable to allow himself to be possessed by *kairos*. The ego is not, despite all its claim to "activity," an acting subject; he is a procrastinating subject. Hamlet, no doubt, eventually kills his uncle, but when he does, Schneiderman writes, "it is too late, his act no longer means anything, it no longer has its ethical edge. The murder of Claudius is an afterthought, which Hamlet, as Lacan said, can only accomplish when he is dying, when he will not have to bear responsibility for his act" (153). This is not to say that murder is an inherently ethical act; to conclude so is to miss entirely the problem at hand. Hamlet is an ego and egoist to the end: he acts only to avenge himself (when he learns Claudius is responsible for his impending death) and, with his dying breath, he asks Horatio to tell his story. Hamlet, thus, represents, in Schneiderman's words, "a powerful argument against anyone who would set up such a structure [the mature and adult ego] as a standard for ethical conduct" (154).

Of course, this interpretation proves problematic and perhaps contrariwise to Nietzsche. For in his *Birth of Tragedy,* Nietzsche himself offers a reading of Hamlet that at first glance appears to challenge Schneiderman. It is Nietzsche's argument that Hamlet "in a sense" (60) resembles the Dionysian man. "Both have looked truly into the essence of things, they have *gained knowledge,* and nausea inhibits action; for their action could not change anything in the eternal nature of things; they feel it to be ridiculous or humiliating that they should be asked to set right a world that is out of joint. Knowledge kills action; action requires the veil of illusion" (60).[3] Thus at this point, Nietzsche and Schneiderman's interpretations converge: ethical action requires illusion, requires that one forget one's knowledge of self and of truth.

The argument here is not simply that complete knowledge is impossible—although, of course, we begin with that premise. The argument is that one must forget one's self as an ego as well as forget the

"Truth," which is, of course, the non-truth of truth. With Gorgias, we presume that "if all men on all subjects had <both> memory of things past and <awareness> of things present and foreknowledge of the future" ("Encomium of Helen," 11), we would have no need of opinion. That is, as Gorgias claims in "On Nature," knowledge of what exists is impossible; *doxa* is what appears to be, and it is opposed, according to the philosopher, to *epistēmē* or *apodictic* knowledge. Hence, humans operate in a "slippery" world where certain knowledge is impossible and *doxa* is "slippery and insecure," casting us into "slippery and insecure successes" (Gorgias, "Encomium of Helen" 11). The slippage between *logos* and what is and the slippage between *logos* and *epistēmē* create a rhetorical situation, calling forth "false arguments" *(pseudo logos)* that allow people to act in the face of uncertainty. However, as I argued in the last chapter, because of the instability of language and its impossible relation to being, there are no "true" arguments to oppose the "false."

Then the question arises, how are we to *know* how to act? And with this question, the rhetorical question is forestalled, and ethics is once again subjected to epistemology; rhetoric is once again reduced to persuasive discourse. The "answer" is to construct warrantable beliefs (Wayne Booth, *Modern Dogma*) or socially justified beliefs (Richard Rorty, *Philosophy*) that will provide for ethical action. Rhetoric is epistemic, surely. It can and does function to create and to sustain social beliefs. But Gorgias, Nietzsche, and Baudrillard are attempting to seduce us into resisting to reduce *logos* once again to the demands of philosophic and phallogocentric rhetoric: *logos* in the service of *epistēmē* (however contingent) and in the service of public and political discourse, which as we have seen require (subjected and normalized) subjects. Robert Scott, in his landmark essay, "On Viewing Rhetoric as Epistemic," sets forth the following ethical guidelines for acting "in the face of uncertainty to create situational truth": toleration, will, and responsibility (316). Three principles emanating from the subject. The rhetorical subject is once again the point of origin: a conscious, rationalizing, thinking ego, driven by a will to [contingent] truth.

An Other Ethics: The Unconscious and the Opportune Moment

It is not Hamlet's thinking per se, Schneiderman writes, that is "the culprit [the disease of the ego]; it is rather the 'I think,' the belief that the ego is the center of thinking" (150). It is when I think I am thinking that I am. And it is when I am that I cease to be other. And it is when I think I am thinking that I procrastinate—that is, I do not desire and

I do not act. Ethics require action—at the right time and not when it is too late. But this action knows no master. Desire—not the ego—is the basis of action. Indeed, desire, according to Schneiderman, is the overcoming of "narcissism, because desire is always the desire of the Other, . . . and because desire always seeks recognition by the Other's desire" (22). What is truly ethical, then, is situated on the cutting edges of desire, *kairos,* and the unconscious: that is, in the space left by the death of the ego.

That space is the other, the desire of the other that the ego represses. That space is where that which cannot be totalized by the oppressive and normalizing state exists. This space is the locus of the unconscious. However, let me state that I am not referring to the Freudian, Oedipalized unconscious. By "unconscious," I am referring to all that goes unheard, excluded, or repressed, such as Woman or sophistry, by the totalizing ego (Lacan, *Feminine Sexuality* 165). I do not assume that the unconscious exists extrasymbolically; indeed, Lacan argues that it is structured like a language (*Four Fundamental Concepts* 149, 203). But it does operate according to a logic other than the logic of the ego (which is primarily one of cause and effect and of "meaningful" linkages, sequences, and orders). Schneiderman writes: "The thoughts whose provenance is most clearly unconscious are those that come to me when I do not think to think. These are thoughts that surge forth; they are the stuff of free association" (150). They are the stuff generating in the gaps of language, of meaning, and of intentionality. They are the stuff that is often excluded, in Michel Serres's terms, as "noise." It is all that heretofore has remained unarticulated and unrepresentable.

An "other" ethics, one that would, according to Lyotard, bear witness to what is truly other (again, not the other that is merely the negation of the same), to what is truly different, would—I propose—open up a space for the constitution of a new subjectivity—one in which a subject is not constructed according to the logic of the master/slave dialectic. This is the space opened up by the loss of the ego, or—in Foucault's words—the "death of man." In *The Order of Things,* he writes, "It is no longer possible to think in our day other than in the void left by man's disappearance. For this void does not create a deficiency; it does not constitute a lacuna that must be filled. It is nothing more, and nothing less, than the unfolding of a space in which it is once more possible to think" (342)—and, I would add, to be ethically. Perhaps this new ethical space is none other than the other Other that will accomplish the dispersion of Man's selfsame identity. Of course, Lacan has argued that "there is no Other of the Other" (*Écrits* 311). Indeed, what need would the other have for an other? But we have not yet become sufficiently other, and the Nietzschean challenge partially realized through Zarathustra remains: the letting be of a liberatory space that will free the subjected subject from his prison house of lack, and allow him or her to act according to his or her ethical desires—rather than according to the normalizing and categorical imperatives established by politics in the name of ethics. And this is precisely the point where we must take our leave, our letting be, of Lacan, insofar as he figures Woman across a lack *(manque)* within the logic of negation.

The Master/Slave Morality and Redemption

Nietzsche's critique of the subject also reveals the subject as a composite effect of two "reactive" forces: *ressentiment* and bad conscience. *Ressentiment* is the belief that others are the cause of our sufferings. Bad conscience is the interiorization of suffering—the machine for the manufacturing of guilt. The subject, constituted as such, is rendered (as he argues in *On the Genealogy of Morals*) calculable, regular, and able to make promises; that is, the subject is constituted as a sovereign agent (57). Bred as such, individuals are created and appropriated via, in Deleuze's words, the "social straitjacket" of guilt and debt that organizes the community as such.

The subject, constituted across *ressentiment* and bad conscience, is rooted in what Nietzsche refers to as a master/slave morality. The master and the slave are equally enslaved by the relationship between them. The slave is posited as powerless in order for the master to posit himself as powerful, just as the ego posits a non-ego in order to oppose himself to it in order to posit itself as an ego. It is a relationship of *ressentiment* and a relationship of debt. The slave is indebted to the master; the master is indebted to the slave for his very identity as a master. Culture, as we know it, according to Nietzsche, is modeled on this morality. Christianity most certainly is: the believer, the sinner, the man of bad conscience, is indebted to the master, God, for the redemption of his sins. And yet it is the master whose "perfection" constitutes man across "original sin," rendering man never able to pay the debt.

Such a morality exudes a strong belief in representation: the slave believes that the master is a representative of power; the master believes that he is representing power. As we have seen, Deleuze in *Nietzsche and Philosophy* states that the mania for representation is common to all slaves (81). It is certainly demonstrative of the will to truth, of the desire for certainty and for pinning all signifieds down to a primary mover: its signification, its meaning (that is, its responsibility to meaning, to signification). In *Thus Spoke Zarathustra,* Nietzsche contends that it is the will's antipathy toward the "it was"—a spirit of revenge and *ressentiment* that demands a redemption of the "it was"—a redemption of all suffering. And yet this redemption is an accusation, an act of aggression, with a desire to punish. Instead of seeking redemption, according to Nietzsche, we would be better served if we sought to transform every "it was" into "I willed it thus, so shall I will it." That is, if humankind embraced the concept of the eternal return and *amor fati* (an act of affirmation of all things, not willing them any differently), such a willing would annihilate all "half-willing" (all *ressentiment*, all bad conscience) as Vitanza's *Negation, Subjectivity, and the History of Rhetoric* demonstrates.

It is from this Nietzschean insight, an insight achieved due to his philological origins, that subjectivity is bought at the price of remembrance, the remembrance of one's guilt, just as etymologically truth is specifically that which is not forgotten. In Greek, as was mentioned in the last chapter, truth is *alētheia* (not-forgetting). *Lethe* is forgetting, a forgetting experienced in dreams, madness, unconsciousness, the irrational forces of the dark. The α-privativum renders truth a remembrance, as in a not forgetting. In Plato's *Meno*, Socrates characterizes knowledge of the truth specifically as the evocation of a memory of truth, of the truth which we have merely forgotten. Our subjectivity requires that we remember, that we not forget ourselves, that we remain rational, coherent, speaking beings, that we remember and search for our origins, for our cause, for our paternity. It is the Oedipal impulse—indeed, the Oedipal imperative—of subjectivity: to search out our identity, to uncover our guilt.

But it is Jocasta, a Woman, who attempts to seduce Oedipus away from the truth, from a truth that is destructive and blinding. It is Helen who dispenses the *pharmakon nepenthes*—the drug dropped into the wine at Sparta which purges one of all remembrances of shame, guilt, fear, and hatred. Froma Zeitlin writes that Helen's *pharmakon* belongs "to the poetics of enchantment" (409), foreshadowing Baudrillard's strategies of appearances, of seduction. It is Jocasta's, Helen's, and Nietzsche's insight that forgetting is the ethical strategy, a proactive process that, like art, protects us from our truth, from the tyranny of our metaphysics. There are those who argue that such a forgetting is a denial of the ideological forces that frame our being. Cultural critique as practiced by social constructionists and neo-Marxists argues that the hegemony of Western metaphysics can only be countered specifically by remembering—that is, by uncovering and revealing our constructedness. Certainly, this remembering, this hermeneutic of suspicion, deconstructs one truth but simultaneously reconstructs another truth to take its place. This process of demystification merely results in a remystification. For the act of remembrance is, once again, specifically the memory of a truth, the evocation of guilt, inspired by the twin forces of *ressentiment* and bad conscience. Remembrance achieved via a demystification is just another manifestation of Oedipal obsession, of Ahab's search for the Great White Whale or current critique's search for the Great White Male: the true narrative, the true guilt, the true redemption. The revenge fantasy becomes incorporated as truth.

Woman Is (in) the Act of Forgetting

It is against this revenge-seeking truth, disguised as social critique, that the process of forgetting finds itself. This, then, is Jocasta; this is the figure of Woman. But this is not just any Woman; it is specifically the "Third Woman." The Third Woman to whom I point is identified by Elizabeth Berg in reference to Derrida's three characterizations of Nietzsche's figures of Woman in *Spurs:* The First Woman is the Castrated Woman, the Second Woman is the Castrating Woman, the Third Woman is the Affirming Woman (97). In what follows, I will identify each of these figures in the works of Nietzsche in an effort to argue that to dismiss Nietzsche as a misogynist is to conflate all of his comments regarding women without regard to the fact that he is talking about many different kinds of being. Indeed, some women suffer his condemnation, but the Third Woman claims his praises as the figure of the *Ubermensch*. It is she who overcomes the tyranny of truth and subjectivity, the long reign of reactive forces.

In *Thus Spoke Zarathustra*, Nietzsche speaks of the "Three Metamorphoses" of being (54–56). These three metamorphoses represent the three women, or three possible states of being. The first is that of a camel. According to Nietzsche, the camel is a "weight-bearing spirit"; it longs to be burdened, to be laden with the memory of duty, responsibility, guilt, and truth—a memory that exists as its *raison d'être,* as its constitutive element. The camel packs the values and morals of the time, weighted with the gravity of truth and consequences. Its will is reactive; its desire punitive. He writes "there are those who would lose their whole joy in living if their duty were taken from them—especially the womanly, the born subjects" (*Will to Power* 522).

It is Nietzsche's own sister, Elisabeth, who best represents the First Woman, the woman who wills to be burdened with the value "Thou Shalt" and to offer to society, particularly men, her undying devotion.[4] Of devotion, Nietzsche offers this aphorism, "*Devotion.*—There are noble women who are afflicted with a certain poverty of the spirit, and they know no better way to *express* their deepest devotion than to offer their virtue and shame. They own nothing higher" (*Gay Science* 125). With only the will of public morality and its accompanying demand for revenge to will her, Elisabeth—as this First Woman—offers her devotion to her brother, Friedrich. It is insightful to recall, as does H. F. Peters in his biography of Elisabeth Forster-Nietzsche, *Zarathustra's Sister,* that Nietzsche's pet name for Elisabeth was "Llama." Peters writes:

> In her book on her brother Elisabeth says she was delighted when he called her "Llama" because the description of that animal, which he had found in a book on natural history, fitted her so well. "The Llama," she quotes, "is a strange animal; voluntarily it carries the heaviest burdens, but if it is treated badly it refuses to eat and lies down to die." What she failed to quote was "when a llama does not want to go on, it turns its head round and discharges its saliva, which has an unpleasant odor, into the rider's face." (10)

Such a reaction was identical to Elisabeth's own. Peters tells us that during Elisabeth's violent fits of temper, she would scream at Nietzsche, "pummel him with her small fists in uncontrolled rage; when he turned away in disgust, she would spit at him. That is why he gave her the nickname 'Llama'" (10), his "*faithful* Llama" (10; emphasis mine).

However, Elisabeth's devotion and fidelity was always motivated by her desire to make powerful social connections, to gain influence with the Wagners and Von Bulows of the day, and later to make a fortune off of Nietzsche's work, although she herself remained uninfluenced by his philosophical gospel. Elisabeth married a fiercely anti-Semitic man, Dr. Bernard Forster, a union that troubled Nietzsche greatly. He viewed the marriage as, in Peters words, "a cruel betrayal. It had opened his eyes to the true character of his faithful Llama. She had never understood him, she had not the faintest notion of his philosophy, she had remained what she had always been: a petty spiteful creature imbued with self-righteous middle-class morality" (108).

It was, indeed, ironic that the messenger of *amor fati,* eternal recurrence, and the *Ubermensch* had any relation to this "petty spiteful creature," a woman who throughout her life and Nietzsche's life personified *ressentiment* and the desire for revenge. Elisabeth demonstrated this as she learned of her brother's desire for a young Russian woman, Lou Salomé. Elisabeth did not approve of the reckless ways and amoral habits of Lou. It was no secret that Lou, Paul Rée, and Nietzsche had talked of and planned for an unusual living arrangement, a *mariage à trois*— yet without the marriage. Elisabeth was appalled and jealous, and so, in the name of middle-class morality, she plotted her revenge: to teach Lou a lesson that she would not forget. Elisabeth wrote many poisonous letters to Lou's family, Rée's mother, and the Prussian police. It was Elisabeth's desire that Lou, the woman her brother loved, be expelled from the country (Peters, *My Sister, My Spouse* 143–44). Of his sister's (and mother's) reaction, Nietzsche writes, in a letter to Overbeck, "I have the Naumburg virtue against me" (quoted in Peters, *Zarathustra's Sister* 67).

The faithful Llama weighted with Naumburg virtue, soured with jealousy and spite, is the First Woman. She espouses love and devotion—as did Elisabeth. However, for Nietzsche, the virtues "love and devotion" are degenerative and life-sapping. In *The Case of Wagner* he writes: "In many cases of feminine love, perhaps including the most famous ones above all, love is merely a more refined form of parasitism, a form of nestling down in another soul, sometimes even in the flesh of another—alas, always decidedly at the expense of 'the host'!" (161).

In contradistinction to the First Woman, the faithful, weight-bearing, duty-honoring Llama, is the Second Woman.[5] According to Nietzsche, the second metamorphosis is characterized as such:

> the spirit here becomes a lion; it wants to capture freedom and be lord in its own desert. . . . To create freedom for itself and a sacred No even to duty. . . . To seize the right to new values—that is the most terrible proceeding for a weight-bearing and reverential spirit. Truly, to this spirit it is a theft and a work for an animal of prey. Once it loved this 'Thou Shalt' as its holiest thing: now it has to find illusion and caprice even in the holiest, that it may steal freedom from its love: the lion is needed for this theft. (*Thus Spoke Zarathustra* 55–56)[6]

This "thieving" woman is a woman who says "No" to duty, to the demands of traditional morality and expectations. These are women with whom Nietzsche was familiar, particularly with the grand patroness of the German feminist movement, Malwida Von Meysenberg (it was in her home that Lou Salomé was introduced to Paul Rée). Contemporary feminists are often offended at Nietzsche's condemnation of this Second Woman. Indeed, his criticisms are harsh. For example, in *Beyond Good and Evil*, he writes, "Woman wants to become self-reliant—and for that reason she is beginning to enlighten men about 'woman as such': *this* is one of the worst developments of the general *uglification* of Europe. For what must these clumsy attempts of women at scientific self-exposure bring to light" (162–63). What Nietzsche found reprehensible about the feminist movement was the means and goals of its adherents. What it strived for (and there are certainly modern-day analogs) were the same political rights and privileges that men enjoyed at the time; in short, they sought to attain the state of male being and male subjectivity. Nietzsche argues that these women "imitate all the stupidities with which 'man' in Europe, European 'manliness,' is sick" (*Beyond Good and Evil* 169). The Second Woman's goal is an unhealthy, unethical one. It is Nietzsche's argument that humanism, subjectivity, and politics are sick—diseased with bad faith and *ressentiment*. The goals of "equality" and "de-feminization" are cancerous and motivated by a degenerate will to power. As such, the Second Woman figures as a beast of prey, characterized as a tarantula:

> Your triangle and symbol sit black upon your back[7] . . . [and] revenge sits within your soul . . . you preachers of *equality!* You are tarantulas and dealers in hidden revengefulness! . . . "We shall practise revenge and outrage against all who are not as we are"—thus the tarantula-hearts promise themselves. "And 'will to equality'—that itself shall henceforth be the name of virtue; and we shall raise outcry against everything that has power!" You preachers of equality, thus from you the tyrant-madness of impotence cries for "equality": thus your most secret tyrant-appetite disguises itself in words of virtue. (*Thus Spoke Zarathustra* 123)

Becoming the Third Woman

One woman in particular played an extraordinarily significant role in the life and writings of Nietzsche: Lou Salomé.[8] By any standards, Lou was an unusual woman: brilliant, passionate, attractive, prolific, insightful, creative, and defiant in regards to the cultural restraints that disempower women. A critic of Lou, Dieter Bassermann, describes her this way: "Wherever Lou went she caused whirlpools and currents of spirit and feeling, untroubled like a cataract whether its course would bring blessing or desolation. A mighty, unbroken force of nature, daemonic, primordial without any feminine or indeed human weaknesses—a virago in the sense of the ancients, but lacking in genuine *humanitas,* a being from prehistoric times" (quoted in Peters, *My Sister, My Spouse* 13). It is this Woman who figures as the bridge from the Second Woman to the Third Woman, as the overcoming of the Second Woman. As the Second Woman, she was a beast of prey, a woman who said "no" to duty and the moral obligations of the time. She assumed a position of equality and subjectivity. Yet, although she was very much an independent woman, she was very resistant to the feminist ideals of the militant suffragettes (*My Sister, My Spouse* 190). Situated in a liminal state between the Second and the Third, Lou was not yet able to overcome herself, her castrating desires, her will to power; she was not yet ready to say "yes" to Zarathustra and to become the Affirming Woman (Lou ultimately rejected Nietzsche's thought as she devoted the latter part of her life to Freudian psychoanalysis).[9] And yet, it is her "no" to Nietzsche which engendered the text *Thus Spoke Zarathustra* (*My Sister, My Spouse* 8; Shapiro 128). Thus, paradoxically, it was Lou's reluctance to surrender that resulted in Nietzsche's metaphorical impregnation. (It has been said of Lou, Peters tells us, that she "would form a passionate attachment to a man and 9 months later the man would give birth to a book" [*My Sister, My Spouse* 13; Shapiro 126–28]. But again, the gestational, creative gesture must be understood as separate from the Mother.) Indeed, as Peters states, "it is sobering to reflect that in 1882 the course of Nietzsche's life depended on the yes or no of a 21 year old girl" (*Zarathustra's Sister* 143).

It is Lou's "no" that constructs the possibility for the overcoming of the Second Woman, for the Coming of the Third Woman, the Affirming Woman.[10] According to *Zarathustra*, the Third Woman, the third metamorphosis is to become a child: "innocence and forgetfulness, a new beginning, a sport, a self-propelling wheel, a first motion, a sacred Yes. Yes, a sacred Yes is needed . . . for the sport of creation: the spirit now wills *its own* will" (55). It is this affirmation which is needed for the act of self-creation, of overcoming the reactive forces which define Male subjectivity as such and of which the First and the Second Woman suffer—*ressentiment* and bad faith. Hence, this "self-propelling" wheel/will is markedly different from the philosopher's "unmoved mover." As Nietzsche's critique of metaphysics has born out, the philosopher's unmoved mover is a reactive construction: used to protect the philosopher from the untruth of truth. Becoming the Third Woman is an act of *poiēsis*—a creative act, rather than a reactive act; the Third Woman is an artist; she creates something new—new values, a new ethic, a new way of being through forgetting (*Gay Science* 37; Thiele 119–38). One could say that "becoming the Third Woman" is "becoming Woman" as spoken of by Deleuze and Guattari: "Although all becomings are already molecular, including becoming-woman, it must be said that all becomings begin with and pass through becoming-woman. It is the key to all the other becomings" (*Thousand Plateaus* 277). All becomings require active, not reactive forces. Active forces emanate from the affirmative will to power, prevailing over the reactive forces. The artist is the penultimate product of these active forces. Reactive forces emanate from negation, from the will to nothing. The ascetic man is the lowest example of being, as a product of *ressentiment* and bad faith (Deleuze, *Nietzsche* 111–46). The affirming Third Woman's creative gesture is to create herself as a work of art, to create the *Ubermensch;* yet, unlike the philosophic imperative, this creative

gesture has no representative aspirations, no desire nor intention to create truth. Becoming has no *telos;* it is a process without a goal; it aspires
to (Gorgias's) nothing. Nietzsche writes, "what is truth to woman?
From the beginning, nothing has been more alien, repugnant, and hos-
tile to woman than truth—her great art is the lie, her highest concern
is mere appearance and beauty" (*Beyond Good and Evil* 163). And elsewhere, "Finally *women* . . . : do they not *have* to be first of all and
above all else actresses? . . . They 'put on something' even when they
take off everything. Woman is so artistic" (*Gay Science* 317). It is this
act of dissimulation, this respect for *apatē,* which offers the possibility
for a transfiguration, a transvaluation, of the Western metaphysical tradition that has held us hostage. It is Nietzsche's fundamental argument
that we need art [illusion] to save us from the truth (*Will to Power* 435),
that art is the "great means of making life possible, the great seduction
to life, the great stimulant of life[,] . . . the only superior counterforce
to all will to denial of life" (*Will to Power* 452). He writes:

> we convalescents still need art, [but] it is another kind of art
> [*pace* Wagnerian opera, for example]—a mocking, light,
> fleeting, divinely untroubled, divinely artificial art that, like
> a pure flame, licks into unclouded skies. Above all, an art for
> artists, for artists only! We know better afterward what
> above all is needed for this: cheerfulness, any cheerfulness,
> my friends. . . . There are a few things we now know too
> well, we knowing ones: oh, how we now learn to forget
> well, and to be good at *not* knowing, as artists! . . . We no
> longer believe that truth remains truth when the veils are
> withdrawn. . . . Today we consider it a matter of decency
> not to wish to see everything naked, or to be present at
> everything, or to understand and "know" everything. . . .
> One should have more respect for the bashfulness with which
> nature has hidden behind riddles and iridescent uncertain-
> ties. Perhaps truth is a woman who has reasons for not
> letting us see her reasons? Perhaps her name is—to speak
> Greek—*Baubo?* Oh those Greeks! They knew how to live.
> What is required for that is to stop courageously at the sur-
> face, the fold, the skin, to adore appearance, to believe in
> forms, tones, words, in the whole Olympus of appearance.
> Those Greeks were superficial—*out of profundity.* . . . And
> is not this precisely what we are again coming back to, we
> daredevils of the spirit . . . ? Are we not, precisely in this re-
> spect, Greeks? Adorers of forms, of tones, of words? And
> therefore—*artists?* (*Gay Science* 37–38)[11]

This artistic one is alternately Lou, Ariadne, Helen, and Baubo: she is the power, the force of self-overcoming. According to Deleuze, "Ariadne is Nietzsche's first secret, the first feminine power, the anima, the inseparable fiancée of Dionysian affirmation" (*Nietzsche* 20). Ariadne is in contradistinction to the First Woman, which is, Deleuze continues, "altogether different; negative and moralising, the terrible mother [and sister], the mother of good and evil, she who depreciates and denies life" (20). The First Woman is born of bad faith, of guilt, and of duty. The Second Woman is born of *ressentiment* and the negative. The Third Woman is Ariadne, is she who forgets and thus affirms (see Deleuze, *Nietzsche* 186–89).

"Forgetting" the History of Rhetoric

In his "On the Uses and Disadvantages of History for Life" (in *Untimely Meditations*) Nietzsche discusses three historiographical methodologies which could roughly be compared to his Three Women: the first is the "monumental" method by which history is written as the tale of great actors, as the effects of great individuals. The second methodology is termed the "antiquarian" by which the historian focuses on causes as it produces narratives which demonstrate that the present is not the effect of individual efforts, but the result of interconnecting conditions which render the present an inevitable, not accidental, outcome. The third method is termed the "critical." The critical history, as the Third Strategy, is presented by Nietzsche as antidotal. A critical history comes about as a therapeutic need to "break up and dissolve a part of the past" (*Untimely Meditations* 75). Whereas the first two historical impulses are based on remembrances (that is, the memory of great individuals or the memory of tradition, continuing conditions circumscribing the present), the third history employs forgetfulness. Nietzsche writes in *On the Genealogy of Morals*, "There [can] be no happiness, no cheerfulness, no hope, no pride, no *present*, without forgetfulness" (58). John Poulakos, in "Nietzsche and Histories of Rhetoric," elaborates, "If we are to place history in the service of life, we must rid ourselves of the burdens of the past and strive to create from them materials that are useful, that augment our capacity to live joyfully" (90). For Nietzsche, the burdens of the past must be forgotten if one is to live in the present. Guilt and the constant desire for redemption are symptomatic of the will to death, not the will to life. The burdens of the past anchor the ego, continually refueling its bad faith and *ressentiment*.

Vitanza's version of a historiography that forgets would be "sub/versive." He writes,

the role of the Sub/Versive Historians . . . will be to bring
into realization what has been *displaced*—and that is the Sophistic idea of *Kairos*, not just in relation to the theological
notion of a "moment of crisis" or "a time filled with significance" . . . but more so in relation to the other meaning that
the concept has and upon which I building—namely, *many
competing, contradictory voices*—whether serious or comedic or downright silly or stupid, whether disciplinary or
metadisciplinary or "nondisciplinary," whether *logoi* or *dissoi logoi* or *dissoi paralogoi,* or finally whether commensurable or other/wise. ("Critical Sub/Versions" 60–61)

Steve Whitson's unpublished manuscript "Nietzsche, Deception, and
the History of Rhetoric," could be considered a sub/versive history, an
incommensurable historiography. Whitson outlines Nietzsche's three
genres of history across the questionably penned work *My Sister and
I*—the claimed and dis-claimed autobiographical work written by Nietzsche during his time in the sanitarium in Turin. The book tells of the
incestuous relationship he had with his sister Elisabeth. Whitson points
out Derrida's claim in *Glas* that the incest taboo is the foundation that
permits the Hegelian dialectic to function. This claim, no doubt, elec-
trifies the interpretation of Nietzsche's relationship with all women and
with the history of rhetoric.

What this third position, or Third Sophistic, advocates is becoming
Woman and embracing forgetfulness, and therefore it "forgets" the
philosophical demand for first principles, which believe that "any explanation is better than none" (*Twilight* 51). This is how we will our
nothingness, our will to death. Nietzsche has told us repeatedly that it
is our constant demand for causality, for agency, for subjectivity, that
represents our degenerative being.

Remembering, as a function of subjectivity and of its first principle
of causality, denies its own rhetoricity just as truth denies its own rhetoricity, its being, as in Nietzsche's infamous words, "a mobile army
of metaphors, metonyms, anthropomorphisms, in short a sum of human relations which were poetically and rhetorically heightened, transferred, and adorned, and after long use seem solid, canonical, and binding to a nation" ("On Truth and Lying" 250). Paradoxically, it is the
act of forgetting that embraces rhetoricity—that is rhetoric as Woman,
sophistry, or the instability of language and the incommensurability of
discourse. It is this act of forgetting that makes possible the overcoming
of Man and the coming of the *Ubermensch,* or the being who lives
without revenge, bad faith, and *ressentiment,* the being always in the

process of becoming (*Will to Power* 377), who creates itself as a work of art (*Gay Science* 232). Nietzsche writes, "Becoming as invention, willing, self-denial, overcoming of oneself: no subject but an action, a positing, creative, no 'causes and effects' " (*Will to Power* 331; see also 377–78).

The *Dissoi-Logoi* of Woman: Implications

In *On the Genealogy of Morals,* Nietzsche notes the genealogy not only of good and evil, but also of his "tragic" philosophy. He writes:

> The affirmation of passing away *and destroying,* which is the decisive feature of a Dionysian philosophy; saying Yes to opposition and war; *becoming,* along with a radical repudiation of the very concept of *being*—all this is clearly more closely related to me than anything else thought to date. The doctrine of the "eternal recurrence," that is, of the unconditional and infinitely repeated circular course of all things— this doctrine of Zarathustra *might* in the end have been taught already by Heraclitus. (273–74)[12]

And what is it that Heraclitus will have taught? Heraclitus is perhaps best known for his doctrine of the necessary and inevitable tension of opposing forces. We both are and are not. We both step and do not step in the same river (Freeman 28, 51).

Heraclitus's image of a bow distressed, or of a lyre strung, demonstrates his "paratheory" of opposition. Harmonic music is the result of tension, of an unresolved paradox; the harmony of the spheres is not cosmological. The paradox of the bow is further exemplified by—as a Heraclitean fragment makes a pun of—its name: "The bow is called Life, but its work is death" (Freeman 28, fragment 48). The Greek word *bios* is for life, *bios* for bow. Life comes from death, death from life. Pleasure from pain, pain from pleasure. Yes from no, no from yes. Nietzsche echoes Heraclitus: negating and destroying are conditions of the yes-saying life (*Ecce Homo* 328; see also Kofman's "Nietzsche"). Both are commenting on, both are bearing witness *to,* the paradoxical disorder of things—to the opposing forces at work simultaneously, to the tension that resists resolution. According to Nietzsche, Parmenides (in contrast to Heraclitus) was unable to

> get past the concept of a negative quality, the concept of non-existence . . . can something which is not, be? For the only single form of knowledge which we trust immediately and absolutely and to deny which amounts to insanity is

the tautology A=A. But just this tautological insight proclaims inexorably: What is not, is not. What is, is. And sud-
denly Parmenides felt a monstrous logical sin burdening his
whole previous life. . . . he must hate in his deepest soul the
antinomy-play of Heraclitus. (*Philosophy* 76–77)

Parmenides thus "flees" into the "rigor mortis of the coldest emptiest
concept of all, the concept of being" because he is unable to be enchanted and seduced (80–81).

And thus we return again to Helen, the enchanting seducer, specifically to her bridal tapestry. Homer writes of Helen weaving a tapestry recording the "many contests that the horse-taming Trojans and the
bronze-chitoned Achaeans were suffering for her sake in deadly war"
(*Iliad* 3.125–28). Norman Austin explains the tradition regarding her
tapestry: "Such contests in archaic Greek tradition lead in two directions: to athletic contests, on the one hand, like the celebrated Olympian Games; and to bride competitions, on the other, where heroes
gathered as a woman's suitors and competed for the woman-as-prize"
(39). But Helen's tapestry, unlike Penelope's, will remain forever
unfinished as "the competition in [Helen's] case is perpetually renewed
and perpetually undecided. . . . Helen's privilege is to signify for men
that zone where quotidian being borders being itself, where all meanings are in perpetual dispute, and misinterpretation is death" (Austin
40). Helen's tapestry, therefore, represents "Homer's Contest," a post-
humously published work in which Nietzsche argues that the value of
such contests lies in continued tension created by their ultimate unde-
cidability, by their perpetual *agon*. This tension is played out through
the distance, through the spaces between, in the words of Vitanza, "dis-
logoi and dat-logoi."

Dissoi Logoi, of course, is the title given to an anonymous text
found among the manuscripts of Sextus Empiricus. The *Dissoi Logoi*,
or "Twofold Arguments," is characteristic of the sophistic method, or
perhaps more appropriately, the sophistic movement, whereby opposing
arguments are followed concerning, for example, the "identity and
non-identity of apparently opposite moral and philosophic terms such
as good and bad, true and false" (G. B. Kerferd, *Sophistic Movement*
54). Some have suggested that the *Dissoi Logoi* could have been authored by a member of the Protagoras school, as Protagoras was well
known for this argumentative method. Diogenes Laertius writes of the
doctrine of Protagoras thus: "He was the first to say that there are two
logoi [arguments] concerning everything, these being opposed each to
the other. It was by means of these logoi that he proceeded to propound
arguments involving a series of stages, and he was the first to do this"

(quoted in Kerferd 84). Beyond Protagoras's two opposing arguments, a Third Sophistic, Third Woman counts, as Vitanza does, to "some more" (*Negation* 7)—or, rather, takes no account for the unaccountable.

Kerferd suggests that the point is "not simply the occurrence of opposing arguments but the fact that both opposing arguments could be expressed by a single speaker, as it were *within* a single complex argument" (84). What is at stake here is the virtue of the *logos*. In contradistinction to Eleatic philosophers and followers of Parmenides, *logos* is not coherent and noncontradictory. Again, what is at stake is the virtue of the *logos*. What the sophistic *dissoi logoi* approach demonstrates is the infidelity of the *logos;* that is, the inability of the *logos* to speak one and always the same. Within the space of one argument lies the opposing force, so that a paradoxical *aporia* or tension distances the argument from a stable conclusion. Indeed any *logos,* statement, or position inherently contradicts itself, negates itself. For Ferdinand de Saussure, there is no definitive truth which can be stated in positive terms; "there are only differences" (118). A poststructuralist articulation of this is Jacques Derrida's neologism *"différance"*: difference doubled by deferral *(Speech and Phenomena).* Meaning occurs through the play of *difference*—in the space of a closed system. Meaning occurs through the tension of difference, through the tension of distance—a distance that is always already simultaneously overreached and underreached but never traversed.

One of the opening scenes of Nietzsche's *Thus Spoke Zarathustra*—focuses on a tightrope walker—the man who risks himself constantly—who after strutting his hour upon the stage loses himself and falls and, who in the process of falling, loses consciousness only to regain it for a brief moment before his death. Zarathustra comments, "Man is a rope, fastened between animal and Superman—a rope over an abyss. A dangerous going-across, a dangerous wayfaring, a dangerous looking-back, a dangerous shuddering and staying-still" (43). And that "rope" over the abyss is infinitely divisible. Half the distance between point A and point B is point C; half the distance between point B and point C is point D. The distance can be divided endlessly; there is a space between each point that can never be traversed. Each point, therefore, is distanced by a gap, a fissure. A line is mostly space: empty, endlessly divisible space.

Furthermore, a line is a fiction; that is, what we think of as a continuous line is no more than a series of points, a series of gaps. Even a point is a fiction, as a subatomic particle, like an electron, is mostly space. Likewise, a community is a fiction. The polis, the political body, is a line drawn to circumscribe the fluid nonpoints, the "wavicles" called "citizens." A line is a logical convenience, a rational connection—just as the "community" is a totalizing and safe dot-to-dot picture that ignores the abyss of difference that exists between each dot. Deleuze and Guattari explain, "one does not reach becoming or the molecular, as long as a line is connected to two distant points. . . . A line of becoming is not defined by points that it connects, or by points that compose it; on the contrary, it passes *between* points" (*Thousand Plateaus* 293).

In contradistinction to the traditional political virtue of *sōphrosynē*—that is, literally, safe ways of being, of thinking—Nietzsche argues in *Beyond Good and Evil* for the tightrope walker who "lives 'unphilosophically' and 'unwisely,' above all *imprudently*, and feels the burden and the duty of a hundred attempts and temptations of life—*he risks himself constantly*, he plays the wicked game—" (125; emphasis mine). Likewise, the "unwise"—if such a concept could be thought—is the one who risks the tightrope, risks the whole, risks "consensus," in a sophistic and "kairological" way (Sloterdijk 21), rather than in a logical and traditionally "political" way. Can we then even speak of "politics" in a paradoxical world? Of course. Perhaps the better question is: Can we speak of a politics or of a political being that acknowledges gaps, distance, and *différance*? Nietzsche indeed speaks of such a self and offers, not really a model, but perhaps what could best be called a "pathos." The self not constituted through and by the herd mentality risks the self by risking the gaps, the fissures, and the distances of infinite possibilities moment by moment by moment. It is, paradoxically, by risking the self that one gains an ethical self. It is the danger itself, according to Peter Sloterdijk, that constitutes the self: "Every essential historical moment is . . . a 'moment of danger,' and it is this danger that mediates all subjectivity. Thus, one can also say—presuming a slight taste for dark formulation—that it is not the thinker who is engaging himself and thinking. Rather, it is this danger that engages itself and thinks through him" (*Thinker on Stage* 21).

As the tightrope is nothing more than discontinuous gaps, falling is inevitable. The fall of man is a fall into Woman—into the space of space, into the abyss, into the tragic space, or—in Julia Kristeva's lexicon—into the *chora*. Zarathustra proclaims: "It is not the height, it is the abyss that is terrible! The abyss where the glance plunges *downward* and the hand grasps *upward*. There the heart grows giddy through its two-fold will" (164; emphasis his). It is the fall into the abyss that constitutes the twofold will: the *dissoi logoi* of subjectivity. Again, the invention of the self requires the "frenzy of disintegration" (Sloterdijk 28), the annihilation of the self which echoes the Heraclitean bow of life and death.

The necessary fall into the "cavern of eros" (Sloterdijk 28) is a fall, however, that defies gravity. The fall is a fall without gravity in that it is a fall without *telos*—the momentum is not directed toward any end, any closure, or any possession. The fall is generated by a desire that desires itself—not an object of desire (*Beyond Good and Evil* 93). The fall is also without gravity in that it is not a grave fall (nor a fall toward the grave, toward death), but it is a light and weightless fall characterized by laughter and, Nietzsche writes, a "certain divine frivolity, an 'upward' without tension and constraint, a 'downward' without condescension and humiliation—without *gravity!*" (*Beyond Good and Evil* 106). The ethical subject risks the fall—and laughs at the fall. He/she risks the self by laughing at the self as it falls into the space of Woman.

Again, this space is not extrasymbolic. It has no nostalgia for the real. The ethical subject seeks not to escape from language (which is the metaphysical desire to inhabit Plato's "blessed isle" referred to in the *Gorgias*), but rather to fall into language, into the vertiginous possibilities of the not-yet articulated. The ethical subject seeks not to control language, but rather to let it be. This is, according to Heidegger, the act of venturing language ("What Are Poets For?"), of risking the game, of dualing/dueling the cast of the die.

This is the difference between the discourse of the ego and the discourse of the Third Woman: the ego is a function of deliberative discourse—of establishing a "course of action," of ethical/political action (Aristotle, *Rhetoric* I.4–8). But, as we have seen via Hamlet, deliberative rhetoric is a procrastination technique that allows the ego to not act—or to act only when it is too late. Deliberative rhetoric is based on Aristotelian assumptions about the nature of language as communicative, informational, and communal. A Third Sophistic praxis is, contrariwise, "dicastic": that is, every utterance is a new cast of the die (Deleuze, *Nietzsche* 25–27). It is neither probabilistic nor predictable. Dicastic discourse is seen, by philosophic standards, to be lacking in self-restraint like Woman or the dark horse: excessive, intemperate, desire-driven.

Whereas sophistic rhetoric seduces one away from one's self, deliberative rhetoric produces the self, the self-identical ego. Deliberative rhetoric, with its fixed and stable subject positions (speaker and listener; I and you), is the ideological *technē* whereby subjects are produced. Althusser writes:

> individuals [are transformed] into subjects . . . by that very precise operation which I have called interpellation or hailing, and which can be imagined along the lines of the most commonplace police (or other) hailing: "Hey, you there!" Assuming that the theoretical scene I have imagined takes

place in the street, the hailed individual will turn round. By this mere one-hundred-and-eighty-degree physical conversion, he becomes a *subject*. Why? Because he has recognized that the hail was "really" addressed to him, and that "it was really him who was hailed" (and not someone else). (*Lenin and Philosophy* 174–75)

Deliberative rhetoric is also the pedagogical discourse, the purpose of which is to construct "civil servants." Nietzsche writes: "'What is the task of all higher education?'—To turn a man into a machine. . . . 'Who is the perfect man?'—The civil servant" (*Twilight* 83–84).

Woman and the Pathos of Distance

In *Thus Spoke Zarathustra,* truth personified laughs at the male philosopher who believes in Woman and truth: "Although you men call me 'profound' or 'faithful,' 'eternal,' 'mysterious' . . . I am merely changeable and untamed and in everything a woman, and no virtuous one" (131–32). Truth, Nietzsche contends, is the great lie, the great deceiver. Truth is a woman, veiled and fickle—a shallow surface of mere appearance and beauty. When "truth" is embraced as a deception, when we allow ourselves to be seduced by Woman—rather than positing either as eternal, stable verities—we fall into a space of style and invention that affirms difference—not the Hegelian difference that opposes merely to assert the selfsame.

Woman is a riddle, a paradox, an *aporia*. Woman is pregnant with possibility (*Thus Spoke Zarathustra* 91). Woman is pregnant with the indeterminable, the unknowable. It is impossible, therefore, to predict what Woman may bring forth. The "rough beast" that will come can only be known in and through Woman. It can never be known in itself, despite Socrates' rather premature claim that it was possible for him, as he was the midwife who could distinguish the "wind egg from the genuine birth" (Plato, *Theaetetus*). But the genuine birth never comes—only a series of aborted attempts. Woman is pregnant with the possibility of birth (of truth), and simultaneously pregnant with the impossibility of giving birth (to truth), the impossibility of bringing forth truth, of making truth present or presentable.

Thus Woman maintains the distance between us and truth. Of this distance, Sloterdijk writes, "We maintain an irrevocable distance from [truth], a distance that so radically determines our everyday existence in the world that, even with the staunchest will to truth, *we are not at liberty to distance ourselves from this condition of distance.* As a rule, it is impossible to survive the final dissolution of the distance that exists between us and the unimaginable reality of the terrible truth" (39, emphasis mine). And what is this terrible truth? That truth is not; that it is Woman. Woman is all style, no substance; or, rather, Woman's style is her substance. As style, she operates as a veil, as the distance between what is not and what is. Woman is the uncrossable chasm, the untraversable space—the distance that can never be overcome: "One thirsts for her and is not satisfied, one looks at her through veils, one snatches at her through nets" (Nietzsche, *Thus Spoke Zarathustra* 132). But one can never embrace her, never feel, see, nor taste her—although one may fathom her unfathomable depths—because she is not. She is always just out of reach, seducing from an unbearable and constantly deferring distance.

This is Aspasia's distance. As you recall, Aspasia was one of the well-known *hetairai* of the classical age.[13] But she was not a citizen of the Athenian polis as she was an immigrant from Miletus. Although she was denied the full citizen rights due to her birth and gender, she was a highly influential member of her community. Plato's *Menexenus* states that she was once a teacher of Socrates, giving him rhetorical guidance and instruction. The work also suggests that it was she who wrote Pericles' funeral oration. Of course, traditional readings have claimed that Plato was not completely serious here (Plutarch 151). But, all accounts considered, including Plutarch's and Cheryl Glenn's *(Rhetoric Retold)*, it is obvious that Aspasia, as long-time companion to Pericles, was a woman to be taken seriously by virtue of her intelligence, wit, and charm—and part of her charm was perhaps attributable to her rhetorical style, which was said to have resembled Gorgias's (Philostratus, *Epistle*, reprinted in Sprague 41–42). Although Pericles gave her the unofficial status of common-law wife, she belonged to no one. Although she was not a legitimate member of the polis, she had great influence. Her salon entertained Socrates, Democritus, and Anaxagoras, among others, who examined their system of government and criticized its faults. The citizens of Athens charged that Aspasia had influenced Pericles for the injury of the state and that she had instructed him in unspeakable and indescribable vices. Aspasia maintained a distance from men, from the polis, from traditional notions of marriage and protocol. This is Lou, this is Ariadne, this is Helen; she was charged a nihilist—an anarchist, and yet she constructed, created a polis of sorts that was interested in new ways of thinking, new ways of maintaining relationships. A pathos of distance created by a woman.

Metaphorically, it could be said that it is her distance that accounts for her power and charm. This is precisely what Nietzsche argues, that "the enchantment and the most powerful effect of woman, is, to use the language of philosophers, an effect at a distance, an *actio in distans;*

there belongs thereto, however, primarily and above all—*distance!*" (*Gay Science* 124). Woman is, in effect, distance itself.

It is necessary to maintain the distance. Nietzsche is interested in the "genuine" philosopher—in the philosopher who no longer believes in truth or Woman and who is, hence, neither "genuine" nor a "philosopher" (*Thus Spoke Zarathustra* 144). This Third Woman/Sophist knows only that she/he has fallen in and out of the spaces of woman, abandoning herself/himself moment by moment, and like Zarathustra has danced upon the tightrope, the rope that was infinitely more space than line—and has fallen time and time again through the gaps into the abyss of the *chora*. She/he is the yes-sayer who affirms life, who begets life, who creates beyond herself/himself (145). Thus, for Nietzsche, the notions of distance and the "tragic pathos" become the *"pathos of distance"*—a pathos based not on consensus, not on the collapse of difference, not on the slow metabolism that puts *différance* on ice, but rather a pathos based on dissensus, difference, distance. In *Will to Power*, Nietzsche argues that the will to power (the active, nonreactive force) is not a being but a pathos. And what the will wills is to affirm difference. In *Beyond Good and Evil*, Nietzsche defines the pathos of distance as the ingrained difference between strata and as a craving for an ever-new widening of distances, including distances within one's self— a process of self-overcoming. The pathos of difference lies in contradistinction to the notion of community that has been defined—as total identity (Habermas, Aristotle).

Woman, as this difference, this distance, resists identity, representation, and truth. Indeed, Woman questions our will to truth, our will to represent, our will to stabilize all becoming as being. The Third Woman reveals this will as a sickness, as a will to nothingness. Nietzsche states in *The Gay Science* that every metaphysics, every philosophy that knows some final state is motivated by sickness (*ressentiment* and bad faith) (34). To overcome this sickness engendered by metaphysics and truth, we overcome ourselves, our subjectivity; we become the Third Woman. This becoming is a process, not a state, not an identity, not a political program. This is why, Graybeal writes, the "great feminine figures reappear throughout [*Thus Spoke Zarathustra*], to undermine and unsettle any pretense Zarathustra makes of coming up with a program, a plan, a new symbolic structure which would only issue again in nihilism" (76). Against this nihilism, Nietzsche offers the Third Woman as an affirmation—the "Yes-saying pathos *par excellence*" (*Ecce Homo* 296) in order to create possibilities of being, political or otherwise, within her distance, within the space of invention, within the space of forgetting.

4

Après l'orgie: Baudrillard and the Seduction of Truth

> We immoralists . . . A powerful seduction fights on our behalf, the most powerful perhaps that there has ever been—the seduction of truth—"Truth"? Who has forced this word on me? But I repudiate it; but I disdain this proud word: no, we do not need even this; . . . The spell that fights on our behalf, the eye of Venus that charms and blinds even our opponents, is *the magic of the extreme,* the seduction that everything extreme exercises: we immoralists—we are the most extreme.
>
> —Nietzsche, *The Will to Power*

> Is not Zarathustra in view of all this a *seducer?*—But what does he himself say, as he returns again for the first time to his solitude? Precisely the opposite of everything that any "sage," "saint," "world-redeemer," or any other decadent would say in such a case.—Not only does he speak differently, he also is different—.
>
> —Nietzsche, *Ecce Homo*

In 1983, more than two thousand years after Gorgias's "On Nature" and a hundred years following Friedrich Nietzsche's *The Birth of Tragedy,* Jean Baudrillard, responding to the orgiastic tendencies of the political, sexual, and social revolutions of the 1960s, published a small piece with the provocative title "What Are You Doing after the Orgy?" His title comes from the brief anecdote in which, during an orgy, a man whispers this unexpected question into a woman's ear. This anecdote encapsulates Baudrillard's theoretical strategy: to ask what comes after the obscene; to wonder what lies beyond the banality of truth, meaning, and representation; to question the joint project of modernism, humanism, Marxism, psychoanalysis, hermeneutics, semiotics, philosophy, criticism, and all other systems of production, which have attempted to master, to dominate, to appropriate the unrepresentable and thus render it obscene, he writes, by "materializing [it] by force" (*Seduction* 34). Baudrillard argues that "obscenity is a vulgar offering; it is fundamentally naive and sentimental in terms of what it considers to be the material truth of things without taking into their complexity and subtlety of appearances" ("What Are You Doing" 45). Mas'ud Zavarzadeh and Donald Morton in "Theory as Resistance" describe this process as such: "Things become 'something' when they are used in a culturally senseful way, that is to say, when they are situated on a cultural grid of intelligibility in a social location. It is the process of such situating—the use of discourses to enunciate them—that produces a 'thing' as (socially) 'something' (32). This "thingification," this overzealous production of meaningful somethings is what Baudrillard calls "obscene" and "pornographic." In the midst of this pornographic production frenzy, Baudrillard's words come to us as a seductive whisper, and if we had ears to hear him, we would accept his challenge to seduce ourselves beyond the current orgy of meaning.

After the orgy, or *après*-modernism, for Baudrillard, doesn't evoke connotations of temporality or historical, linear, or traditionally metonymic sequencing. What is *"après"* for Baudrillard is, rather, metaleptically understood, just as for Jean-François Lyotard postmodernism precedes any modernism (*Postmodern Condition* 79). Lyotard explains that a postmodern artist's *oeuvre* displaces traditional aesthetic criteria and past rules by formulating the rules

> of what *will have been done*. Hence the fact that work and text have the character of an *event;* hence also, they always come too late for their author, or, what amounts to the same thing, their being put into work, their realization *(mise en oeuvre)* always begins too soon. *Post modern* would have to be understood according to the paradox of the future *(post)* anterior *(modo)*. (81)

Thus, generated in a ambiguous temporal frame of "always already" and yet "not yet," the postmodern artist becomes, as in Nietzsche's case, a "posthumous man," and the postmodern moment appears, as Gorgias suggests, "kairotic." For Baudrillard, then, what will have followed the orgy—the orgy of meaning, truth, and representation—is seduction, and what will have preceded the orgiast—the philosopher—is Woman. Woman and/as Seduction is what will have survived/resisted the modernist assault on the enchanted world and its denial of the play of appearances—an assault and denial accomplished via the tyranny of truth, subjectivity, and communication. Using Gorgias's tripart argument or "tragedy of knowledge" as explored in chapter 2 as a model, this chapter will explore Baudrillard's response to the following very modern notions that (1) truth exists—the real exists and somehow coheres with and correlates to its representation; (2) the truth, the real, or what is, can be known, understood, and interpreted—in fact, there exists an epistemological imperative to indeed know all, to wrest from nature her secrets, and to dredge the soul for truth; (3) the function of language is to serve as a medium of communicating these truths and understandings and to thereby constitute a community of like-minded peers who will work together in harmony and peace.

Much work has been done within postmodern and deconstructive theoretical works to reveal the phallogocentric underpinnings of the Enlightenment project. Baudrillard leaves this work to others although his writings clearly represent an understanding of the philosophical tradition. His "attack" on this tradition takes place within a different sphere. For where others attempt to deconstruct the phallus in order to privilege the womb or to deconstruct Kantian ideals and Platonic truths in order to establish consensus-seeking social-construction notions of knowledge, Baudrillard places both enterprises—phallogocentric philosophy and negative deconstruction—within the same universe of "production." Both groups are planted firmly within the tradition that assumes being (whether *a priori* given or socially constructed), that assumes the necessity for meaning, and that assumes the efficacy of language to guarantee such. Now all these assumptions find themselves fulfilled within a very particular universe—the universe of production. The question Baudrillard poses is not whether truth exists but why we insist that it does.

The Tyranny of Truth

As we established in our discussions of Gorgias and Parmenides, Nietzsche and Hegel, the debate over the existence of being—truth, what is, the real—is a perennial argument. It is an argument for which the stakes are insurmountable; those stakes being, namely, who has the power to decide what is and according to what standards such a decision is to be made.

Baudrillard's earliest attacks on truth were articulated by his resistance to Karl Marx and Sigmund Freud. Despite their historical reputations as "hermeneuts of suspicion" and as theoretical revolutionaries who worked to debunk the great truths of their time, they were, according to Baudrillard, the two greatest prophets and profiteers of production. Neither, Baudrillard has argued, was able to escape the mirror; that is, neither was able to avoid the modernist error of representation—the beliefs that, at bedrock, there is some referent, some principle of truth, and that one's purpose is to reflect it accurately and to find one's self in that reflection—one's meaning, one's truth, one's cure, one's liberation. The modernist goal, then, is to somehow "get to the bottom" of a reflection in order to find truth, the "kernel," the final turtle.[1] This drive to represent, therefore, is complicit with the metaphysical impulse. It is a familiar impulse. We recognize it with Parmenides and his Goddess, with Plato and his allegory of the cave and his belief in ideal forms. More recently, since the seventeenth century, according to philosopher and pragmatist Richard Rorty in *Philosophy and the Mirror of Nature,* the mind has been compared to a mirror that reflects reality; accurate reflections constitute knowledge. Such a premise relies on a centered conception of self and on very firm dichotomies of subject and object, of reality and appearance, of fact and value. The prevalent conception of reality—otherwise known as the world, the universe, things, nature, or truth—is an inheritor of Plato's world of ideas; it is based on the notion, Rorty writes, "common to Democritus and Descartes, that the universe is made up of very simple, clearly and distinctly knowable things" (*Philosophy* 357). This, according to Baudrillard in "Symbolic Exchange and Death," is symptomatic of metaphysics that requires the distinction between appearance and reality. He writes,

> The problematic of the "natural," . . . becomes the characteristic theme of the bourgeoisie since the Renaissance, the mirror of the bourgeois sign, the mirror of the classical sign. Even today, nostalgia for natural reference survives, in spite of numerous revolutions aimed at smashing this configuration. ("Symbolic Exchange" 137)

This nostalgia for natural reference is bolstered by the seventeenth-century idea of the self, the mind, as comprised of a mirror and an inner eye. Both elements working together allow the self to reflect and to internalize the universals, the meaning of external reality. It is this mirroring and reflecting ability which, in terms of the neoclassic philosophy of the Great Chain of Being, earns men a higher hierarchical footing than women and the animals. It is that which evidences man's rational ability; it is that which makes man human. This ability makes it possible to know an absolute and accessible external reality, making existence a series of "visual" and physical encounters of self with objects (including metaphysical objects—or "ideas") and knowledge the result when such encounters have been accurately reflected. The prerequisite of "accuracy" requires that the object possess inherent meaning and that the mind be capable of making "privileged representations" defined by Rorty as representations which are "automatically and intrinsically accurate" (*Philosophy* 170).

According to such a conception of reality and of self, the subject (seeking to know) engages in a visual quest to represent. This quest can be characterized by the fable of Narcissus. That is, the subject seeks to gaze upon and to reflect upon the mirror, unaware that what he sees is merely an image of himself. For the logic of representation works according to similarities and correspondences. The mirror is mimetic: it copies, it coheres, it renders the same—the selfsame—upon a smooth, continuous, totalizing surface. It cannot reflect what is truly other and, thus, what remains radically different. What it recognizes and thus reflects is what it has seen before and what it wishes to see. The mirror's gaze reflects an "ideal image."

Here I am invoking psychoanalyst Jacques Lacan's notion of the mirror stage. In *Écrits*, Lacan posits the mirror stage as "*an identification*" with an "Ideal-I" (2). Lacanian theory posits that

> somewhere between the ages of six months and eighteen months the subject arrives at an apprehension of both its self and the other—indeed, of its self *as other.* This discovery is assisted by the child seeing, for the first time, its own reflection in a mirror. That reflection enjoys a coherence which the subject itself lacks—it is an *ideal* image. (Silverman, *Subject of Semiotics* 157)

But it is also an image alienated from the subject. Unable to assimilate the image, the subject (as Narcissus) nevertheless attempts to appropriate the reflection and continues to gaze into the mirror in order to sustain his identity. For the subject comforts and deludes himself into thinking that as long as he sees himself, he exists as a subject and possesses the proper identity as a subject. Thus the logic of identity is founded on a mirror reflection, on a projected image.

Baudrillard claims that both Marx and Freud constructed theoretical frameworks complicit with this mimetic impulse. *The Mirror of Production* is the title of Baudrillard's major, but certainly not only, critique of Marx. His critique of Freud was to bear the title *The Mirror of Desire;* and, although he never produced such a text, his treatment of Freud can be found in other, penned works. Because others, especially the work of Mike Gane (*Baudrillard: Critical and Fatal Theory* and *Baudrillard's Bestiary*), have previously and satisfactorily outlined Baudrillard's major arguments against Marxism and psychoanalysis in greater detail, I will only briefly sketch the issue as it relates to the greater purposes of this chapter. It is not my intent to present Baudrillard's specific arguments in order to definitively justify them, but rather to acknowledge them as exemplary of Baudrillard's attack on systems of production.

It is Baudrillard's argument that Marxism is not the revolutionary breakthrough prophesied. Because Marx took production as a given and the subject (as *homo faber* or "productive man") as a given and thus extrapolated the issues of alienated and nonalienated relations of production, he fell prey to the very logic of capitalism itself. Jonathan Culler, in *Ferdinand de Saussure*, explains that "Marx distinguished the use-value of a commodity (its true usefulness to an individual) from its exchange value (its value in the economic system of exchange)" (136). Because Marx insisted on use value as the first principle, as the unquestioned value, Baudrillard argues that Marx "contributed to the mythology (a veritable rationalist mystique) that allows the relation of the individual to objects conceived as use value to pass for a concrete and objective—in sum 'natural'—relation between man's needs and the function proper to the object" (*For a Critique* 134). That is to say, Marxism, with its nostalgic belief in representation, in a representational relation and correlative relation between signifier and signified, is trapped in its ideal image, caught in the mirror of (capitalist) production, fossilized in the amber of truth.

Freud, likewise—according to Baudrillard's critique—was caught in the mirror of desire, another manifestation of the processes of production. Freud's guiding first principle and theoretical foundation is based on desire (on its topographical playground, the unconscious)—desire as the production of memories, the production of repressions, the production of neuroses, psychoses, and genders. Baudrillard's main argument against psychoanalysis is its conflation of the symbolic with primary processes or the unconscious. Again, Baudrillard resists any theoretical formulation which posits a necessary, motivated, and thus "metaphysical" correlation between signifier and signified and/or sign and referent (symptomatic of the processes of production and consumption). Baudrillard theorizes

> that the exclusion of the referent in Saussure's separation of the sign (signifier-signified) from the world entails a "metaphysical representation of the referent." Baudrillard demonstrates this by criticizing Emile Benveniste's relocation of the arbitrariness of the signifier-signified relation between that

of the sign (signifier-signified) and the referent. This reloca-
tion is possible only by reviving the sign's initial separation
from the referent and by repairing it with what Baudrillard
calls the "supernatural" provision of motivation (it matters little whether motivation is affirmed or denied). Motivation parallels the concept of need in political economy.
Need is a function of the capitalist system, just as motivation is a function of the sign system. (Genosko, *Baudrillard
and Signs* 5)

In an interview conducted by Judith Williamson, Baudrillard argues
that Marx's fundamental privileging of use value is analogous to theories of signification's privileging of the referent. He posits his theoretical
challenge as such:

My criticism of use-value or of the referent is of course a
challenge to reference, a challenge to the material world, or
rather, a challenge to the *principle* of reality, because the reality principle is at some level a principle of reference. In order for there to be a reality, there has to be a principle of
reference, a principle of signification, a principle of reality.
Yes, I do contest it. . . . [I]n a way I'm also doing a critique
of the use-value of language. (Williamson 17)

Thus, according to Baudrillard, both Marx and Freud, while attempting to turn metaphysics on its head, fell into the metaphysical trap
of representation—that is, they failed to be suspicious enough, as it has
been said; they failed to question the "reality principle" and the referential fallacy. The joint systems of production and representation begin
with the chief assumption that there is truth—that is, that there is
something to be represented, for example, sex, meaning, power, desire,
the social relation, the citizen. This assumption, harkening back to at
least the Gorgian and Parmenidean argument and Plato's infamous "allegory of the cave," tears the fabric of the possible into the dichotomous
terms of being and not being, reality and appearance. In order to assert
being, the other must be negated. It is this negation that characterizes
the realm of production and representation. Baudrillard writes, "Philosophy is based on the negation of the real. There is at the heart of
philosophy a primordial act regarding the negation of reality; and without that negation there is no philosophy" (*Evil Demon* 51). That is to
say, without negation there is no truth, no production, no subjectivity,
no representation.

Baudrillard has prophesied that the "end of philosophy" is near, just as Nietzsche has proclaimed that "God is dead." These proclamations refer to the "crisis of representation" that characterizes the postmodern condition (Lyotard, *Postmodern Condition*). This "crisis" erupts as seemingly natural systems of representation begin to unhinge, that is, as the first principle that guarantees the efficacy of the representation begins to dissolve. Thus, with the death of God and philosophy (cohorts and coconspirators in the production of truth), it becomes impossible to effect the primary negation that ensures and sustains truth. Baudrillard writes:

> All of Western faith . . . [is] engaged in this wager on representation: that a sign could refer to the depth of meaning, that a sign could *exchange* for meaning and that something could guarantee this exchange—God, of course. But what if God himself can be simulated, that is to say, reduced to the signs which attest his existence? Then the whole system becomes weightless, it is no longer anything but a gigantic simulacrum—not unreal, but a simulacrum, never again exchanging for what is real, but exchanging in itself, in an uninterrupted circuit without reference or circumference. (*Simulations* 10)

Within this crisis of representation, the seemingly self-evident "referent" and heretofore unproblematic "signifier" come to be seen as the fictions that they are, the constructed illusions (as in Gorgias's notion of *apatē* and Nietzsche's "army of metaphors") which order our lives. These various illusions, according to Baudrillard, can be historically classified as "stages of simulation." His purpose here, as is Michel Foucault's in *The Order of Things* and as is Nietzsche's in "History of an Error" (*Twilight* 40), is to demonstrate the constructedness and historicity of systems of representation. His purpose, furthermore, is to demonstrate not only the constructedness of every representation and every ratiocination of that representation but also the belatedness of them. Gane writes:

> Baudrillard's aim here is to show that no adequate analysis of systems of representation can, simply, refer to the "real" world (the referent), as if this was unproblematic. . . . What tends to happen, he argues, is that in each phase of representation a former, dominant conception of the "real" is taken as the reference model of a "current" reality, always already out of date. For example, in discourse today it is possible to find reference to a nature that is above any social

practice: this is comprehensible only as a reference to assumptions produced in a previous period, which still have a
current effectivity. (*Baudrillard's Bestiary* 95)

The Tyranny of the Knowing Subject

Within each stage of simulation, there exists a presupposition of the
nature and being of the real, the referent, and of its appropriate representation, as well as the presupposition of a particular subjectivity
which apprehends each simulation. Baudrillard argues that the subject, as a presupposition, is paradoxically simultaneously constituted in
that moment. Thus the subject, the Cartesian project, is based on the
rational principle and "on the promise of a world which can be con-
firmed only in terms of its own reality" (*Evil Demon* 43). Baudrillard
writes: "The problematic of the subject implies that reality can still be
represented, that things give off signs guaranteeing their existence and
significance—in short, that there is a reality principle" (*Forget* 70). The
presupposition of the reality principle, of the efficacy of faithful representations, engenders a subjectivity based on a dialectical relationship
with the object. Baudrillard states:

> We have always lived off the splendor of the subject and the
> poverty of the object. It is the subject that makes history, it's
> the subject that totalizes the world. Individual subject or
> collective subject, the subject of consciousness or of the un-
> conscious, the ideal of all metaphysics is [the subject]. . . .
> The fate of the object . . . is not even intelligible as such: it is
> only the alienated, accursed part of the subject. . . . In our
> philosophy of desire, the subject retains an absolute privilege,
> since it is the subject that desires. (*Fatal Strategies* 111–12)

And what this subject desires is the mastery and possession of the object. Equipped with an accumulative and acquisitive will, the subject is
the collector *par excellence*—just as the justification of history has been
that production is accumulation (of facts, of knowledge, of wisdom, of
use value). Baudrillard writes, "The collector is possessive. He seeks exclusive rights over the dead object. . . . [H]is love of the object, the amo-
rous stratagems with which he surrounds it, display a hatred and fear
of seduction" (*Seduction* 122). Constituted and justified within the
realm of production, the subject is condemned to will, never to be
willed, that is, seduced. Baudrillard continues, "He prefers the monoto-
nous fascination of the collection, the fascination with dead differences,
this obsession with the same, over the seduction of the other. . . . be-

cause he is logical, motivated by an irreversible logic. To seduce without being seduced—without reversibility" (*Seduction* 123). In *Seduced and Abandoned*, André Frankovits writes that the subject's necessity for mastery requires that he condemn seduction as that which undermines his mastery:

> In the classical sense of simulacrum (which is not strictly Baudrillard's) the workings of seduction, of turning astray, are (effected through) the inclusion of the point of view of the subject—*qua* spectator or auditor—in the simulacrum. It is precisely for this reason that seduction and simulation are condemned: the subject, so taken in by the effects of illusion, is no longer in a position of mastery—unable that is, to gauge the distance between the real and its double. Which is to say, that, if abolition of this distance there be, it is due to the subject's filling the gap. (39–40)

The irreversible logic, evidenced by (cause/effect) rationality and hierarchical values, produces the glory of the subject and the enslavement of the object, in accordance with the Great Chain of Being, as identified by Lovejoy. Baudrillard characterizes this metaphysical totem pole as the

> long chain in which all the conditions of despotic high-handedness are in play which enchain beings one to another, from one species to another—from cruel divinities to their sacrificial victims, from masters to slaves . . . , [beginning with] an all-powerful simulacrum, like the masked divinities which men themselves invent to justify this wretched chain. (*Cool Memories* 116)

The Tyranny of Communication

This "wretched chain" also links a signifier to a signified, enslaves language to a communicative duty. From Parmenides and Plato through Jürgen Habermas, indeed, the entire history of rhetoric can be read as the desire to codify, systematize, and control language, to reduce it to *logos,* to enslave it in the service of truth (certain or probable). For example, St. Augustine mastered language's rhetoricity as he attempted to systematize exegesis. He discovered that evidently sheer fabrics weren't the rage when God designed truth's habit. For as he encountered hermeneutical difficulties, Augustine, one of our first hermeneuts, noted that words do not always mean what they say—or say what they mean.

There are signs and symbols and all sorts of obstructions to the truth. But these ambiguities are accounted for as a conscious, purposeful, and thus logical choice made by the author (that is, God) in order to combat pride and to promote faith. Likewise Peter Ramus attempted, in Walter J. Ong's words, to

> tie down words themselves . . . in simple geometrical patterns. Words are believed to be recalcitrant insofar as they derive from a world of sound, voices, cries; the Ramist ambition is to neutralize this connection by processing what is of itself nonspatial in order to reduce it to space in the starkest way possible. (*Ramus* 89)

The Ramists set about granny-knotting language into systematic charts and dichotomized tables and geometric designs. Thus the "method," the *technē*: dialectic. Ramus writes, "Dialectic is the art or way of teaching *correctly, in order* and *lucidly*" (quoted in Ong 159; emphasis mine).

But there is something about language that doesn't like a method. Ramus knew that; the scholastics, the elocutionists, the nominalists, all knew that. But just as Aristotle, Augustine, and Ramus wanted to pin language down, so too has philosophy (and the philosophic interpretation of rhetoric—that is, the anti-sophistic interpretation of rhetoric) willed language to stop turning, to stop its protean behavior, and to march forward without looking back, just as Ramus wanted eloquence to proceed in "steps" and "forward motions" (Ong 272).

The will to pin language down finds its logical fulfillment during the seventeenth century, with the Royal Society of Science's attempts to create a pure, universal language—a language with which sign would unequivocally equal referent. Thomas Sprat dedicated his life to the endeavor. He is reputed to have gone insane, for he tried to make language do what language refused to do: to stand still, to be clear and distinct, to be faithful to its referent, and to go about her (objective and mathematical) business naked (Ong, *Ramus* 213). This is symptomatic of logocentrism, which, Culler explains, opposes "a reality, a foundation—an order of truth, logic, reason, in short the *logos* . . . —to appearances, accidents, contingencies" (128). Thus, he continues, "signifiers are conceived as standing for or providing access to" this order of truth—which is "in principle independent of" those very signifiers (129). The communicative theory propounded by Habermas demonstrates this fundamental belief as he propounds reason as the means to legitimate knowledge in the face of a postmodern crisis. Habermas adopts modernist presuppositions in formulating his concept of "universal pragmatics"

for universal understanding in discursive practices (*Communication*
1)—that is, ideal speech acts. Habermas's universal pragmatics require
a notion of subjectivity that begs the question of liberation, understanding, and subject production.

Habermas, as well as the modernist enterprise per se, is operating
out of an preeminent conception of language that has been termed the
"conduit metaphor" conception of language by Michael Reddy. He
identifies the major characteristics of this conception of language: (1)
language transfers thoughts from one person to another, (2) written
language or spoken language is invested with the thoughts or feelings
of the subject, (3) words accomplish this transfer, (4) the listener/reader
extracts the meaning from the words. This whole metaphor, in addition to failing to recognize that language is no mere conduit but is,
rather, the very dimension of our being, places too much emphasis on
the subject—on the speaking/writing subject. It is his/her job to put
his/her feelings/thoughts into words so that the reader/listener may
"pick" up on them. This implies a subjectivity that is (1) master and
cause of feelings/thoughts, and (2) master of language (is able to find
the right words for the right feelings, and is able to put them into a
meaningful sequence).

In *Classical Rhetoric and Its Christian and Secular Tradition from
Ancient to Modern Times,* George Kennedy states, "Rhetoric is a form
of communication. The author of a communication has some kind of
purpose, and rhetoric certainly includes the ways by which he seeks to
accomplish that purpose" (4). From its very inception, Kennedy would
argue, language has been primarily communicative (in fact, he defines
so-called secondary rhetoric as "commonplaces, figures of speech and
thought and tropes" which are used when language is not being "used
for [its] primary oral purpose" of communication [5]). Rhetoric, thus
defined, guarantees the authority of the speaking/writing being and assumes a very passive, Aristotelian audience. James Kinneavy, Lloyd
Bitzer, and Wayne Booth ("Rhetorical Stance") would all concur with
Kennedy's depiction of the rhetorical project—that is, speaker speaking, knowledge transferred, listener receiving. Kinneavy, despite his
elaborate classifications, really has only one communicative model, the
triangle: an encoder, a decoder, and a signal. Bitzer adds the situation
as exigency. Booth adds an element of "good reason" and "warrantable
beliefs" to the equation. But still the traditional elements of the communication triangle remain unproblematically speaker, listener, signal.
And still the end of communication remains the same: understanding,
that is, the transmittance of knowledge.

The emphasis on communicating knowledge is symptomatic of the

Enlightenment project—the progressive accumulation of facts as universal laws—and symptomatic of the insecurity of some disciplines
(generally the human and social sciences) which sense the shadow of
positivism. David Russell suggests that the metaphors of knowledge are
revealing—that they reveal that knowledge is thought of as a thing, in
physical terms, as a commodity. For example, we speak of "the store-
house of knowledge" (Russell), and we say "I get it" when we have
understood. Writing must be justified as an activity—a productive activity, producing exchangeable goods.

No Degree Zero: Challenging Production

It is Baudrillard's argument that we are on the other side of the crisis of
representation. We have entered a new stage of simulation, a stage in
which faithful referents and Habermasian efforts at legitimization are
passé, impotent, superfluous, and irrelevant. Gane writes,

> The reality and certainty of the dialectic has gone, to be re-
> placed by genetic codes and random combinations. Even
> critical theory and political revolution become things of the
> past, and belong to the old order . . . Against the new order
> a strategy of dialectical transcendence is of no avail. The sys-
> tem has effectively neutralized all first order (natural sys-
> tems) and second order (dialectic) strategies. (*Baudrillard's
> Bestiary* 78)

This new stage, according to Baudrillard, is the "fractal stage" or "viral
stage," wherein there is no longer any referent at all and wherein "value
radiates in all directions, filling in all interstices, without bearing reference to anything whatsoever except by mere contiguity)" ("Transpolitics" 15).

The challenge, then, for critical theory is how to combat production—our current social universe inhabited by the living dead, by referents, discourses, and values unaware of their death—a world, profoundly obscene and pornographic, that has lost its "natural" referent,
that has produced simulacra at such speed that it now precedes the real
(*Evil Demon* 13) "like those dolls," Baudrillard writes, "adorned with
genitalia, that talk, pee, and will one day make love. And the little girl's
reaction: 'My little sister, she knows how to do that too. Can't you give
me a real one?' " (*Seduction* 34).

Critical theories fail today because they operate out of a nostalgia
for a natural referent, they emanate from the subject (by taking subjectivity as foundational), and they assume language is communicative—
all assumptions of an antiquated stage of simulation. Thus grounded in

such assumptions, they remain forever entrapped by the terms of the very system of representation (that is, production) from which they are supposedly emancipating themselves. Although Baudrillard would never claim to offer a revolutionary program or agenda for liberation — for such claims are fraught with the totalizing impulses of modernism — he has, however, suggested that within the realm of seduction (vis-à-vis the realm of production), we may find ways to resist the dialectical violence of truth, subjectivity, and communication.

According to Baudrillard, the rapacious violence of the dialectic insistence on truth has rendered our world pornographic. (His definition of pornography vastly differs from, say, that of Catharine MacKinnon's.) He writes,

> A pornographic culture *par excellence;* one that pursues the workings of the real at all times and in all places. A pornographic culture with its ideology of the concrete, of facticity and use, and its concern with the preeminence of use value, the material infrastructure of things, and the body as the material infrastructure of desire. (*Seduction* 34)

This pornographic impulse, that is, the will to represent, abducts becoming by forcing it to become visible being *(alētheia)*.

It is this will to represent, fueled by the master/slave dialectic, which sustains the truth, the subject — the master of the world of appearances who enslaves the other. However, the ideal subject (as Nietzsche and Foucault have shown us) is the enslaved, or subjected, subject. Indeed, we have not escaped terrorism and abduction. To repeat Baudrillard, it is our subjectivity (our identity, our relationship to truth)

> whose hostages we are: called upon to assume it, to answer for it with our own lives (this is called security, occasionally social), called on to be ourselves, to talk, delight, realize ourselves . . . it calls on you to reveal yourself as you are [as a sign]. It is always blackmail by identity (and thus a symbolic murder, since you are never that, except precisely by being condemned to it). (*Fatal Strategies* 40)

Subjectivity, identity, posited as a real and true ethos with a one-to-one correspondence (as self-identical) has, in its murder of illusion, inspired terror — just as "*all meaningful discourse seeks to end appearances*" (Baudrillard, *Seduction* 54; emphasis his) and requires the exclusion, the annihilation of the "third." "Meaningful" discourse — that is, the rational coupling of signified with signifier — has as its aim the annihilation of the magical world of illusion and irrational couplings (Baudrillard,

"Fatality" 279).[2] Just as the positing of identity requires the negation of the other, the erection of truth necessitates the negation of illusion and appearance. To protect ourselves, our ethical beings, from this act of violence, Baudrillard suggests, "Against the true of the true, against the truer than the true . . . we must remake illusion, rediscover illusion, this power . . . to tear the same away from the same, called seduction" (*Fatal Strategies* 51).

Seduction; Or, the Feminine

Baudrillard distinguishes production from seduction as follows:

> The original sense of "production" is not in fact that of material manufacture; rather, it means to render visible, to cause to appear and be made to appear: *pro-ducere*. . . . To produce is to force what belongs to another order (that of secrecy and seduction) to materialize. *Seduction* is that which is everywhere and always opposed to *production;* seduction withdraws something from the visible order and so runs counter to production, whose project is to set everything up in clear view, whether it be an object, a number, or a concept. . . . this is . . . the project of our whole culture, whose natural condition is "obscenity." (*Forget* 21–22)

To return to Helen: figured within production as either object of desire or subject of desire, she is condemned. But if we figured the case against her differently, not with a dialectical difference of the selfsame, but with a difference of difference (that is, in terms of seduction), what will we have found? Bear in mind, we are not asking the question: was Helen seduced? For this question presupposes, as does all other philosophical questions, the logic that positions subjects and objects. Again, we are figuring seduction with a difference.

It was this difference which escaped Freud, which he failed to be seduced by. It is a commonplace in psychoanalytic history that Freud originally developed a theory to explain hysteria that argued that the disturbed women had been, at some point in their lives, traumatized— that is, sexually seduced by their fathers (or father figures). However, as Freud's relationship with Wilhelm Fliess developed, he abandoned (in approximately 1897) his seduction theory in favor of the Oedipal story. Although Jeffrey Moussaieff Masson offers in his *Assault on Truth* (as well as in his more disturbing *Dark Science*) an insightful and passionate study of Freud's abandonment of the seduction theory, he nevertheless casts seduction in terms of production (that is, he posits seduction as abduction). This is not to say that "real women" (and men) do not get raped and are not otherwise sexually abused, but this rape occurs within the universe of production where terror and violence sustain the representations of our truth, our identity, and even our sexuality. Freud's abandonment of the seduction theory, thus, was an act of production. Baudrillard writes, "Freud abolished seduction in order to put into place a machinery of interpretation, and of sexual repression, that offer all the characteristics of objectivity and coherence" (*Seduction* 57). Freud was interested in the metonymic logic of ego construction, of neurotic and pathologic developments. His will to knowledge insisted, demanded, that he construct a theory that offered a logical account, that situated subjects. And thus his answer, his grand narrative: Oedipus.

The Oedipal narrative produces an account, proffers a definitive solution to the Sphinx's riddle (to the riddle of ambiguity, of Becoming):[3] Man. Against Freud, Baudrillard argues that the Oedipal story "imposes a history upon us," a history, he writes, "of repression and unconscious work, a psychological history of complexes and mourning, of the always altered and mortifying rapports with the Father, the Law, and the Symbolic Order" (*Fatal Strategies* 138). This narrative, this history, has produced us—our truth, our subjectivity—as representations of the grand referent: our sexuality (that is, anatomy is destiny). According to Freud, the prime mover is sexual desire, which he characterizes as "half-tamed demons" (*Dora* 131). When these demons are allowed free rein (or free reign), hysteria results. Hence, for Freud, as for Plato, sexual desire left unchecked is *the* cause of all problems of the self: all neuroses, all psychoses. He writes, "Sexuality does not simply intervene, like a *deus ex machina* [a revealing analogy] . . . but that it provides the motive power for every single symptom, and for every single manifestation of a symptom" (*Dora* 136). The cure, by implication, is regulated sexuality, checked desire, rationality. Hence Freud lays Dora on his couch in order to order Dora. Freud's normalizing therapy, like Plato's (in the *Phaedrus*), relies on limiting the excess, on rationalizing the irrational, on making conscious the unconscious. Consciousness is, according to Freud, the way to control the unconscious: "Psychoanalytic treatment . . . brings to light . . . so many hidden psychical factors" (*Dora* 139).

Freud was able to produce Dora, but failed to seduce Dora or to be seduced by her. He was able to situate her within a particular narrative, to force her to represent Oedipal sexuality, to hermeneutically predetermine the events involving Herr K. The failure of psychoanalysis, according to Baudrillard, is its blind insistence on laying bare the truth, the truth of one's sexuality, and inscribing it within a particular narrative. Thus psychoanalysis—despite its claims to the contrary—

will never be able to liberate subjectivity, but only to produce it. The Oedipal narrative as prescriptive, according to Baudrillard, can never liberate one, therefore, but merely enslave one to subjectivity and sexuality. Baudrillard writes, "*We were all once produced, we must all be seduced.* That is the only true 'liberation,' that which opens beyond the Oedipus complex and the Law, and which delivers us from a stern psychological calvary as well as from the biological fatality of having been sexually engendered" (*Fatal Strategies* 138; emphasis mine).

We have our *Critique of Pure Reason* (Kant); what we need now, according to Baudrillard, is a critique of sexual reason (*Seduction* 37). It is Baudrillard's argument that the blind spot of psychoanalysis is its axiomatic insistence on sexuality. The psychoanalytic project, motivated by "sexual reason," manufactures sexuality and gender (masculine/feminine), and therefore is symptomatic of the realm of production. As an alternative to production, Baudrillard offers "the order of the feminine":

> understood outside the opposition masculine/feminine, that opposition being essentially masculine, sexual in intention, and incapable of being overturned without ceasing to exist. . . . One may catch a glimpse of another, parallel universe (the two never meet). . . . A universe that can no longer be interpreted in terms of psychic or psychological relations, nor those of repression and the unconscious, but must be interpreted in the terms of play, challenges, duels, the strategy of appearances—that is, the terms of seduction. A universe that can no longer be interpreted in terms of structures and diacritical oppositions, but implies a seductive reversibility—a universe where the feminine is not what opposes the masculine, but what seduces the masculine. (*Seduction* 7)

It is important to establish immediately that "the feminine" is, to Baudrillard, not a representation of gender, sex, or sexuality. It is not a "marked" term; and it would certainly not lay claim to any truth of its own, specifically a sexual truth. The feminine does not exist in "nature" (it bears no relation to "mother nature"); but, rather, exists (if it can be said that it is) in the space of simulation, artifice (Baudrillard, *Seduction* 2, 11). Therefore, we have avoided the essentialist problem of arguing from *physis* as do some feminists. The feminine is nothing, Gorgias's *apatē;* but, this is her strength, just as it is *apatē*'s strength to answer to *kairos* and disrupt the dialectic stronghold (Baudrillard, *Seduction* 14). The feminine does not lie in opposition to the masculine. Only within the realm of production will you find the binary opposition masculine/feminine (Baudrillard, *Seduction* 16). "The feminine" operates in a different sphere: that of seduction.

Like the Sphinx, the feminine is insoluble. Is it Woman? Is it Lion? Bird? Again, it lays no claim to truth, especially to the truth of its own being, for it is not, it is becoming: a series of transmogrifications, metamorphoses, and rhetorical tropings. It is not a known term; it is not a gender; it is a challenge, a challenge to the comfortable binaries which sustain truth, a challenge to our social, gender coding (Baudrillard, *Fatal Strategies* 127). It is best not to conflate "the feminine" with androgyny (that is a position of neither/nor); "the feminine" is both/and, an excess of gender that causes the sexual poles to waiver. Within seduction there are no more marked terms, the given representations can't hold, the metaphor is liquidated (Baudrillard, *Fatal Strategies* 121).

The Seduction of Truth

Finally, there is no referent. The ambiguity of the signifier has cut the signified loose. Seduction is a challenge to the stability of the Signified/signifier chain, the presumed clarity and the givenness of truth. Seduction is the space of artifice, the realm of simulation, and nothing more. That is, there is nothing beyond, behind, beneath the artifice.[4] There is no bottom turtle upon which the world rests. Within production, the goal is to strip the truth (and the subject) of its illusions, of its veil of rhetoricity, to lay bare, to unconceal, to render naked. Within seduction, the veil is all. Baudrillard writes:

> There is . . . never any nudity, never any nude body that is simply nude; there is never just a body. It is like the Indian said when the white man asked him why he ran around naked: "For me, it is all face." In a non-fetishistic culture (one that does not fetishize nudity as objective truth) the body is not, as in our own, opposed to the face, conceived as alone rich in expression and endowed with "eyes": it is itself a face, and looks at you. It is therefore not obscene, that is to say, made to be seen nude. It *cannot* be seen nude, no more than the face can for us, for the body is—and is only—a symbolic veil; and it is by way of this play of veils, which literally, abolishes the body "as such," that seduction occurs. This is where seduction is at play and not in the tearing away of the veil in the name of some manifestation of truth or desire. (*Seduction* 33)

This is where epistemology has failed us, Baudrillard argues. It has produced knowledge and, by extension, has produced us as subjects, insofar as we strip the veils of appearance, of style, of illusion, in order to reveal the truth. It is this abduction of that which is not by that which is (the *cogito*—the thinking being) that defines epistemology as such. The Cartesian subject takes as its primary foundation the presupposition that there exists an "objective" world, comprised of, for example, so many "bodies" in need of stripping bare. For Baudrillard, the subject/object dichotomy, which sustains humanist subjectivity and "the principle of the real," is a futile dichotomy, symptomatic of the obscene and pornographic impulses of the realm of production. Within seduction, truth and subjectivity have no claim to objectivity, and thus the dichotomy of illusion/reality becomes meaningless. Within seduction, Baudrillard argues, there is

> no possibility existing at all of reconciling the "illusion" of the world with the "reality" of the world. And I have to say this once again: here the "illusion" is not simply irreality or non-reality; rather, it is in the literal sense of the word (*il-ludere* in Latin) a *play* upon "reality" or a *mise en jeu* of the real. It is, to say it one more time, the issuing of a challenge to the "real"—the attempt to put the real, quite simply, on the spot. . . . I do not believe in the possibility of "real-ising" the world through any rational or materialist principle. (*Evil Demon* 46)

The Seduction of the Subject

Likewise, with seduction, there is no possibility of "real-ising" the subject. Let me explain by returning once again to Helen: we have no desire to vindicate her as object of desire. To do so would be to assume the woman-as-victim subject position, a popular position but, nevertheless, a reactive one. Further, we have no desire to vindicate her as subject of desire. To do so would be to assume the woman-as-humanist subject position, an ethical dead end. Whereas production supposes and imposes mastery, seduction presumes that no player can be greater than the challenge (as in Nietzsche's "Homer's Contest").[5] Baudrillard writes,

> each one knows that triumph is not definitive, for *no one will ever occupy* the blind spot around which the battle is arrayed. Wanting to occupy it, wanting to take the empty space of stratagem (like wanting to annex the empty heart of truth), is madness and an absolute misunderstanding of the world as play and ceremony. (*Fatal Strategies* 176–77)

There is will in seduction, but it is a will with a difference. It is the will to will willingly *(amor fati)*. It is the will of which Martin Heidegger writes in "What Are Poets For?" It is the will not of "wanting, coveting, or seeking power, but only [of] 'giving' or 'creating'" (Tomlinson xii)— but definitively not of "producing." Such an affirmative and inventive will wills difference and chance—not probability, nor predictability, but difference and chance.

The question is not does Helen will—that is, does Helen possess a will? But rather, does Helen figure in the will to affirmation which simply wills eternally without a synthesizing stay of the same? Yes, Helen figures in seduction as the "feminine." Helen is thus neither subject nor object; she is neither an active subject who imposes her will on the real, nor is she a passive victim of another's will. For, Baudrillard stresses, "There is no active or passive mode in seduction, no subject or object, no interior or exterior: seduction plays on both sides, and there is no frontier separating them. One cannot seduce others, if one has not oneself been seduced" (*Seduction* 81). And what seduces one's subjectivity, Baudrillard posits, is

> the passion of playing and being played, it is the passion of illusion and appearance, it is that which comes from elsewhere, from others, from their face, their language, their gestures—and that which bothers you, lures you, summons you into existence; it is the encounter, the surprise of what exists before you, outside of you, *without you*—the marvelous exteriority of the pure object, of the pure event, of what happens without your having anything to do with it. What a relief—this alone is enough to seduce you; we've been so solicited to be the cause of everything, to find a cause for everything . . . being doesn't give a damn about its own being; it is nothing, and exists only when it is lifted out of itself, into the play of the world and the vertigo of seduction. (*Fatal Strategies* 139)

The Seduction of Discourse

To experience the "play of the world and the vertigo of seduction" requires a radically new relationship to language. Heretofore, as we have noted, the subject's relationship to language has been modeled on the Platonic myth of the charioteer, as demonstrated in the *Phaedrus*. The subject whips and spurs language (and the so-called irrational elements of being—that is, desire and wantonness) into obedience and temperance. Once again, his team consists of a noble horse, white in color, which needs no whip but "is driven by word of command alone" (*Phaedrus* 253), is driven by *logos*, by reason. The other horse, the dark horse, however, is an insolent, desire-driven, "jumble of a creature" which is "shaggy-eared and deaf, hardly heeding whip or spur" (253). But heed it must. It must be violently brought to its haunches in fear and awe. It must be controlled—bridled—by the noble charioteer. This conception of our relationship to language—to control its excesses, to bridle its ambiguities—reflects a theory of discourse as emanating from the subject. That is, within the realm of production, the aim of the speaking subject is to make language articulate truth, to "real-ise" being, in all its clarity and simplicity, to indite (and indict) its meaning.

This is evidenced by production's two chief meaning-making machines—machines well-oiled to create obscenity via language, to create pornographic discourse, to produce an orgy of meaning and understanding. We know these hyperactive machines as hermeneutics and semiotics. Within production, hermeneutics (the study of understanding) and semiotics (the "science" of meaning) are two sides of the same coin. They are fashioned of the same metal: rationality (in *logos* we trust). Their imprints are different, but it is their differences which posit each's identity. Whereas semioticians analyze language as the constitutive basis of the signifying system in an effort to show how and why signs relate to each other, hermeneuts—in contrast—attempt to demonstrate how language is constitutive of being itself. Rather than the endless referential nature of the semiotic conception of language, the hermeneutic conception views language as a process of disclosing not language but being itself. Yet despite their differences, they remain concerned with the production of meaning, understanding, and/or being.

Baudrillard is suggesting that we allow language to seduce meaning, understanding, and being, "to go beyond its intentional operation and get caught up in its own dizzy whirl" (*Illusion* 37). To seduce and to be seduced by language is to send a sign (for, after all, we must write—he is not advancing political quietism, silence, or extralinguistic mysticism) but to do so with no expectation of return (understanding) and with no demand for meaning (for real-ising being). What must be challenged, according to Baudrillard, are the assumptions that there exists some necessary referential relation between language and "reality" and that language's raison d'être is to reproduce—that is, "communicate"—that reality. Baudrillard has written, "Communication is to language what reproduction is to sexuality" (*Cool Memories II* 52). Certainly, within production, communication takes place. But the "dizzy whirl" or ecstasy experienced in/by being led astray (that is being seduced) by language "corresponds to the libertine phase of a sexuality without reproduction"—without reproducing the real (*Cool Memories II* 52). Seduction's radical ethic is to forget the real, to offer no explanation, and thereby to affirm the "shiny surface of non-sense" (*Seduction* 54) rather than to force out meaning, interpretation, and understanding. Baudrillard is calling for a letting-be, a laissez-faire, of the not-yet said, to allow it to remain unsaid, undisclosed, and without meaning. Although I am invoking Heidegger here, we perhaps would do well to forget him as well. For, as a hermeneut, he is straining his ear to hear what has not been said and in so doing is committing violence against, in Baudrillard's term, the "secret" or that which does not circulate via "communication" (Baudrillard, *Cool Memories* 118; and *Fatal Strategies* 61, 65). Heidegger's "letting-be" may very well be guilty of wrenching "what is" from the clearing, rather than letting it exhaust itself in its own dizzying whirl of ecstasy.

Again, it is important to rearticulate that Baudrillard's conception of "nonsense" is not simply the "irrational"—or that which opposes the rational. Nor does Baudrillard's notion of "illusion" oppose that which is the True. These oppositions are symptomatic of the principle of the real and the realm of production. As we have already pointed out, it is precisely this relationship of opposition, of binaries, of dichotomies, which—via the negative—sustains the production of truth, subjectivity, and communication. For Baudrillard, seduction implies a radically different relationship which would treat "signs in terms of their seductive attraction, rather than their contrasts and oppositions . . . , [w]hich would break with the specular nature of the sign and the encumbrance of the referent. . . . For seduction supposes that minimum reversibility which puts an end to every fixed opposition and, therefore, every conventional semiology" (*Seduction* 103–4).

The seductive attraction of signs resists the logical coupling, the shotgun wedding that conventional semiology, rational discourse, and communication imposes. Within seduction, signs indeed combine, but without causal links. These new, noncausal linkages are the effect of an encounter between "fragments of language, unknown to each other" who meet "as if by enchantment and discover with delight that they were neither one nor the other" (Baudrillard, *Fatal Strategies* 135). Baudrillard writes, "[E]verything is linked and connected, but never with a connection of meaning—always a connection of appearances" (*Fatal Strategies* 176). The term fatal has nothing fatalistic or apocalyptic about it. Rather, the fatal is situated between the determined and the aleatory.[6] In this way—by not setting up a rational/irrational dichotomy—Baudrillard escapes the traps of binary thinking and the Aristotelian first principle of noncontradiction. Fatal relations suggest that things or words are indeed linked—but perhaps not rationally as our subjectivity has supposed us to assume. Rather, things or words are linked contiguously, not causally. By employing fatal strategies, Baudrillard's writing challenges these radically contiguous linkages, following them as far as he can go, in order to participate in what might appear.

For Baudrillard, seduction in language operates as a challenge and is thus radically different than communication or rational, consensus-seeking discourse. This is so, according to Baudrillard, because the challenge "creates a nondialectic, ineluctable space. . . . [I]t opposes its own space to political space. It knows neither middle-range nor long-term; its only term is the immediacy of a response or of death. Everything linear, including history, has an end; challenge alone is without end since it is indefinitely reversible" (*Forget* 56). The linear, synthesizing drive of the dialectic thus finds its challenge in seduction whereby each term, each dialectical opposition, finds its position malleable, ambiguous, slippery, and reversible.

It is this reversibility in seduction, its desire to trope nondialectically, which characterizes the feminine. The feminine abolishes the trope of identity, of representation, the metaphor ("which is the mode of language, the possibility of communicating meaning" [Baudrillard, *Forget* 75]); and in its place is metamorphosis, which is "the radical point of the system, the point where there is no longer any law or symbolic order. It is a process without any subject, without death, beyond death, beyond any desire, in which only the rules of the game of forms are involved" (Baudrillard, *Forget* 75). It is at this radical point of metamorphosis at which one is "Becoming Woman" according to Gilles Deleuze (although Baudrillard has often told us to "forget" Deleuze, on this point he heartily concurs [*Forget* 75]). It is this possibility of transmutation, such as Nietzsche propounds in *Thus Spoke Zarathustra,* whereby truth is challenged by the false than false, whereby subjectivity is challenged by the object (not the passive object of the dialectic, but the object as an active effect) and discourse is challenged by fatal linkages and thereby turned from its truth and meaning, that can liberate being from its being, from its representation, and offer us an ethical revolution *après l'orgie.*

Seducing Revolution

Current critical practices, emanating as they are from the subject and from an antiquated order of simulation, offer no relief from the terror of truth to which we have been subjected for more than two thousand years. It is Baudrillard's argument that to achieve "liberation," one must radically rethink the conception of "liberty" and "empowerment." Baudrillard, despite the stereotypical criticisms of "quietism" and "apoliticism" aimed his way, is indeed interested in a "revolution." But he is not interested in constructing a revolution within the terms of production. Baudrillard's aim is to proffer a revolutionary critique but without a revolutionary subject. Gane explains that Baudrillard is influenced by Louis Althusser's argument that if there is such a thing as true practice, true revolutionary critique, it is the result of work in the "more-than-true, of *effects at a distance*, with the aim of positional displacement" (Gane, *Baudrillard* 28). Althusser writes, "[O]ne must think in extremes which means within a position from which one states borderline theses, or, to make thought possible, one occupies the place of the impossible" (*Essays in Self Criticism* 170). Baudrillard's conception of a revolution involves the seduction of truth, subjectivity, and discourse in order to think the impossible, the unrepresentable—that which has not yet been thought, or rather, to think that which will have been thought. Baudrillard writes, "[N]o one knows what relation can be established between elements that are outside representation. This is a problem of which our epistemology of knowledge permits no resolution since it always postulates the medium of a subject and of language, the medium of a representation" (*In the Shadow* 52). If there is to be a revolution, if we are to realize new, ethical ways of being—beyond the dialectic, beyond production and representation—our epistemology must be seduced.

And so must our notions of community, solidarity, and consensus be seduced. Current critical practices and calls for revolution are operating out of an antiquated notion of "the social." According to Baudrillard, in our current fractal stage of simulation, we have already suffered "the death of the social" and of the social contract.[7] But, Baudrillard reminds us, to say the "death of the social" is not to say the "end of the social." In place of phatic notions of community and solidarity, which are no longer possible to realize in this age of the "transpolitical," Baudrillard offers us, as Nietzsche does, a pathos of distance, that is, the feminine that is the "irony of the community" (*Seduction* 5–6). Seduction, a radically different register of challenges and contingent linkages, implies a new sociality. According to Baudrillard:

> The players . . . are not separate or individualized: they are instituted in a dual and agonistic relation. They are not even solidary—solidarity supposing a *formal* conception of the social, the moral ideal of a group in competition. The players are *tied* to each other; their parity entails an obligation that does not require solidarity, at least not as something that needs to be conceptualized or interiorized. The rule has no need of a formal structure or superstructure—whether

> moral or psychological—to function. Precisely because rules
> are arbitrary and ungrounded, because they have no refer-
> ents, they do not require a consensus, nor any collective will
> or truth. They exist, that's all. And they exist only when
> shared, while the Law floats above scattered individuals.
> (*Seduction* 136)

The current orgy of meaning, representation, and articulation is
governed by the Parmenidean desire that has constituted the metaphysical tradition and its by-products: truth, subjectivity, and rational communication. The seduction of these terms is our only hope for An/other
ethics, for a space of being that will have been truly different, and
would—I propose—open up a space for the constitution of a new subjectivity, within the space of seduction—one in which a subject is not
constructed according to the logic of the master/slave dialectic. This is
the space opened up by the loss of the ego and its sexual, Oedipal
imperative/narrative, or—in Foucault's words—the "death of man" as
he "Becomes Woman." This is the Baudrillardian possibility offered by
seduction, by becoming Woman. He writes,

> Every *positive* form can accommodate itself to its negative
> form [the dialectic], but understands the challenge of the *re-*
> *versible* form as mortal. Every structure can adapt to its sub-
> version or inversion, but not to the reversion of its terms.
> Seduction is this reversible form. Not the seduction to which
> women have been historically consigned: the culture of the
> gynaeceum, of rouge and lace, a seduction reworked by
> the mirror stage and the female imaginary, the terrain of
> sex games and ruses. . . . But seduction as an ironic, alterna-
> tive form, one that breaks the referentiality of sex and pro-
> vides a space, not of desire, but of play and defiance.[8] (*Seduc-*
> *tion* 21)

5

Seduction and the "Third Sophistic": (Femme) Fatale Tactics Contra Fetal Pedagogies, Critical Practices, and Neopragmatic Politics

We must become traitors, practice faithlessness, and always relinquish our ideals.
> —Nietzsche, *Human, All Too Human*

Domination does not replace the desire for recognition [that is, love]; rather it enlists it.
> —Jessica Benjamin, *The Bonds of Love*

They did not want to look on the naked face of luck (tuche), so they turned themselves over to science (techne). As a result, they are released from their dependence on luck; but not from their dependence on science.
> —Hippocratic treatise, *Peri Technes*

We in cities rightly grow shrewd at appraising man-made institutions—but beyond these tiny concentration points of rhetoric and traffic, there lies the eternally unsolvable Enigma, the preposterous fact that both existence and nothingness are equally unthinkable. And in this staggering disproportion between man and no-man, there is no place for purely human boasts of grandeur, or for forgetting that men build their cultures by huddling together, nervously loquacious, at the edge of an abyss.
> —Kenneth Burke, *Permanence and Change*

"To teach writing," according to James Berlin, "is to argue for a version of reality, and the best way of *knowing* and *communicating*" that reality ("Contemporary Composition" 766; emphasis mine). It is Berlin's point that pedagogies are sustained and motivated by, in Jean-François Lyotard's terminology, "grand narratives" that tell the story of how things "really are" and how things "should be" — that is, pedagogies are never ideologically innocent. To teach writing, Berlin has further argued, is to compose writing subjects who will serve that ideology, that particular narrative of reality. This assertion, made by Berlin in the early 1980s (as well as by the work of Patricia Bizzell, David Bartholomae, Greg Myers, Victor Vitanza, John Schilb, John Clifford, and John Trimbur), struck the discipline of composition as a radical and challenging idea, even though the Marxist critique of ideology and subjectivity had been underway for more than twenty years through the work of the Frankfurt school theorists and the French poststructuralists. What troubled, and what continues to trouble, teachers of writing is this Foucauldian claim that subjects are constituted via discourse strategies that maintain power/knowledge relations, this claim that writing/speaking subjects exist only insofar as they are written, as they are subjected. Such a claim seriously problematizes traditional notions of the writer, of the text, of authorial intent, and of the meaning-making process and further problematizes composition studies by politicizing the pedagogical act of teaching writing.

For example, Berlin, in "Rhetoric and Ideology in the Writing Class," describes how writers are variously composed according to the major schools of thought within composition studies. The cognitive process of writing, as propounded by Linda Flowers and John Hayes, in Berlin's estimation, constructs writing subjects constituted as productive, goal-directed, and focused individuals who have mastered the problem-solving model, who will "create a commodified text . . . that belongs to the individual and has exchange value" (483), who will "realize goals, not deliberate about their value" (482), and who will thus be easily appropriated by the corporate, capitalist state. The self-expressive school, represented by Ken Macrorie, William Coles, and Peter Elbow, argues that truth can be learned, but cannot be taught; that coming to truth is a private experience. And that truth is ultimately a truth about the self. The rhetoric of self-expressivist pedagogy, according to Berlin, can be used to reinforce the entrepreneurial virtues capitalism most values: individualism, private initiative, the confidence for risk taking (487). That is to say, the emphasis on the individual merely recomposes subjects who are subjected to the corporate, American myth of equal opportunity with its inherent blindness to material conditions of inequality, which deny that very opportunity to many.

In response to such "inner-directed" pedagogies that emphasize the self and its problematic attendants, authenticity and truth, since the early 1980s, there has been a growing interest in composition theory in so-called outer-directed pedagogies. Outer-directed theorists, according to Bizzell, argue that inner-directed pedagogies are epistemologically and politically naive: first because they take the writing subject as given and as the primary site of language production, and secondly because they do not question how that self is itself a site of symbolic and ideological production. Therefore the so-called outer-directed theorists focus on the social and ideological processes of language use and acquisition. Berlin identifies these theorists as practitioners of a new rhetoric that he terms "social-epistemic" and that others have termed "social constructionist." Although there are many different practices and constitutions of this rhetoric, they generally share a fundamental belief in the socially constructed and dialectical nature of truth. That is, unlike the self-expressive practitioners who assume that truth, and particularly the truth of the self, exists a priori and thus merely needs to be discovered or voiced, social-epistemic theorists assume that truth is, in the words of Richard Rorty, "socially justified belief" (*Philosophy*). That is to say, truth and knowledge are rhetorical, social constructs, not foundational, not preexisting givens.

Hence the claim that composition classrooms should become sites of creating "critical consciousness" regarding those social constructs that have been taken as foundational, that reify and propagate injustices (see Jarratt, *Rereading the Sophists;* Freire; Shor; and Aronowitz and Giroux). Thus critical theorists claim that their pedagogies, methodologies, and nonfoundational stance construct subjects who are not ideologically duped and thus subjected to the injustices of the corporate state, but who are emancipated through the process of the development of a critical consciousness (and conscience). The emphasis on the revealing of false consciousness or, in Freire's terminology, "consciencization," demonstrates a underlying faith in rationality as the goal; "consciencization," is to make rational what has been hidden in the structures of society. Despite all this pick and shoveling in order to reveal ideological presences, such "emancipatory" pedagogies carefully avoid striking at the rock-bottom foundation of their own enterprise: reason. What goes un-demystified is rationality itself. Rationality cannot be so easily divorced from its master, truth. Nietzsche's question "What will remains hidden in reason?" needs to be asked by such "critical" theorists. That is, whose truth is being revealed via the process of consciencization— via rationalization—via the process of "coming to know"?

Almost twenty years later, Berlin's critique, now accepted as a commonplace, has in many ways obscured the more radical problematization offered by poststructuralist and postmodern theory and by the post-modern condition of the late twentieth century. For although Berlin and others justifiably criticize inner-directed theories of composition as re-producing individuals in order to reify the political horrors of our time, and as being *grounded* in Western metaphysical assumptions about and traditions of subjectivity, truth, and language, and although they simul-taneously espouse "anti-foundational" theories and rigorous "critical" methodologies, they incipiently and insidiously reinvoke those very no-tions and foundations that have sustained the metaphysical tradition, namely reason and logic. This is not to say that emancipatory pedagogy and critical theory does not have its value; this is not to say that it should not be taught. There is value in making students think critically about racism and sexism, for example. And, furthermore, I have no doubt that it does empower its students and proponents. Any educa-tion—to greater or lesser degrees (according to its hidden curriculum and material resources)—likewise empowers students as it initiates them into and equips them with a discourse that constitutes them and gains them admittance into a discourse community. However, this edu-cational process in no way liberates the subject from the process of sub-jectification, the process of becoming subject, of coming to know, to be, and to have an identity. Therefore, what these critical theorists have demonstrated so forcefully to me is that there is no metalanguage or paraposition with which or from which one can establish a critique that is not implicated in the humanist, Enlightenment project—the terms of which Parmenides and Plato set up long ago.

Critical pedagogy claims to have dumped this metaphysical bag-gage by questioning the foundation of truth and being as *a priori,* and by establishing truth and being as socially, discursively constructed. Yet herein lies the social-epistemic and critical pedagogies' insidious foundationalism: the presuppositions that (1) there must be something: ideology, the social, "material" conditions, the individual, individual rights, freedom, the dialectic, (for example), and (2) it must be able to be known (thus rational), and (3) it must be able to be communicated (thus language and subjects are already presupposed to be rational). Re-member, Berlin wrote, "To teach writing is to argue for a version of reality, and the best way of knowing and communicating it." What Ber-lin has done, therefore, in the name of liberation and emancipation, is to argue for a version of reality and the best way of knowing and com-municating it. Again, Berlin obscures what is at stake here, as does the title of Michael Bernard-Donals and Richard Glejzer's coedited *Rheto-ric in an Antifoundational World*. Rhetoric is not "in" an antifounda-tional world, it is *constitutive* of it: the world's simultaneous possibil-ity and impossibility. Recall Gorgias's so-called tragedy of knowledge:

Nothing exists; even if it did exist, you couldn't know it; even if you could know it, you couldn't communicate it. The world is rendered foundationless because there is no way to found being and knowing extradiscursively or divorced from *logos*. Thus rhetoric is both the foundation of any being and knowing (as in Aristotelian rhetoric) and its impossibility (as in [Third] sophistic rhetoric). When Bizzell writes "there is no foundational knowledge, no knowledge that is necessary or self-evident. Whatever we believe, we believe only because we have been persuaded" ("Beyond" 261), she presumes an Aristotelian discursive world with Aristotelian rhetors who persuade and who are persuaded. Furthermore, when she argues that we should "get over" antifoundationalism by positing "nonfoundational" programs that will "help our students, and our fellow citizens, to engage in a rhetorical process that can collectively generate trustworthy knowledge and beliefs conducive to the common good" ("Beyond" 271), she is arguing for Aristotelian foundations against sophistic rhetoric's instability. Of course, Bizzell is not a lone voice; she echoes all the voices of the rhetorical tradition, which has established foundations in the face of antifoundationalism by requiring rhetoric to keep its sophistic tendencies in check. Further, when Bizzell argues that we should "aver provocatively that we intend to make our students better people, that we believe education should develop civic virtue" ("Beyond" 271), she is again echoing the rhetorical tradition, which has required rhetoric to serve the polis, and which has required the teaching of rhetoric to be in the service of *paideia*—the construction of suitable, that is, guilty, subjects.

I am arguing, contra Bizzell, that what is at stake is not whether we can establish foundations in a foundationless world. For we have proved to be able to do so; we have being doing it—very well, I might add—for more than 2500 years (I'm leaving the "we" purposely ambiguous). The foundations that have been built, I would wager, have been built with "good intentions" to establish a civic body. I doubt very strongly that Peter Elbow or Linda Flower would aver that they are not trying to help their students, that they are not trying to help construct writing subjects that can serve the polis. This is the point that Berlin (and others) make: foundations are rhetorically constituted, which produce subjects who "will not only see [these foundations] as acceptable, but perceive [them] 'precisely as the way things are, ought to be, and will be'" (Zavarzadeh and Morton, "Theory Pedagogy Politics" 2). And again, we have been very good at rhetorically constructing foundations. Thus to profess antifoundationalism, according to Stanley Fish, "says nothing about what we can now do or not do; it is an account of what we have always been doing and cannot help but do . . . —act in accordance with the standards and norms that are the content of our beliefs and, therefore, the very structure of our consciousness" ("Consequences" 114). For many, Fish states, "the consequences of antifoundationalist theory are disastrous and amount to the loss of everything we associate with rational inquiry: public and shared standards, criteria for preferring one reading of a text or of the world to another, checks against irresponsibility, and so on" ("Consequences" 113). Yet, he continues, soothing the fear, antifoundationalism "is an argument for the situated subject, for the individual who is always constrained by the local or community standards and criteria of which his judgment is an extension" (113). That is, within the foundationless world in which we operate, we have always already posited foundations, which dictate norms for our behaviors and structure our consciousness. What is at stake, then, is *resisting* such foundations. Fish would characterize this as evidence of my antifoundationalist "theory hope," which reasons that "since we now know that our convictions about truth and factuality have not been imposed on us by the world, or imprinted in our brains, but are derived from the practices of ideologically motivated communities, we can set them aside in favor of convictions that we choose freely" (113). I do not, despite Fish's insistence, have this "hope." Indeed, Fish's representation of antifoundationalism reveals his own "theory hope": a foundational faith in a rational and (however locally and situationally constrained) grammatical subject. His claim that it is my hope to have the subject "freely choose" to be unsubjected presupposes, once again, a theory of will emanating from a subject. Therefore, Fish has not risked the abyss of antifoundationalism. Nor have we as writing teachers. The question then becomes: what is our will to "help" our students, to construct "fellow citizens," to program the common good? What is our will to produce subjects as such?

The past chapters have attempted to demonstrate what will is hidden in such attempts to produce subjects, programs, politics, knowledge, and the real—in short—truth. I have argued that the will to truth and the will to represent truth have exacted too high a price: nothing short of our subjection and the negation/expulsion of all others. Therefore, to repeat myself, insofar as our pedagogical goal remains within the realm of production, we remain modernists, subject to the program of modernism, complicit with the epistemic violence (which does affect "real" bodies) of such. To repeat Baudrillard's radical ethic: "*We were all once produced, we must all be seduced. That is the only true 'liberation'*"—from the imperatives of truth and its required, sustaining representations (*Fatal Strategies* 138; emphasis mine).

But, you may say, to allow ourselves to be seduced—is this not just a "flight into language" (Eagleton) away from the "real," political, and material concerns of today? On the contrary. I am arguing, have been arguing, that I should prefer that political and material conditions were otherwise. But there is no foundation I can appeal to, extradiscursively, to found things as otherwise. In what follows, I will argue that seduction (or what I have been calling "Woman" or "sophistry") can address what will have been otherwise. But first I want to address two recently offered antidotes to our antifoundational, postmodern, rhetorical world. The first is offered in the name of Woman: the "feminization" of composition studies through the figure of the Mother. The second is offered in the name of a Third Sophistic: neopragmatism. I will demonstrate that neither alternative is Woman enough or [Third] Sophistic enough.

Panic Masculinity and Agent Mother: Fetal Pedagogies

A recent trend in composition studies, instigated by gender, social, and political concerns, has been a call for the "feminization" of composition pedagogy in order to redistribute power and to give women a voice.[1] Working against traditional male-gendered rhetorical models (that is, Platonic or Aristotelian) and bolstered by Rogerian rhetoric,[2] social-constructionist bases, and the moral psychology studies of Carol Gilligan[3] and Mary Belenky et al.,[4] collaborative learning proponents have sought to reconstruct the classroom as a site of social cooperation, connectedness, and nurturance (values not traditionally associated with masculinity). They have reenvisioned composition as an act of understanding rather than of agonistics. Sally Gearhart in "The Womanization of Rhetoric," for example, characterizes this new classroom as a "womblike matrix" (199)—that is, as Susan Jarratt in her critique characterizes it, a "dialogic context for [the] exchange of ideas" ("Feminism and Composition" 107). Catherine Lamb, in "Beyond Argument in Feminist Composition," argues that the feminist composition classroom would foster negotiation, mediation, and resolution by practicing what Sara Ruddick calls "Maternal Thinking"—that is, attentive love. The goal of such a pedagogy appears to be, according to Alison Ainley, to return to the Mother "as the embodiment of [the] idealized virtues of forbearance, fortitude, care, and patience" (53).

It is my argument that this theoretical tack and pedagogical strategy is a dangerous one, with potentially explosive and damaging repercussions—for masculinity and femininity, for "real" men and women. The hope is to temper masculinity's excesses (as institutionalized in patriarchy, warfare, and phallogocentrism) with this new "feminizing" pedagogy through the figure of the Mother. Yet, as Nancy Chodorow, Dorothy Dinnerstein, and Adrienne Rich have argued before me, proponents of the figure of the Mother deny a compelling "reality": that this Mother is a function of patriarchy, that the Mother is the pedagogue that reproduces masculinity, and that the Mother is complicit in the construction of male narcissism and fetishization, two psychological neuroses that are easily pathologized by our "New War" mentality, which prescribes "hyper-masculinity," sexism, violence, and a paranoid and paramilitary way of being. Thus, in what follows, I aim to identify the crisis of masculinity and to demonstrate in what ways the pedagogy of the Mother (as a figure in institutionalized Motherhood) is in a large part historically responsible for masculinity as such and, therefore, cannot represent a remedy.

In *Warrior Dreams,* James William Gibson analyzes the current paramilitary phenomena in America, complete with paintball aficionados, soldiers of fortune, vigilantes, and pistol-club members preaching a "philosophy of violence" (174). Granted, not all men are gun-toting, Rambo-aspiring warriors, yet the fear motivating these new warriors is a sense of impotence that informs American masculinity today. This sense of powerlessness is specifically sensed as the result of cultural emasculation. Although the excesses of masculinity have long been associated with war and violence, today's warrior is specifically a paramilitary warrior. The Vietnam War experience, which severed our national record of military victory and prowess, according to Gibson, disrupted our cultural identity: If America was no longer a winning warrior, what was it? (10–11). This devastating loss, coupled with civil rights and feminist movements and exacerbated by significant economic changes (for example, becoming a debtor nation), mark our current definitions of masculinity (11). The backlash against women and homosexuality reflects a desire to settle into a comfortable masculinity, where power relations are uncontested. In response to this crisis of masculinity, some feminists have suggested that we send in the Mothers. But how can we look to the Mother to rectify the very situation she helped to create? If the battle is against the Mother (against dependency), what possible efficacy could she have in a peacekeeping mission? It is my fundamental presupposition, informed by psychoanalytic theory, that the Mother is an agent who constitutes masculinity as such.

Further, it is my conviction, informed by feminist readings of ideology, that the Mother is an agent of patriarchy; thus how can we separate the figure of Mother from her patriarchy-serving role? Although I am not eager to agree with Tania Modleski, generally, I agree with her on this point: "[F]eminism," she reminds us (echoing a particular feminist sentiment),

> has emphasized from the beginning the oppressiveness of the ideology of compulsory heterosexuality and the institution it supports—that of the nuclear family. The family is the structural unit keeping women economically and physically

dependent on men; separating women from other women; and, in extreme (but by no means uncommon) cases, providing the space in which men may abuse women with impunity. (13)

Although a new wave of feminism faults previous generations of feminists for too harshly condemning the family (see for example, Elizabeth Fox-Genovese), to critique the institution of Motherhood in no way forecloses the possibility of negotiating new definitions of family. However, instead of "new definitions," we get a tired rerun featuring the same all-nurturing Mother. Once again, however strategically, we risk the reification of the "maternal instinct," the "God-given" justification for her uncompensated work bearing and rearing children. How can we separate the figure of the Mother from the traditional assumptions regarding her nurturing role? The Mother as nurturing agent fulfills the ideological need of the industrial revolution, evidenced by the doctrine of "separate spheres" (see Wolff 12–33; Fineman 14–22; and Chodorow 173–90). The mother-child dyad fostered as a loving (and often "natural") ideal, Badinter writes, "legitimizes the exclusion of fathers, which reinforces the myth" (*XY* 63).

Even if we underscore the constructedness of this nurturing ability, if we continue to accept it as women's mode and function, we are complicit in its reification (see Looser, "Composing" and Culley et al.). Our insistence on valuing "women's ways" of knowing, being, writing, and loving must be challenged, if only because these are the very characteristics that have been taken as instinctual and as suiting us "by nature" to the mothering of children, relegating women to the private sphere, barring women from the public sphere, and demanding that women be totally self-sacrificing. As Janis Tedesco reminds us, "women's ways of knowing" are *primarily* women's ways of *adapting* (252). Chodorow, in *The Reproduction of Mothering*, provides an analysis of the various discourses, including socio-biological, socio-anthropological, and socio-psychological, that "naturalize" concepts of nurturing in order to debunk the reasons given as to why women must/should/do Mother. She points to the work of Margaret Polatnick, whose research agenda asks "not how women come to mother, but *why men do not.* . . . [She concludes that women's] mothering reinforces and perpetuates women's relative powerlessness" (31; emphasis mine).

We have recognized for some time, along with Susan Suleiman, that the "good and even the good-enough (Winnicott) mother is characterized . . . not only by tenderness and the 'masochistic-feminine willingness to sacrifice' but above all by her exclusive and total involvement with her child" (355). The Mother's love is offered in exchange for her self-denial and effacement (see Benjamin), suggesting that women's ways of mothering should be scrutinized, not unquestionably embraced, because these are the very values and qualities that have disempowered women. That women are cast as nurturing Mother is patriarchy's most subtle and ingenious tool. Some might argue that I am merely throwing the baby out with the bathwater. I would respond that the unquestioned acceptance of Mothering as a value and importing it into the composition classroom is a case of drowning the baby in the bathwater, or perhaps, more (in)appropriately, in the amniotic fluid.

Woman is not necessarily a Mother or prone to Mothering: we've demonstrated this. Or have we? Still the conflation continues: Woman equals Womb; Woman's Work equals Loving, Mothering. Consider the following statements made by proponents of a nurturing pedagogy. I am struck by the rhetorical ways in which "woman," "feminine," "feminist," and "mother" get conflated. For example, Louise Wetherbee Phelps, in her "Becoming a Warrior: Lessons of the Feminist Workplace" (she evidently has warrior dreams of her own), argues that "*the composition workplace is always already feminist*" (302; emphasis hers). She comes to this conclusion because teachers of writing are "predominantly female" and these female teachers "already have some degree of power," specifically "discursive power," within this workforce (302). She continues, "A writing classroom headed by a woman teacher is a microcosm where she sets the work agenda and exercises various kinds of control, over who speaks and is heard, what writing or talk is valued, what is read, who passes with what grades, and in what terms (intellectual frameworks, social purposes, language) these things are interpreted and understood" (302). And, she further argues, these power-wielding women (who are thus "feminist") teach via "feminine principles" — that is, "'women's ways' of knowing, acting, speaking, writing, reading, and educating" (303). These "feminine principles" or "women's ways" include a "parentlike caring for students' development," — that is, Mothering (303). Although Phelps does note the possible sites of controversy and contention regarding these "feminine principles," she does use interchangeably words such as "feminist," "woman," and "feminine." Sue Ellen Holbrook's "Women's Work: The Feminizing of Composition" also reflects this conflation. According to her informative statistical analysis, the teaching of composition remains "women's work" — that is, statistically, more women than men teach composition. She concludes, therefore, that composition is being "feminized" — "a process made possible by its low status and women's" (209). Again, it is assumed that "real women" are "feminine" and engage in some activity that necessarily produces "feminizing" results. Susan Hunter's "A Woman's Place *Is* in the Composition Classroom," likewise, conflates "woman" with "mother" (234) and "woman" with "feminist" (242). Quoting Nancy Hartsock, Hunter constructs the equation: "Female Experience" equals "Mothering" equals "Woman" equals "Feminist" equals "Liberation" (234). Of course, this raises obvious questions: Can "men" not be feminists? Can "men" not nurture? Can "men" not participate in this liberating pedagogy? Apparently not; apparently woman's place is in the nursery/composition classroom.

Collaborating with the Phallus

The figure of the Father—as the law of the father, as the patriarchal model, as the wielder of the phallus, and, thus as the controller of the Symbolic—has been the primary target for many feminists (and/or others) aiming to deconstruct the power/knowledge matrix which has sustained gender inequities. The dismantling of the Father's power has tempted many to try to place this displaced power onto the Mother. Although the figure of the Mother will certainly, as Elinor Gadon's *Once and Future Goddess* suggests, "resacralize"—that is, "remystify"— woman's body and sexuality, it will never be able to upset the binary constructions of Western thought, the very binaries which have justified patriarchy for so long. The worship of "feminine principles," thus, is merely a deconstructive act of depriviledging one side of the binary (that is, patriarchy, the father, masculine), while repriviledging the other (matriarchy, the mother, feminine). According to Benjamin, "To idealize maternal nurturance . . . only confirms the dualism and denies historical reality. To accept the old ideal of motherhood—even as an ideal—is to remain inside the revolving door of gender polarity" (206). The simple reversal of the terms has in no way offered us a breakthrough or a breakdown of the Hegelian master/slave dialectic. Baudrillard reminds us that this is the brilliance of the dialectic, that it can "accommodate itself to its negative form" (*Seduction* 21), to the inversion of its terms.

I question the efficacy and ethics of such a goal, of realigning "the figure of woman as mother" as a new, liberating, equalizing paradigm for ethical relations—either between writer and reader, or teacher and student. Margo Culley and colleagues claim that

> the feminist classroom may become the place where the cultural split between mother and father may be healed. The feminist intellectual appropriates the *word* for herself and its power to name the manifestations of patriarchy. It may be that as women academics we have become the fathers, entered into the realm of history which men have always

controlled. Yet, in a more profound sense feminism repudi-
ates the law and order of the father and transforms history
by bringing to it what we know about being mothers and
being mothered. (18)

Is such a pedagogy—coined "gynagogy" by some (Gore 3)—truly an
empowering model? Is "love," the Mother's love in particular, a viable
technē for liberation? It is my argument that, on the contrary, love—
and the Mother's love in particular—prescribes a set of relations and
a process of subject constitution which insidiously reinvoke Western,
metaphysical, political, and patriarchal traditions. Not only does this
Mother's love paradigm secure the traditional relations within the so-
called nuclear family, but it also secures the Oedipal construction of
consciousness and conscience as well as perpetuating the master/slave
dialectic that sustains subjectivity.

This construction is based on a castration anxiety fueled by sexual
differentiation. Freud argues in "Some Psychical Consequences of the
Anatomical Distinction Between the Sexes" that "normal" male subjectivity is dependent on an insistence of the "visible" lack of his sexual
other. That is, by projecting onto the female (primarily the Mother) a
lack, by constructing the Mother, psychically, as the symbol of lack,
he protects himself from the threat of lack. The formulation reads
like a syllogism: She is Lack; She is different from me; Therefore, I am
not lacking. He needs the Mother to sustain his disavowal. Yet he is
"equipped," you say; how and why can he be possibly lacking? This is
because, Jacques Lacan argues in "The Signification of the Phallus," the
little boy's "equipment" is not the phallus. This is the state of symbolic castration wherein he finds himself. Judith Butler explains that
the "threat [of castration] institutes and sustains the assumption of the
masculine sex in relation to the 'having' of the phallus, whereby the
feminine 'sex' is assumed through embodying that threat as the 'being'
of the phallus, posing as the 'loss' with which the masculine is perpetually threatened" (*Bodies that Matter* 197). Therefore, to be male is to
be in a state of perpetual anxiety regarding an imaginary threat of loss.
This, then, is how he (mis)recognizes himself as masculine, as not lacking. And it is the Mother's voice that first "recognizes" the child; it is
the Mother's voice that first introduces the child to the Symbolic; it is
the Mother's voice and hands that first territorialize the child's body.

Proponents of a maternal pedagogy, however, don't envision the
maternal voice and hand as being implicated in the demands of the
Symbolic. The presupposition is that the Mother's voice is fundamentally a pure communication, untainted by the ideology of phallogocentrism. Therefore, according to Lamb, the goal and methodology of a

patently feminist composition pedagogy should be to counter "mono-logic" forms of argumentation by emphasizing the supposedly mater-nal skills of negotiation and mediation that will culminate in a "reso-lution of conflict that is fair to both sides" (11)—a resolution which will lessen the distance between the parties via "loving attention" or empathy, which suspends any existing hierarchy (15), and thereby guar-antees a "mutual recognition."[5] Such a pedagogy obviously has its foundation in the processes of collaborative learning, which is, accord-ing to John Trimbur, "the process of intellectual negotiation and collec-tive decision-making" with the aim of reaching "consensus through an expanding conversation" ("Consensus and Difference" 602).

The danger of such a consensus-seeking pedagogy is its potential to glorify the discursive production of knowledge while ignoring how that production sustains hierarchical systems of power. Greg Myers writes, "[T]he ideas of *consensus* and *reality* . . . , though they seem so progres-sive, are part of the structure of ideology" (156). Evelyn Ashton-Jones, in her "Collaboration, Conversation, and the Politics of Gender," fur-ther argues that collaborative learning has not undergone the necessary scrutiny but has been, nevertheless, largely adopted by feminists as somehow integrally a "feminist" action. She cites, for example, Cynthia Caywood and Gillian Overing's *Teaching Writing: Pedagogy, Gender, and Equity*, which claims that collaborative learning is "compatible with feminism, if not feminist in and of itself" (quoted in Ashton-Jones 8). Ashton-Jones argues that the "interactional dynamics of writing groups" inevitably and demonstrably reproduce the ideology of gender and that the unexamined valorization of collaboration "unwittingly colludes in the reproduction of gender structures that feminists seek to disrupt" (7). Thus, to "portray collaborative pedagogies as pedagogies of equity, . . . is to perpetuate and collude in the silence that helps to conceal the reproduction of gender ideology" (17).

Trimbur, I wager, would concur with this critique, as he has pre-viously argued that intellectual negotiation and discourse should aim for revealing differences, as in Victor Vitanza's notion of a rhetoric of *dissensus* ("Critical Sub/Versions"), rather than solidifying identifica-tions (Trimbur, "Consensus and Difference"). This demand for main-taining difference is an extraordinarily significant one. For what are normalized, consensual discourse communities but a community of peers who have been accepted into that community only insofar as they have abandoned their differences—only insofar as they have accepted the status quo of that community: its language, its discourse, its values? What differences have been sacrificed to attain consensus, to achieve identification? And whose voices have been silenced through consensus? This is Susan Jarratt's argument in "Feminism and Composition: The

Case for Conflict." She writes, "For some composition teachers, creating a supportive climate in the classroom and validating student experience leads them to avoid conflict [and] . . . leaves them insufficiently prepared to negotiate the oppressive [and silencing] discourses of racism, sexism, and classism" (106). And this conflict-free, hierarchically neutral classroom may in fact strengthen, not eradicate, masculine values and impulses. Benjamin argues that "the lack of manifest authority intensifies the pressure to perform independently, to live up to the ideal without leaning on a concrete person who embodies it. The idealization of masculine values and the disparagement of feminine values persist unabated even though individual men and women are freer to cross over than before" (172).[6]

It appears that reconstituting the composition classroom as a site of maternal care potentially reterritorializes power relations, specifically the power relations of mother and child, male and female, public and private, master and servant. Nevertheless Jim Corder argues in "Argument as Emergence, Rhetoric as Love" that in order to understand we have "*to know* each other, *to be present to* each other, *to embrace* each other" (23). It is just such a love that describes the Hegelian, negating process of subject constitution. Love is a demand: "love me; recognize me; identify [with] me" and thus remains a fetal strategy, a pathos of unity and consensus. Hegel argues that the demand for recognition is the fundamental demand for consciousness of one's self. In *The Phenomenology of Spirit,* Hegel posits that one's identity is dependent on recognizing one's self as being recognized by the other. Yet this relationship is not based on a mutual (that is, equal) recognition, as the one attempts to prove identity through domination, through the negation of this other.[7] This is the fetal strategy whereby we, in Baudrillard's words, murder the other, the object of love (for in love, the other is always objectified). And it is in this sense that the student becomes an object of the Mother's love—that is, "embraced" in a relation of mastery.

I'm Mother, You're Son: Who's Innocent?

A so-called maternal classroom seems to perpetuate the American cultural myth of a mother country with outstretched, loving arms, guaranteeing opportunity and equality for all. This is the myth of the melting pot: that is, putting students in collaborative relations is like putting a bowl of Velveeta cheese and salsa in the microwave to create a delightful dish to be consumed. As Ashton-Jones, Jarratt, Myers, and Trimbur have argued, there is value in sustaining conflict and encouraging differences, and to strive for consensus is a problematic endeavor and ideal. To seek consensus in the name of the Mother is even more so, for it is my argument that essentializing and reidealizing the so-called maternal love instincts and nurturing capacities potentially blinds us to the power of the Mother, to the hierarchical relationship between mother and child, and to her gendered and trained incapacities. Didn't Gilligan remind us that it is women's special knack not to resolve conflict, but to avoid it altogether? What does a mother's lullaby serve but to silence the disgruntled child's cry? And if mothers are so well-versed in conflict resolution, then why are mothers always deferring negotiation by telling their children to "just wait until your father comes home"?

What disturbs me is that proponents of "gynagogy," "maternal thinking," and "nurturing classrooms" often justify their positions via the rhetoric of victimage. They seem to suggest that there exists an original, innocent "feminine realm [that has been] corrupted by phallic" evil (Benjamin 223). The advantages of such a rhetoric are many and obvious: It provides a sense of moral orthodoxy, a special mission, and a superior insight. Ruddick, for example, argues that a "feminist standpoint" is "a superior vision" (quoted in Lamb 16). It is Ruddick's argument that this moral superiority has been gained at the price of oppression and victimization. This process of casting one's self as victim and then claiming moral superiority is a powerful justification for victimizing others. Most well-known histories of our American frontier, for example, cast the pioneer as the victim of natural forces and Indian savagery. Such innocence and victimization justify "Manifest Destiny": the "taming" of the West and the brutal acts of genocide against the Native American population. My point is that claiming innocence is never innocent.

This is Shelby Steele's argument in "I'm Black, You're White, Who's Innocent?" He posits that the racial struggle in America "has always been primarily a struggle for innocence" (5), that "[b]oth races [white and black] instinctively understand that to lose innocence is to lose power (in relation to each other). To be innocent someone else must be guilty" (6). By claiming power through their innocence, women can use their victimization as an entitlement to "power over," not just "power together." This, of course, is not to say that "real" women are not victimized. But to claim power by virtue of one's victimization is, in Steele's words, "a formula that binds the victim to his victimization by linking his power to his status as a victim" (14). For example, Maxine Hairston identifies composition practitioners as the "female partner in an abusive marriage and composition theorists who turn to deconstruction as "the intimate enemy" that must be rallied against (273, 277). Therefore, as Hairston's allegory forcefully demonstrates, women must continue to assume the role of the victim in order to maintain the

power achieved through their innocence (see Reichert's "A Contributing Listener and Other Composition Wives"). Therefore, "empowerment" is achieved at too high of a price. Furthermore, claiming victimization can blind us to the ways in which we are complicit with our
oppression. Foucault has argued that power is successful in proportion
to its ability to hide its own mechanisms (*Discipline and Punish* 187).

Christiane Olivier in *Jocasta's Children* offers a corrective to this
rhetoric of innocence and victimage by suggesting that Jocasta—the
mother in the Oedipal narrative—is perhaps guiltier than Oedipus himself (2). Estela Welldon, in *Mother, Madonna, Whore,* likewise dismisses
the Mother's natural innocence. She writes:

> It looks as though we have all become silent conspirators
> in a system which, from whatever angle we look at them,
> women are either dispossessed of all power or made . . . sex-
> ual objects and victims. . . . We do not accord them any
> sense of responsibility for their own unique functions, deeply
> related to fecundity and motherhood, and liable at times to
> manifest themselves perversely. Why should Jocasta, when
> both she and Oedipus learn the facts of their incestuous re-
> lationship, be the one to promptly commit suicide? (86)

Olivier argues that—beyond Jocasta and Oedipus—it is the Mother's
love that has constituted our patriarchal society as such, and warns that
"the spider's web that [mothers] have woven around the little boy is the
very web" in which we find ourselves—as women—trapped (89). Now,
it is not my purpose to cast blame nor to demand guilt, but rather to
acknowledge women's—the Mother's in particular—profound complicity in systems of domination and oppression. But, as Jessica Benjamin writes, "[T]o reduce domination to a simple relation of doer and
done- to is to substitute moral outrage for analysis. Such a simplifica-
tion, moreover, reproduces the structure of gender polarity under the
guise of attacking it" (9–10).

It is my purpose to acknowledge the Mother as neither innocent
nor guilty, but as an active agent of a child's subject constitution. It is
the very relation to the Mother—in our Western culture—that constitutes a child's gendered subjectivity as such (see Olivier 86). In terms of
the Oedipal model of development, Benjamin reminds us, "[A]ll infants
feel themselves to be like their mothers. But boys discover that they cannot grow up to *become* her; they can only *have* her. . . . Male children
achieve their masculinity by denying their original identification or oneness with their mothers" (75) and by denying and denigrating "the
feminine." Girls, on the other hand, "gain a sense of self by protecting
the all-good, all-powerful maternal object, at the price of compliance.

She becomes unable to distinguish what she wants from what mother wants. The fear of separation and difference has been transposed into submission" (Benjamin 79).

The relation to the Mother, then, is tinged with fear and an infantile acknowledgment of the power inequities within that relation. Furthermore, that fear is exacerbated by the fact that a Mother's love is itself not distributed evenly or "democratically." Olivier states, "Girls are for the most part weaned earlier than boys. Mothers stop giving the bottle to girls, on average, in the twelfth month, and to boys in the fifteenth. The feed is longer for boys: at two months, forty-five minutes, against twenty-five minutes for girls" (54). Now we see that within this idealized Mother-child relationship, this nurturing love, there exists inequities and sexism. It is this inequity, this unequal distribution of the Mother's milk, that instills in women a sense of oral desperation that becomes sublimated into "love." Olivier writes:

> And so [this] excess of "emptiness" and desire for "fullness"
> will take the woman into the kitchen where she will take up
> her position somewhere between the fridge and the cooker,
> by way of the sink. . . . [S]he will be told that this is the place
> that has been planned for her since the dawn of time, that
> this is her kingdom. . . . What a sham it is, what an infernal
> circle, in which mothers provide for whole families so that,
> by this round-about route, they can feed the hungry little
> girl they carry inside them! . . . By the mechanism of projec-
> tion, each woman imagines that everyone else is like her and
> therefore famished, and, herself insatiable, feels obliged to
> feed them till they can eat no more. In the lives of women
> an unprotected, empty inside cohabits strangely with a gen-
> erous outside. Women, it seems, tend to mix up "loving"
> and "feeding." (56)

Women love only because they have been loved—that is, left for nothing, as nothing. Denied their clitoral identity and thus not yet able to identify with the reproducing vaginal mother, girls were/are nothing for the first twelve to thirteen years of their lives. This, then, is a mother's love. I am reminded of Kenneth Burke's acknowledgment that a shepherd will love, nurture, care for, and act in the best interest of the sheep. But he or she may very well be raising them for market—to be bought and sold (and slaughtered) as commodities (*Rhetoric of Motives* 27). These commodities will serve the polis as gendered subjects who will faithfully reproduce the family structure which creates misogynist men and submissive women. Is the idealization of the Mother another example of the conservative backlash against women? Is this

Mother truly the one who will lead us out of Egypt? Is this truly the emancipatory pedagogy we have been waiting for?

If Freud is correct in asserting that our primary relations determine our subsequent relations, then we must question how maternal pedagogues avoid merely reinscribing within the composition classroom the same set of relations that each student had to his or to her mother. If gynagogy proposes to deconstruct traditional hierarchical and phallic relations between student and teacher—that is, by attempting to disperse the teacher's authority while "empowering" students—how can they counteract or disperse the very real and threatening power of the Mother? How can proponents of a nurturing classroom apologize for the Mother's power and desire? For behind the nurturing mother lie the threats of being engulfed by her and of being denied her love. (And sometimes, as the Susan Smith story attests, the Mother's "love" manifests itself in tragic ways. A Mother's "instinct" can also be murderous [see Melanie Klein]).[8] How can gynagogy answer to the charge that the Mother is a necessary player in the son's Oedipalization? According to Chodorow's reading of the Oedipal relationship,

> When individual women—mothers—provide parenting, total dependence is on the Mother. It is aspects of the relationship to *her* that are internalized defensively; it is *her* care that must be consistent and reliable; it is *her* absence that produces anxiety. The infant's earliest experience and development is in the context of, and proceeds out of, an interpersonal relationship to its mother. This relationship, however, is not symmetrical. (60–61)

Just because our freshman composition students have (most probably) survived high school, it doesn't mean they have survived the Oedipal relation and are able to deal with their ambivalent feelings toward the Mother.

The mother-child dyad is not an intersubjective and thus ideal relationship; it is not an example of "collaboration" and equitable connectedness. It is my argument that Mothers in the classroom potentially infantilize our students and encourage narcissism by replaying the Oedipal scenario. And, furthermore, casting the composition classroom as a nursery never adequately addresses how these composition teachers-cum-Mothers are going to negotiate masculinity's war against the Mother. According to Chodorow, "For children of both genders, mothers represent regression and lack of autonomy. A boy associates these issues with his gender identification as well. Dependence on his mother, attachment to her, and identification with her represent that which is not masculine; a boy must reject dependence and deny attachment and identification" (181). Chodorow reminds us, once again, that masculinity requires a Mother to push against. How, exactly, is a collaborative and maternal pedagogy going to resolve this tension? Furthermore, how is this maternal pedagogy going to answer the ethical question it sidesteps in the name of "feminine principles"? The ethical issue is this: we are teaching "real" men and asking them, in subtle and not-so-subtle ways, to stop being men, and thereby we are denying them the only identity that they have (n)ever known. To tell them that "masculinity" is something they need to be purged and cured of has ethical implications. We feminists claim that we have been denied our identity as women, yet must we, likewise, deny men theirs, by telling them to become more like us, more like women? Naomi Wolf offers us this disturbing image: "Many of the behaviors now under criticism are so embedded in the sense of masculinity learned by many men from infancy on that the thought of excising them from one's identity must feel like being asked to scrape away a skin. What would be left? What would one be but bleeding, mute, unrecognizable? Is that a Man?" (22). These are, of course, difficult and complicated issues, which—I am suggesting—need to be scrutinized before we embrace the Mother.[9]

In contradistinction to compositionists who plead for more mothering, Gibson, Chodorow, Dinnerstein, and Olivier (among others) suggest less mothering in conjunction with more fathering. This will aid our daughters as well as our sons. According to Janice Hays,

> a study done in the 1970s . . . found that women college students who had reached the highest levels of moral development often came from families in which mothers were not overly involved with their children's welfare but had busy and active lives of their own and even, on occasion, voiced their annoyance at having to extend themselves on their children's behalf—a posture contrary to usual maternal stereotypes. (176)

Thus, perhaps we do not need Mothers or "Good Enough" Mothers in the classrooms, but revolutionary pedagogues who realize that the excesses of masculinity are a function of the excesses of femininity, and vice versa. What is needed, according to Benjamin, is to move beyond the Mother/Father binary, to acknowledge their relation of supplementarity. She writes:

> it is necessary to criticize not only the idealization of the masculine side, but also the reactive valorization of femininity. What is necessary is not to take sides but to remain focused

on the dualistic structure itself. . . . The point is to get out
of the antithesis between mother and father, this revolving
door between the regressive maternal warmth and the icy
paternal outside. (9, 177)

It does not follow, however, that the pedagogical imperative becomes the deployment of maternal/paternal tag-team teaching. For although the kinship restructuring argument posed by Chodorow and
others could alleviate masculinity's fundamental need to distance itself
from the maternal, it does not necessarily solve the problem of sexual
differentiation, of symbolic castration. The family has experienced significant restructuring since the time Chodorow wrote her proposal more
than twenty years ago. Yet, despite these changes and despite the acceptance of alternative families (other than the so-called nuclear family),
hypermasculinity continues to be reproduced. According to Gilles Deleuze and Félix Guattari, "the problem is not resolved until we do
away with *both the problem and the solution*" (*Anti-Oedipus* 81). That
is, the "problem" is Oedipalization; the "solution," according to psychoanalytic theories of self-development, is successful Oedipalization;
thus the Oedipal triangle exists as a "no-exit" scenario. Can we, then,
truly "cure" the excesses of masculinity within the double-bind presented by familial care? Perhaps the pedagogical task at hand is the de-
Oedipalization of the classroom. For as long as we embrace each other
in maternal ways, we participate in the arming of our New War warriors, who know that virility demands a victim. It is just such a fetal subjectivity that demonstrates the necessity of moving beyond the Mother's
love. This is not a prescription for dispensing with all that goes by the
name of "love." It is, rather, a challenge to understand the ways and
means whereby love heretofore has been dispensed and signified: the
practices through which love has constructed our identity, the manner
in which love reproduces masculinity and femininity, and the strategies
by which we psychically invest our very subjectivity in the notion and
act of love.

If Not the Mother, Then Perhaps the Cyborg? Seduction and/as the Third Sophistic

Viewed from the political right or the political left, America is seen as
experiencing a crisis of democracy, evidenced by the inequities lived according to race, class, gender, and sexual orientation, by the fact that
all people are, thus, not viewed as created equally before the law, by the
fact that our so-called elected political representatives don't accurately
represent their constituencies, by the fact that education—the so-called

guarantor of democratic citizenship—is not equally dispensed. Certainly all would agree—although many would dispute the causes or the evidences of such—that we have found ourselves in a state of crisis. Whatever the origin of our present tense—whether it is somehow congenital, resulting from a democracy conceived during a time of blatant racism, classism, and sexism, or whether incipient, resulting from post-Fordist and pan-capitalist economics—the crisis can only be attended to, I am suggesting, *rhetorically.* That is, a political crisis instantiates a rhetorical crisis. This claim is, of course, a commonplace for anyone familiar with the mythology attending the "origin of rhetoric," where rhetoric appears simultaneously with a "catastrophic breach in the social order," in the "hiatus between the political orders of tyranny and democracy" (Farenga 1035). Plato dismissed rhetoric precisely because of its political nature; Aristotle codified his rhetoric as a model of civic discourse. More recently, many theorists and practitioners of rhetoric and composition have attempted to create rhetorical and pedagogical practices that would answer to the political crisis of our time, including Linda Flower, "Literate Action"; Elizabeth Erwin, "Encouraging Civic Participation"; Ellen Cushman, "The Rhetorician as an Agent of Social Change"; and James Klumpp, "The Rhetoric of Community at Century's End." Indeed, Jasper Neel argues that it is our personal ethical charge to do so; he writes, "I regard the 1992 LA riot as a personal failure. Because composition is the doorway subject, the enabling, authorizing agent, and because the LA riot grew directly out of alienation and despair, I must confront the responsibility I bear for not having found a way to deliver my pedagogy to those who need it most" (*Aristotle's Voice* 133). That is, for Neel, LA's political crisis was a rhetorical crisis fueled if not caused by a pedagogical crisis. In a parallel fashion, Chantal Mouffe's call for a rhetorical formulation of citizenship is a call for a *Return of the Political* or a "democratic *ethos,*" which she defines as the "mobilization of passions and sentiments, the multiplication of practices, institutions, and language games that provide the conditions of possibility for democratic subjects and democratic forms of willing" (*Deconstruction* 5).

However, as Neel's reading of Aristotle argues, not all rhetorics or "language games" prescribe, enable, or preserve a democratic ethos or civic body. Jeffrey Walker reminds us that

> Aristotle's preferred term for "deliberative" discourse is *symbouleutikon* . . . which is better translated as "advisory," invok[ing] the image of the *symboulos,* the "advisor" or "councilor," speaking in a relatively small meeting . . . suggest[ing] that Aristotle's image of an ideal speech-situation

is a relatively small group of councilors, or magistrates—not the popular Assembly, nor the popular jury-courts, of the Athenian democracy. (post to H-RHETOR)

Walker further notes that, in contradistinction to Aristotle's rhetoric, "The preferred term [for "deliberative" discourse] for sophistic manuals . . . is usually *demegorikon*." Aristotle's "representative" democracy/rhetoric is, thus, not the radical democracy as envisioned by Mouffe and others. A growing recognition of the inadequacies (including the inherent classism and racism) of Aristotelian rhetoric has led many to re-evaluate sophistic rhetoric as a discursive practice, as a "New Rhetoric" for the people, that could encourage democratic practices in our multicultural America. Sophistic rhetoric, consequently, has been identified as a democracy-building alternative to Aristotelian rhetoric. John Poulakos writes:

> Contrary to what some of their critics have said, the sophists' motto was not the survival of the fittest but fitting as many as possible for survival. In this sense, the sophists can be said to have helped strengthen the recently instituted democracy by forging a mentality aware of the centrality of persuasion in the coordination of sociopolitical action and the resolution of human conflicts. (*Sophistical Rhetoric* 14)

It is this understanding of sophistic rhetoric, this contra-Platonic rehabilitation, that is further developed by Susan Jarratt in *Rereading the Sophists* and by Neel in *Plato, Derrida, and Writing*.

As Poulakos's eloquent reading of the sophists argues, the sophists of the fourth- and fifth-century BCE Athens were a product of *that* time, answering to the cultural demands of that moment; likewise, a sophist or a sophistic rhetoric that intends to respond to our milieu must contend with the postmodern conditions of a loss of history, of a loss of temporality. Thus when Steven Mailloux calls for a "Rhetoric 2000" to answer to "current cultural conversations, relevant social practices, and constraining material circumstances of its historical moment" (*Rhetorical Power* 134; see also *Reception* 192), he assumes that our postmodern historical moment can be real-ised and represented rhetorically. In a postmodern world, however, Mailloux's assumptions are symptomatic of a very unpostmodern *nostalgia*—indeed, a *nostalgia* for the year 2000 and for a rhetoric to represent it. Yet our postmodern crisis is precisely a crisis of representation. Therefore, contra Patricia Bizzell, who argues that it should be our pedagogical purpose to assume "the project of restoring a sense of history" ("Fredric Jameson" 485) whether it be the past or the future, I am suggesting this is an untimely and impossible goal. It is my argument that these "New Rhetorics" still fail to answer to the crises of postmodern America and that what is at stake is the necessity of practicing an intense rhetoric, of forging a newer-than-new rhetoric, which will have been a Third Sophistic rhetoric embodied in the postmodern, posthuman, post-Aristotelian figure of the Cyborg.

The remainder of this chapter will address this posthuman, Third Sophistic civic body, particularly in the face of a postmodern age, when the current conditions of possibility have rendered dubious or groundless many of the foundations—albeit contingent ones—of rhetoric. Specifically, the contention that must be questioned is Aristotle's presupposition that rhetoric has three functions: exhorting or dissuading, accusing or defending, and praising or blaming. He defines these functions according to the proposed audience of each—judges of things to come, judges of things past, or mere spectators—and according to the temporal setting of each: the future, the past, and the present (*Rhetoric* 1358b1–6). This rhetoric serves to construct and maintain the civic body, the body politic. Although these temporal and functional definitions of rhetoric may have accurately represented classical discourse, they now—at the dawn of the twenty-first century—strike us as lacking, particularly since the advent of the technological age. The postmodern challenges to history, to politics, to communications, to political agency, along with our increasing digital and virtual experiences, have radically altered our conceptions of time, place, and rhetorical purpose and have led us to question the form of a body politic that rhetoric (a body of discourse) constructs. What, then, are the prospects for rhetoric when the terms of the triad (including "speaker" [*ethos*], "audience" [*pathos*], and "message" [*logos*]), which have long since defined rhetoric, are rendered referentless? What are the prospects for rhetoric when historical temporality (that is, "past," "present," and "future") is challenged? Such prospects have been addressed by Tharon Howard, Johndan Johnson-Eilola, Gregory Ulmer, and Diane Davis, among others. My attempt here is to join that discussion by linking the figure of the Cyborg with the sophist, and by proffering this Third Sophistic Cyborg not as a rhetorical subject/political agent in any traditional sense but rather as a rhetorical figure that embodies postmodern rhetorical practices.

Yet, if we are willing to face this sophistic challenge, we must do so on its terms—not on Plato's. Plato, as we know, condemned sophistry precisely because it was not a *technē*: it offered no rational account or *logos*, neither of the good, the true, and the beautiful nor of its own machinations. Rather than attempting to codify and rationalize a sophistic practice, I am suggesting that we should ignore such

Platonic sophist-baiting and stop trying to prove that sophistry is a *technē*. Rather, we could consider sophistry as *mētis*, a sophistic quality that eludes Platonic hunters. *Mētis* is a knowing, doing, and making not in regards to truth (either certain or probable), but in regards to a "transient, shifting, disconcerting and ambiguous" situation such as our postmodern condition (Detienne and Vernant 3).

Re-Figuring Temporality/Troping History

Baudrillard argues that we are on the other side of the crisis of representation. We have entered a new stage of simulation, which is—according to Baudrillard—the "fractal stage" or "viral stage" wherein there is no longer any referent ("Transpolitics" 15). Within the fractal stage, temporality itself has lost its sense of reference. Fredric Jameson begins his book *Postmodernism: Or, the Cultural Logic of Late Capitalism* with this characterization: "It is *safest* to grasp the concept of the postmodern as an attempt to think the present historically in an age that has forgotten how to think historically in the first place" (ix, emphasis mine). Although I question his desire for safe ways of thinking, his characterization of the postmodern world foregrounds our "troubling relationship to history" (Halberstam and Livingston 3). According to Judith Halberstam and Ira Livingston, "Speed and its possibilities—the speed of the new, the speeds of potential futures colliding with the fast approaching past—create a crisis in the category of 'history' and the narratives it inspires. History is inefficient as a method of processing meaning; it cannot keep up" (3). Therefore, given today's ahistorical epistemological framework and the temporal, historical grounding of the new rhetorics, it seems strange that such rhetorics are so advocated. Aristotle claims that there are three species of rhetoric: deliberative, forensic, and epideictic. Each of these has its own "time":

> for the deliberative speaker, the future (for whether exhorting or dissuading he advises about future events); for the speaker in court, the past (for he always prosecutes or defends concerning what has been done); in epideictic the present is the most important; for all speakers praise or blame in regard to existing qualities, but they often also make use of other things, both reminding [the audience] of the past and projecting the course of the future. (*On Rhetoric* 1358b)

Yet, according to Jean-François Lyotard, with the collapse of the "grand narratives" that guarantee temporality, sustain history, and give meaning to the story of the past, the context for our present, and the trajectory for our future, how can we distinguish along with Aristotle the species and functions of rhetoric? After the crisis of representation, rhetoric cannot represent or appeal to any event, guarantee its existence, its occurrence, or its remembrance. This is demonstrated by the current contestability of any history—from claims that the Holocaust didn't exist to arguments that our origins are out of Africa or not out of Africa to debates concerning women in history and out of history. These revisionary claims are not guaranteed by any meta-temporality; there is no past, present, or future to end the polemics. There is no past, no future; we can't even, Baudrillard argues, properly claim that there is a "present" or "real time."[10]

It is Baudrillard's argument that our "future" is already our "past"—that in a certain sense the year 2000 has already happened *(Illusion)*. This strange statement can only be understood outside of routine notions of temporality or historical, linear, or traditionally metonymic sequencing, and suggests that our "future" can only be constructed outside of the Aristotelian conceptions of the "past," the "present," and the "future." This "future" (which cannot be properly understood as a future) can be framed in terms of the future anterior, or "what will have been" (Lyotard, *Postmodern Condition* 81). This future anterior doesn't deny that there is a past, doesn't dismiss the work of historical materialism; nor does it deny that there is a present, doesn't dismiss the "reality" of social and political lived conditions; this future anterior doesn't deny that there is a future, doesn't dismiss the harbingers of radical democracy. Rather, it attends to the transpolitical moment of this postmodern age via a transrhetoric—a rhetoric to come (I will more carefully articulate such below)—and thereby services a "democracy to come" (Derrida, "Remarks"): "not a democracy that claims to instantiate justice here and now, not an apologetics for actually existing liberal democracy (but neither a dismissal of the latter), but a democracy guided by the *futural* or *projective* transcendence of justice" (Critchley 36). The future anterior (or what I will associate below with a Third Sophistic rhetoric [Vitanza]) is *not* a utopian pronouncement or dispensation but rather, according to Derrida,

> happens in the singular event of engagement, and when I speak of democracy to come *(la démocratie à venir)* this does not mean that tomorrow democracy will be realized, and it does not refer to a future democracy, rather it means that there is an engagement with regard to democracy which consists in recognizing the irreducibility of the promise when, in the messianic moment, "it can come" *("ça peut venir")*. . . .

> This is not utopian, it is what takes place here and now, in a
> here and now that I regularly try to dissociate from the pres-
> ent. ("Remarks" 83)

Such a "here and now" is akin to a kairotic moment, which exists simultaneously in and out of time—always the "opportune moment" yet
often adecorous and therefore inappropriate (see Poulakos, *Sophistical
Rhetoric* 61, 62). The rhetorical agent or political subject of such a moment doesn't precede the moment *a priori*, but is rather called into being within the moment—and thus the citizen and the political body, in
a Third Sophistic manner, exists rhetorically in a rhetorical moment as
a rhetorical trope or figuration.

As Donna Haraway reminds us, "Figures do not have to be representational and mimetic, but they do have to be tropic; that is, they
cannot be literal and self-identical. Figures must involve at least some
kind of displacement that can trouble identifications and certainties"
(*Modest* 11). That is, the citizen/rhetor as discursive event escapes
the modernist trap of self-identity (citizen/subject) and representation
(politics/the social)—traps of the Enlightenment as we have seen that
have been offered to us as truths or rather, according to Nietzsche, as a
"sum of human relations which were poetically and rhetorically heightened, transferred, and adorned, and after long use seem solid, canonical, and binding to a nation" ("On Truth and Lying" 250). What traditional rhetorics have are rhetors and/as citizens as part of a standing
army—tropes as troops/truths (see Mailloux, "Afterword"; and
Ronell). What new rhetorics have attempted is a mobilization of tropes
in order to rotate the troops/truth (Mailloux, "Afterword" 301).

One such attempt at rotating the troops/truth is made by radical
pedagogues such as Henry Giroux, Peter McLaren, and Susan Jarratt.
Another is made by neopragmatists such as Richard Rorty and Steven
Mailloux. Both of these projects have sought to regenerate public and
political discourse without reestablishing the foundational truths of liberal humanism. McLaren, for example, argues that the "tension between multiple ethnicities and the politics of universal justice is the ur-
gent issue of the new millennium" and requires the construction of
an "*ethos* of critical responsiveness" that is "not grounded in transcendental or ontological principles" (11). This, of course, echoes neopragmatism's antifoundationalism. But I am advocating here a third op-
tion, a postmodern rhetoric, or what I'm calling a "Third Sophistic
postmodern posthuman transrhetoric(s)." I mark it as a third and separate category even though both of the previously mentioned options
(radical pedagogy and neopragmatism) have been identified in various moments as "postmodern" and as sophistic—even as "Third So-

phistic" (Crowley, "Plea"; Jarratt, *Rereading the Sophists;* Mailloux, "Sophistry"). I argue that a postmodern/Third Sophistic rhetoric should be understood in terms that Victor Vitanza offered: a "Postmodern/ParaRhetoric" as an "'art' of 'resisting and disrupting' the available means (that is the cultural codes) that allow for persuasion and identification: the 'art' of not only refusing the available (capitalistic/socialist) codes but also of refusing altogether to recode, or to reterritorialize power relations" ("'Some More' Notes" 133). Because both radical pedagogy and neopragmatics do indeed attempt to recode power relations, I am distancing them from what Vitanza calls a Third Sophistic or a Postmodern/ParaRhetoric and what I am calling a Third Sophistic postmodern posthuman transrhetoric(s).

I realize that my offer, here, of postmodern rhetoric(s) as a *pharmakon* for our state of political, social, and cultural crisis will be taken—most generously—as an oxymoron. The terms "postmodern" and "rhetoric" have most often in our discipline been taken to cancel each other out. That is, rhetoric is taken to be primarily political, and postmodernism is constantly attacked as being apolitical. And, indeed, to be called apolitical these days has become the gravest insult. Postmodernism has thus been dismissed as "ludic" (Ebert)—as laughable/absurd or as only being interested in the laughable or the absurd or as responding to public and legitimation crises with laughter ("the death of the social!"—ha, ha; "the death of the subject!"—ho, ho). The big joke, then, to many is postmodern theory. I am reminded here of Milan Kundera's novel *The Joke,* wherein the protagonist pens a postcard as a joke, but it is (mis)interpreted as being deadly serious, and as a result he is expelled from the Party, expelled from the University. Similarly, if today's postmodern theorist writes a deadly serious analysis of twentieth-century rhetoric, she will most likely be (mis)interpreted as a joke and subsequently dismissed from the (feminist) party. As we can see, these descriptives "ludic" and "serious" are woefully inadequate. My point is that the stakes are very high indeed. These are serious times, more serious than we may be able to acknowledge. We have experienced a crisis of representation, a loss of history. But although postmodernism is serious, it is so without gravity. That is, it seeks no redemption nor revenge (see Vitanza, *Negation*). Although I am not interested in offering another apology here for postmodernism, I am interested in suggesting that the answer to our moment of crisis is not to construct a rhetor/citizen as *Homo seriosus* (Lanham, *Motives of Eloquence* 6). That was modernism's answer. Instead, the postmodern response is to couple with *Homo rhetoricus* who, as does the sophist, "threatens the serious at every point" (6). Therefore, just as Athenian democracy needed fewer philosopher kings (*Homo seriosus*) and more sophists (*Homo rhe-*

toricus), so too does twenty-first-century American democracy need a sophistic rhetorical practice. It needs, specifically, a Third Sophistic practice to answer to our postmodern conditions.

Again, I want to distance my conception of a Third Sophistic from both radical pedagogy and neopragmatic practices. Because Vitanza's "A Feminist Sophistic?" has already addressed radical pedagogy, I won't repeat his arguments on that score. Instead, I will briefly gloss neopragmatism's relationship to sophistry as it has been convincingly articulated by Mailloux in his introduction to *Rhetoric, Sophistry, Pragmatism,* as well as in *Reception Histories,* but argue, contra Mailloux, that neopragmatism—despite its sophistic elements—is not a *Third* Sophistic practice. There are, to appropriate Mailloux, sophistics, and there are (Third) Sophistics—just as a rose by any other name is not a rose but a ruse (Mike Rose 61).

Speaking Pragmatically . . .

Rorty offers us the following "slogans" of neopragmatism: (1) it is anti-essentialist in regards to "notions like 'truth,' 'knowledge'" (*Consequences* 162); (2) it assumes that there "is no epistemological difference between truth about what ought to be and truth about what is, nor any metaphysical difference between facts and values" (163); and (3) it assumes that "there are no constraints on inquiry save conversational ones" (163). These "slogans," of course, echo Plato's condemnation of rhetoric: that it betrays truth or the search thereof by dealing only with *doxa* or public opinion; that it can pass the weaker case off as the stronger; that it can seduce us by charm and wit. Neopragmatically inclined Stanley Fish writes, "To the accusation that rhetoric deals only with the realms of the probable and contingent and forsakes truth, the sophists and their successors respond that truth itself is a contingent affair and assumes a different shape in the light of differing local urgencies and the convictions associated with them" (quoted in Mailloux, "Sophistry" 16). Therefore, Mailloux argues, although "it would be nice to have theoretical, transcendental protection against the use and abuse of all historical instruments, including rhetoric, . . . no such theory or metanarrative seems to have worked, and now in the 'postmodern condition' all such foundations are more and more often being called into question" (20; *Reception* 40). Thus, to answer to these postmodern questions, Mailloux offers us neopragmatism "as a postmodernist form of sophistic rhetoric" ("Sophistry" 2).

Indeed, Mailloux's characterization of our postmodern world as a foundationless one and his characterization of nonfoundational, neopragmatic practices and/as sophistic rhetoric confirm that they form a compatible couple. However, the basic foundation here that is allowed to remain unquestioned is that third slogan: Rorty's assumption that our only constraints—insofar as we are not constrained by truth—are "conversational ones"—those "provided by the remarks of our fellow inquirers" (*Consequences* 163). Rorty both says more and less than he intends here. Yes, indeed, we would acknowledge with him that our only restraints are conversational or discursive ones. But no, we would not reduce conversational restraints to instances of "remarks made." Rather we would need to examine conversational possibilities that are rendered possible precisely by way of determining restraints. This point is, of course, made by Foucault in his "Discourse on Language" (*Archaeology of Knowledge* 218, 222–24), and it is the neopragmatic node that Jarratt notably unhinges in her piece "In Excess." Jarratt asks: "How is 'conversation' structured so as to ask some questions and not others? How do power differentials written into the social order determine rules for speaking? At the limits of current neopragmatism the issue becomes how to speak (of) differences" (209).

But I would push Jarratt's insight one step further in order to argue that the limits of neopragmatism as sophistic are that in addition to its failure to theorize the terms of the conversational "we," it further fails to take the sophistic challenge seriously. For although it dispenses with the demand for truth and with reason as the only suitable mode of inquiry, it still figures language as a tool, as communicative in function. And as such, it requires a disciplined language, constituted across a series of exclusions, particularly (as Jarratt argued) of not only who can speak and when, but also what can possibly be said—not just, of course, in terms of a conversational "content," but in terms of the threatening elements of language itself, which I have been calling sophistry and/as Woman. It is this latter exclusion that leads me to argue that neopragmatic rhetorical practices are not and cannot be exemplary of Third Sophistic practices.

Rorty's discussion of "normal" and "abnormal" discourse bears this out. In *Philosophy and the Mirror of Nature*, Rorty (building on Thomas Kuhn's distinction between "normal" and "revolutionary" science as set forth in *The Structure of Scientific Revolutions*) writes:

> normal discourse is that which is conducted within an agreed-upon set of conventions about what counts as a relevant contribution, what counts as answering a question, what counts as having a good argument for that answer or a good criticism of it. Abnormal discourse is what happens when someone joins in the discourse who is ignorant of these conventions or who sets them aside. *[Epistēmē]* is the product

of normal discourse—the sort of statement which can be agreed to be true by all participants whom the other participants count as "rational." The product of abnormal discourse can be anything from nonsense to intellectual revolution, and there is no discipline which describes it. (320)

Although Rorty has previously distinguished hermeneutics from epistemology as the difference between assuming that "all contributions to a given discourse are commensurable" (an epistemological assumption) and struggling "against this assumption" (a hermeneutic approach) (316), he appears unable to allow for the incommensurability to continue. That is, hermeneutics (what he offers in place of epistemology), by his definition, "is the study of an abnormal discourse from the point of view of some normal discourse—the attempt to make some sense of what is going on at a stage where we are still too unsure about it to describe it, and thereby to begin an epistemological account of it" (320–21). As we have seen, *epistēmē* is the "product" of normal discourse, but *epistēmē* is also the "product" of abnormal discourse—when the incommensurable is finally rendered commensurable with normal discourse, when it is finally normalized—after hermeneutics has "made some sense" of it. Hence, Rorty's hermeneutic pragmatism protects us from the "madness" of abnormal discourse (366).

We could, in Michel Serres's terms, figure abnormal discourse as "noise" or "the set of phenomena of interference that become obstacles to communication" (*Hermes* 66). He writes, "*To hold a dialogue is to suppose a third man and to seek to exclude him;* a successful communication is the exclusion of the third man. The most profound dialectical problem is not the problem of the other, who is only a variety—or a variation—of the same, it is the problem of the third man. We might call this third man the *demon,* the prosopopeia of noise" (*Hermes* 67; emphasis his). "Noise" is what must be excluded in order to make abnormal discourse commensurable with normal discourse. And, although Rorty takes great pains to differentiate his neopragmatism from Jürgen Habermas's "communicative action," he shares with Habermas the quest for "undistorted communication" (Mouffe, *Deconstruction* 7). Thus, neopragmatism by its very definition excludes sophistry insofar as it seeks to exclude "noise," as it seeks to construct a noise-proof or "airtight case" (Rorty, *Philosophy* 157).

Neopragmatic rhetorical practices serve, then, once again (in the name of antifoundationalism) to stabilize language. According to Mailloux, "A pragmatic rhetorician must grant that *in specific times and places* perhaps an appeal to foundationalism might work 'to limit the abuse of language power'" (*Reception* 40). Again, the rhetorical stance offered here emanates from a rhetorical subject who controls language, who can choose to abuse it or not—or to abuse others *via* its power. Indeed, Man is the measure. And he measures out rhetoric and Woman according to his will, protecting us from the radical indeterminacy of language. Tom Cohen argues that American neopragmatism has served "a fairly pragmatic role" as a prophylactic against invading foreign bodies, transmitting poststructuralist theories of language (95).

My contention here, after acknowledging the value of neopragmatic practices, is that although neopragmatism may share certain common characteristics with sophistic rhetoric, it is not sophistic enough; it is not demonstrative of a Third Sophistic as I am defining it, following Vitanza's lead. A Third Sophistic rhetoric resists any recodification (especially of language), thus, insofar as this communicational process is a recodification of the social/cultural codes, it serves to maintain the boundaries and limits of a particular discourse and is motivated by the desire of the "we" to colonize every "they."

Although neopragmatic rhetorics are released from ontological foundations, metaphysical presuppositions and truth, they are not released from their dependence on *technē*. So although as Kenneth Burke reminds us, we huddle loquaciously at the edge of the abyss, we protect ourselves pragmatically from the abyss (of sophistry) with *technē* (*Permanence and Change* 351). This of course echoes the primal tensions which have defined rhetoric from its inception: *technē* vs. *tuchē* (method vs. chance), *physis* vs. *nomos* (nature vs. convention), being vs. not being (reality vs. appearance). Indeed, the entire history of rhetoric can be read as the attempt to deal with the problem of the "third man" by codifying language, to ensure rhetoric's being as a "true *technē*" (a true art or method) rather than a "false" one—that is, sophistry.

The "communicational process" is a territorialization accomplished through the exclusion of the third man or sophistry. For example, "academic discourse" is characterized by "clarity" and "coherence" in order to ensure that the "message" is easily commodified and therefore exchangeable—that is, communicable. Furthermore, to teach "academic discourse" is not only to "invent the university" (Bartholomae), but also to ensure its survival and the survival of those other institutions which operate in conjunction with the university. Rorty argues that the function of an education is to inculcate students into "normal" discourse (*Philosophy* 365) and that the purpose of a freshman English course is "just to get them to write complete sentences, get the commas in the right place, and stuff like that—the stuff that we would like to think the high schools do and, in fact, they don't" (Olson, "Social Construction and Composition Theory" 6). This is precisely why *technē*, or method, has been so highly valued within the history of rhetoric and why composition pedagogy has sought to control language (see Sharon Crowley's *Composition in the University* for a "modest proposal" to answer Rorty's concern). This is precisely why sophistry has been excluded from the university, disparaged and decried. "What this institution cannot bear" Derrida argues, "is for anyone to tamper with language. . . . It can bear more readily the most apparently revolutionary ideological sorts of 'content,' if only that content does not touch the borders of language and of all the [political] contracts that it guarantees" ("Living On" 94–95). Many of those political contracts do indeed guarantee empowerment, but many have served to justify and to perpetuate the disempowerment of others. All this power has been sustained by maintaining the borders of language: through the use of *technē*. Therefore, when I propose a Third Sophistic praxis, I am suggesting that we not reproduce via "conversation" current political relations and ideologies, but rather that we stretch the borders of language, render the code liquid, in order to free us, sophistically, from philosophy's demands for faithful reference and undistorted communication and communities.

But lest we fall prey to the false dichotomy of the opposing binaries that Plato offers us (*technē/tuchē;* philosophy/rhetoric), a Third Sophistic employs a third term. Therefore, I offer the third (sophistic) term *mētis* rather than the pragmatic *technē* (although, certainly the pragmatic *technē* is not Platonic, but Protagorean). In what follows, I hope to distinguish a Third Sophistic from a neopragmatic sophistic, by contrasting Gorgias (a Third Sophistic figure) with Protagoras (a sophist). Protagoras, if you will recall from our discussion in chapter 1, was identified by E. M. Cope to be representative of the Greek school of sophistic thought; whereas Gorgias was representative of the Sicilian school. Cope argues that ultimately the Greek school became more popular because the nature of Gorgias's sophistry was unsuitable for the machinations of the polis. Thenceforth rhetoric existed only insofar as it was appropriate for political discourse and insofar as it consequently excluded sophistry (as seen in Platonic and Aristotelian rhetorics). Furthermore, as discussed in chapter 1, it was Protagoras, presented by Mailloux as an exemplary neopragmatic sophist, who fixed gender and genre. That is, he policed the borders of language in order to police the polis.

Therefore, Rorty parallels Protagoras when he writes, "For even if we agree that languages are not media of representation or expression, they will remain media of communication, *tools* for social interaction, ways of *tying oneself* up with other human beings" (*Contingency* 41). Rorty presents us here with a conversational model that instantiates social bondage. A Third Sophistic conception of language, contrariwise, acknowledges that we are already tied up, networked in fact, but seeks to challenge the social bond, to repeat, by " 'resisting and disrupting' the available means (that is, the cultural codes) that allow for persuasion and identification" (Vitanza, " 'Some More' Notes" 133). Furthermore, the kind of "tying up" that neopragmatism advocates reproduces an antiquated notion of community and civic discourse. According to Baudrillard, in our current fractal stage of simulation—which we have inhabited since the construction of the "hyperreal," made possible by the creation of new technologies, notably television, and now, virtual reality and cyberspace—we have already suffered "the death of the social" and of the social contract. What may be called "the social" today is "the silent majority" as demonstrated by the decline of public discourse (Halloran) and the inefficacy of communicative reason.

To claim, as does Baudrillard, that we have already suffered the death of the social is to claim that the "social" is "nothing but the organized and mobilized residue of symbolic exchange" (*In the Shadow* 72), given that there is no way to represent the social, that there is no grand narrative that guarantees that the signifier "the social" represents the signified "the social"—just as there is no way for elected officials to "represent" their constituencies (see Levin 88–97). This of course does not mean that one cannot reference the social today or witness its effects (or vote, for that matter). This is because, according to Baudrillard, we "have reached the time of political hysteresis" (*Illusion* 238). In physics, Charles Levin explains, "hysteresis is a phenomenon in which a physical effect on a body lags behind its cause" (275). Thus we witness effects of the social ("such as the panic about 'national identity' and 'foreign investment' " in America [Levin 93]) as an effect which lags behind its cause, much as, according to Baudrillard, fingernails and hair continue to grow on a corpse (*Illusion*). Thus the invocation of antiquated notions of the social to resuscitate political discourse within our current stage of simulation will produce a rhetoric which will always arrive too late—dead on arrival. It will always reference a time, a place, a sociality, that has preceded our current state, and thus will be references constructed via nostalgia for a time that never was, that cannot be represented, except through a "synthetic memory," constructed "with the help of many advertising images" (Baudrillard, "Revolution" 234). Thus politics and political discourse nostalgically advocated are ineffective because they are dependent on "two cultural constructs, the social and the discrete individual subject" (Goshorn 216)—both constructs that cannot be real-ised in our postmodern world.

But just as neopragmatism is not advocating a "vulgar relativism," I am not denying the possibilities of/for politics, community, public discourse, or agency. Rather, I am arguing that a business-as-usual rhetoric ("normal discourse") cannot answer to our current simulacra culture, to our present tense. We need a posthumanist transrhetoric ("abnormal discourse") that erupts in "powerful new tropes" (Haraway, "Ecce Homo" 86). The citizen or the denizen of a "democracy to come" must become a trope, a troping figure. And, according to Haraway, the figure of the Cyborg is perhaps the embodiment of our future anterior, the conjugation of ourselves into an [in]tense rhetoric that is already, yet not yet, thereby creating a tension such as Heraclitus's bow, with which we can "forge" the prospect of a rhetoric in the twenty-first century and beyond. The figure of the posthuman occupies "the overlap between the now and the then, the here and the always: the annunciation of posthumanity [of the Cyborg] is always both premature and old news" (Halberstam and Livingston, *Posthuman* 2–3). Thus, Haraway's "Manifesto for Cyborgs," now more than fifteen years old, is both old news and a premature call.

Risking the Abyss: Writing (as) a Third Sophistic Cyborg

Haraway proposes the Cyborg as an answer to the dualisms "ordering discourse in the West since Aristotle still ruled" ("Manifesto for Cyborgs" 205). She writes, "The Cyborg is a kind of disassembled and reassembled, postmodern collective and personal self. This is the self [we] must code" (205). This "coding," however, is resistant to Aristotelian/Platonic rhetorics—the Cyborg-as-speaker is not fixed, temporally, spatially, or bodily. The Cyborg-as-audience is likewise not fixed historically. Or more to the point, both are situated but neither knows where they are in advance (Gary Olson, "Writing, Literacy, and Technology" 9). How then can we classify/codify rhetoric? Is the rhetoric of the Cyborg deliberative? Forensic? Epideictic? How could we say? Why would we try?

My rhetorical purpose is not epideictic. I am neither praising nor blaming the Cyborg, merely suggesting that we are already, yet not yet, Cyborgs; as such, we remain "wedged between two tenses" (Barthes, *Lover's Discourse* 15). We acknowledge that the Cyborg is not, somehow, an essentially transgressive figure, but rather a figure profoundly complicit with the machinations of power and the technologies of the self. The Cyborg is indisputably a "socially and technologically contested site" (Johnson-Eilola, "Control" 391). Unlike many theorists of the electronic age, I do not posit that the Cyborg presages a glorious future, that the Cyborg is necessarily a "liberatory" figure. Along with its detractors, I agree that we "may be [re-]colonizing ourselves and others as we begin to write, read and live with (and within) electronic information spaces such as hypertext" (Johnson-Eilola, "Control" 383), that we may be constituting an electronic panopticon, and as Anne Balsamo argues, we may be obscuring "the disciplining and surveillant consequences of these [bio-]technologies—in short, the biopolitics of technological formations" (5). Additionally, William Covino argues that the Cyborg is "hyperconventional rather than an infidel" (370).

Others have justifiably argued that we cannot overlook the obvious—that "access capital is the poll tax for would-be virtual citizens" (Lockard 220) of a "virtual class" (Kroker and Weinstein). I agree that access to networked environments is entangled with the properties of class and economics. But again, I am not, as Lockard claims "tout[ing] the Internet as democracy actualized," and therefore "liv[ing] with class blinders in a muddle of self-delusion" (220). Rather I am suggesting that hard facts such as those presented by Lockard are not rationales in and of themselves for ceasing to theorize a rhetoric and a democracy to come. Such facts, rather, are arguments for a modern form of democracy that operates out of a grand narrative, the grand nostalgia for some unfettered public sphere and unfettered individualism (see Stratton 266). In a postmodern political scene, nostalgia for modern democracy may be morally edifying, but not particularly useful. Thus, I am in complete disagreement with Rorty when he says: "As a citizen of a democratic state, I do not think that metaphysics-bashing [referring to a Derridean deconstruction of politics] is—except in the very long term—of much use" ("Response" 46). Such a claim, to my mind, presumes that one can bracket the postmodern milieu, that one can continue to enact and to realise a modernist democracy. In contrast, I argue alongside Mark Poster that:

> one can . . . examine phenomena such as the Internet in relation to new forms of the old democracy, while holding open the possibility that what emerges might be something other than democracy in any shape that we can conceive. . . . The Internet resists the basic conditions for asking the question of the effects of technology. It installs a new regime of relations between humans and matter and between matter and non-matter, reconfiguring the relation of technology to culture and thereby undermining the standpoint from within which, in the past, a discourse developed—one which appeared to be natural—about the effects of technology. (204, 205)

Thus when Michael Heim warns that "frequent reading and writing on computers will soon allow us little distance from the tools that trap our language. They will fit like skin" (14), his warning comes too late, and sounds strangely sentimental about preelectronic forms of literacy. Thus, despite all the above warnings and disclaimers, we must acknowledge that we are already Cyborgs and that resistance to the digital world is futile. Haraway explains: "communications technologies and biotechnologies are the crucial tools recrafting our bodies" ("Manifesto for Cyborgs" 205). The Cyborg body, argues Gregory Bateson, is not "bounded by the skin but includes all external pathways along which information can travel" (Bateson, quoted in Balsamo 11). As already constituted by and through these social and information networks, we are Cyborgs. "There are many actual cyborgs among us. . . . Anyone with an artificial organ, limb or supplement (like a pacemaker), anyone reprogrammed to resist disease (immunized) or drugged to think/behave/feel better (psychopharmacology) is technically a Cyborg" (Gray et al. 2). Sandy Stone makes this point when describing physicist Steven Hawking:

> In an important sense, Hawking doesn't stop being Hawking at the edge of his visible body. There is the obvious physical Hawking, vividly outlined by the way our social conditioning teaches us to see a person as a person. But a serious part of Hawking extends into the box in his lap. . . . not to mention the invisible ways, displaced in time and space, in which discourses of medical technology and their physical accretions already permeate him and us. (395)

If we envision the Cyborg, according to Johnson-Eilola, as a "perfect system," we claim that these networks that comprise the cyberspace are "a closed system, a single discourse" by which we are merely spoken ("Control" 394)—and hence the fears expressed by Heim and Covino. Yet, if we view the Cyborg as an effect of power, we acknowledge that we speak "tangent and tangled discourses, simultaneously speaking and being spoken" (394). Thus the Cyborg is "a paradoxical subject/object resistant to perfect communication and control and neat endings" (Johnson-Eilola, "Control" 394). This is the Cyborg of Haraway's manifesto: "Cyborg politics is the struggle for language and the struggle against perfect communication, Cyborg politics insist on noise" (218).

Serres has suggested that "perfect communication" is achieved only by screening out "noise"—the discursive surplus of any given rhetorical situation. Although "noise" can be excluded, it cannot be forever silenced. Although power represses, it simultaneously generates. The Cyborg is not simply a figure of a programmed, integrated circuitry of power and discourse; the Cyborg—as an effect of language—will produce "noise" and will occasionally disrupt the circuit, causing the "perfect communication" to crash. Prophets of perfect communication and of ideal speech acts prescribe a closed system of discourse and a consistent and stable temporality to sustain it. Although pragmatists such as Rorty would disagree with Habermas, questioning the possibility of a communication undistorted by irrationality, they still suggest that to speak pragmatically requires a conventional system of discourse. Rhetoric, therefore, traverses a one-dimensional time line, functioning as the conduit for meanings and messages, guaranteeing the exchange rates of understanding. The Cyborg, contrariwise, experiences language Third Sophistically, as not necessarily controlled by the exchange demands of communication. Language is often "two-headed," pulling in "contrary directions," "oblique and [avoids coming] straight to the point" (Detienne and Vernant 304). As such, rhetoric, rather than proceeding via a smooth circuit and a clear metonymic temporality, moves like a crab—"a double synthesis of opposites: forwards and backwards, left and right. . . . All these characteristics of the crab—its twisted legs, its oblique gait, the double and opposite directions in which it moves— are unmistakably reminiscent of the most famous of Greek blacksmiths, Hephaestus" (Detienne and Vernant 270).

With its crab-like ways, the Cyborg is a preface to Plato and Aristotle, a technological figure which will have preceded, paradoxically, the conception of rhetoric as *techné*. This untimely genealogy is indicative of my purposes: not to prophesy a future but to forge a rhetoric of our future anterior. But first, as my purposes are to speculate on the possibilities of forging "future" rhetorics; I focus your attention on the verb "to forge." One possible meaning is, of course, to counterfeit, to fabricate, to employ artifice. Another meaning is to form metal by heating and hammering, or to form or bring into being especially by the expenditure of effort (Webster's dictionary). Either meaning presumes an artisan; both foreground Hephaestus, whom I mentioned above (see also Macauley and Gordo-Lopez). Hephaestus's power is a function of a

> double and divergent orientation. In order to [work with] shifting, fluid powers such as fire, winds and minerals which the blacksmith must cope with, [those who forge] must possess the qualities of the oblique and the curved—qualities possessed in the highest degree by the crab . . . , the [creature] which half-belongs to the element of the sea with which, for the ancient Greeks, metallurgy appears to have been so profoundly connected. (Detienne and Vernant 272–73)

At our current stage of simulation, we need simulators, not philosopher kings—we need artisans, like Hephaestus. This forging, at once artifice and artisan, is the work of *mētis,* the work of the Cyborg, the work of Hephaestus. And although Plato excludes artisans from crafting the *Republic,* the proper civic body, the myths surrounding the origin of politics and community suggest that artisans, not philosopher kings, were responsible, as in the story of Prometheus stealing the fire. "Human life is thus preserved by an action that is both an artifice and artificial, involving the substitution of a technique for making fire in the place of natural fire, and a trick played on Zeus, which takes him unawares" (Vernant, *Myth and Thought* 239).

Hephaestus, like his sister Athena, is endowed with *mētis,* which, according to Detienne and Vernant, is a combination of "flair, wisdom, . . . subtlety of mind, deception, resourcefulness, vigilance, opportunism" (3). *Mētis* is knowing, doing, and making in relation to "transient, shifting, disconcerting and ambiguous" situations (3), such as metalwork, sea navigation, and life in general. Because the human condition is often characterized by change and the ungovernable forces of nature and fate, *mētis* equips the possessor with the ways and means to negotiate the flux. The goddess Metis is the sister of Tuche, the goddess of chance, who represents the

> individual buffeted by the waves, whirling with the winds, rolling helplessly hither and thither. . . . However, . . . there is also a positive side to her: it is *Tuche* who takes charge of the tiller and guides the ship unerringly to harbour. . . . [In this way,] *Tuche* [also represents] the opportunity to succeed. *Tuche* brings the indiscernible future within the bounds of possibility. . . . *Tuche* [therefore] becomes the model for any form of human endeavour. (Detienne and Vernant 223)

And any human endeavor is further governed by the propitious moment, or *kairos.* Time is, therefore, "not a stable, homogeneous quantity which can be grasped by the mind. Rather it is an active time, a time defined by the opportunity that must be seized, the *kairos* . . . the artisan [or navigator] must recognize and wait for the moment when the time is ripe and be able to adapt himself entirely to circumstances" (Vernant, *Myth and Thought* 291). According to Detienne and Vernant,

> *Tuche* and *Kairos* both emphasise the one essential feature of the art of navigation: the necessary complicity between the pilot and the element of the sea [as between the metal worker and the element of the fire]. . . . Faced with the sea, an expanse where "contrary winds from opposite quarters of the sky can blow within a single moment," the pilot can

only control it by demonstrating that he himself is similarly polymorphic and can take action in as many ways, . . . meet cunning with cunning and [participate in] the fleeting opportunity to reverse the balance of forces. (224–26)

Likewise, Hephaestus, as metal worker, meets the cunning of the fire with the cunning of the artisan, the cunning of Aphrodite with the cunning of the net.

This two-faced and ambiguous yet reciprocal relationship between Tuche and Metis is beginning to be rewritten during the time of Plato's youth, when *tuchē* is increasingly opposed to *technē*. And whereas *mētis* was once praised, funeral orations increasingly replaced the word with *aretē*. Virtue, coupled with *technē*, then, is a "deliberate application of human intelligence to some part of the world, yielding some control over tuche; it is concerned with the management of need and with prediction and control concerning future contingencies . . . four features of techne [are] stressed above all: (1) universality, (2) teachability, (3) precision; (4) concern with explanation" (Nussbaum 94–95).

Therefore, when Plato, in the dialogue *Gorgias*, condemns rhetoric because it is not a *technē*, he is arguing that rhetoric, like *mētis*, is characterized by trickery and stratagem, and remains a stochastic intelligence, not rational, ordered, nor measurable. True rhetoric opposes *tuchē* or chance, rather than negotiates it, as does *mētis*. What Plato prescribes in the *Phaedrus* is a discursive universe in which *tuchē, mētis,* and *kairos* must be controlled and/or excised. Plato's theory and vision of rhetoric presupposes a knowledge and wisdom that is measurable and universal. Of course, Aristotle's system of rhetoric is not so harsh in its condemnation of *mētis*—yet he remains "anxious to make a distinction between prudence, *phronēsis*, and cleverness, *deinotes*," whereas *mētis* had encompassed both qualities (Detienne and Vernant 316).

The challenge, now, for twenty-first-century Cyborgs is to practice a Third Sophistic posthumanist transrhetoric(s), which will radicalize the political, radicalize democracy. Again, this Third Sophistic democracy is not a self-identical civic body, but rather—like the Third Sophist, the Cyborg—is always at least two-headed, at odds. The ends of this rhetoric should never be the resolution of this discrepancy, but rather should be a perpetual engagement with difference. This is the rhetoric to come, which will forge a democracy to come—a democracy of/with difference, a rhetoric of/with difference (see Jarratt, "In Excess" 209). "A democratic society is not just a society that accommodates different groups and beliefs. . . . It is one in which members of society tolerate an *internal* discrepancy between different registers of society. A democratic society does not add up. It is a society of the discontinuous" (Mark Cousins and Parveen Adams quoted in Levin 261). This is how Cyborg rhetoric(s)/politics differs with neopragmatisms: Whereas Rorty prescribes a discursive practice aimed at producing a democratic, conversational "we," which is constructed only insofar as everyone comes "to see other human beings as 'one of us' rather than a 'them'" (*Contingency* xvi), a Cyborg Third Sophistic resists this we-formation, which silences and excludes difference.

A Cyborg, as the embodiment of posthuman transrhetorical practices—what I have been calling "Woman"—is figured as a navigator, endowed with *mētis,* faced with an uncertain future, a postmodern expanse where "contrary winds from opposite quarters of the sky can blow within a single moment" (Pindar, quoted in Detienne and Vernant 225). The Cyborg can only negotiate it by demonstrating that he/she himself/herself is similarly polymorphic and can trope accordingly. Thus the cunning Cyborg (although still a state—now global [Gabilondo]—apparatus, to be sure) can—like Hephaestus—"forge" ahead, or sideways, into virtual spaces and temporalities, crafting a future anterior, an [in]tense rhetorical moment characterized by the forces of *technē,* but also *mētis, tuchē,* and *kairos,* according to the occasion, vacillating moments and opportunities—and by the relativity of argument and truth. In short, different rhetorical moments occasion different rhetorics. The Third Sophist negotiates a rhetorical situation by *mētis* rather than masters it by *technē;* and the cunning Cyborg is the figure (which is not one, but a network) that navigates the postmodern discursive world, characterized by the ecstasy of communication "where meaning is dismembered and scattered to the winds" (Baudrillard, *Illusion* 121) and by civic bodies who, in Gorgias's words "neither remember the past nor observe the present nor prophesy the future" (Freeman 132).

(Non)Composing the Future Anterior of/for Seduction

The problem with current critical theories and pedagogies, according to Baudrillard, is that "the critical spirit has found its summer home in socialism" (*Fatal Strategies* 190). That is, the critical spirit has found a comfortable site to retire—in the production of socialized subjects—and has thus lost its revolutionary potential (as exemplified by Berlin's "Postmodernism" and Faigley's *Fragments of Rationality*). Baudrillard argues that critical theories as practiced remain unchallenging because these theoretical strategies emanate from the subject "and are posed with all the assumptions of the superiority of the subject in its apparent mastery of the world" (Gane, *Baudrillard* 174)—a subject situated within "a cosy world of dialogue[,] human communication . . . [and] rational understanding" (Gane, *Baudrillard* 65)—all banal rhetorical strategies.

A Third Sophistic postmodern posthuman transrhetorical tactic, or what I have been alternately calling Woman and Seduction, on the other hand, assumes that language as trace is more subtle, more ingenious, more critical, more ironic than the subject (Gane, *Baudrillard* 174), or than rhetoric as communication or persuasion, and thus is the only possible tactic left to us that has any chance of subverting modernism's logic and its will to produce and represent. Baudrillard's writing, for example, embodies this tactic as it meets the challenge of radically contiguous linkages, following them as far as he can go, in order to participate in what might appear. As he writes, he encourages "sites of emergence—events, pointed remarks, dream-like flashes of wit, or *witz* . . . [or] the trace . . . : not a meta-language organised around signs, but rather a sort of tracking shot along the line of traces. When this occurs there is no continuity as a rule, and everything begins to move quite quickly" (*Revenge* 24).

This is a writing whose speed surpasses the consumptive appetite of abstractions, concepts, and reasons. This is a radically different view of language and writing than espoused by social-epistemics, radical pedagogies, or neopragmatics. Of this difference, Baudrillard writes,

> By definition, communication simply brings about a relationship between things already in existence. . . . And what is more, it tries to establish an equilibrium—the message and all that. . . . [T]he communicational process has always seemed to me a little too functional . . . as if the only true purpose of things was to [persuade] . . . as if things always exist in a relation of content, be it pedagogical or moral. (*Revenge* 24–25)

Communication—with its postal principle demands of exchange and return—is symptomatic of the pathos of modernity, charged with the whole ideology of liberation and free circulation (Baudrillard, *Fatal Strategies* 105). Communication, like love, is a demand for recognition and thus is a fetal strategy. Fetal strategies will, of necessity, fail because they presuppose a referent that has some relation to the "real." Within our current stage of simulation, however, the "real" has been replaced by the "hyperreal," by the possibility of living in a world that is more real than the real. For example, Baudrillard explains, "freed from the 'true' Mondrian, you are free to produce a Mondrian more Mondrian than Mondrian himself" ("Transpolitics" 14). Baudrillard is suggesting, in effect, a paratheory of the invention of the writing self—an ironic self who, immersed in the instability of language, maintains a distance from truth and all other totalizing theories of unity and community. Indeed, Baudrillard is offering a radical alternative: in place of libera- tory theories he suggests fatal theories, in place of the banality of "love" he offers seduction, in place of the subject he offers the object, in place of a pathos of consensus he offers a Nietzschean pathos of distance. Thus fatal tactics offer the possibility of breaking up the tyranny of truth, being, and identity, which has held us hostage, and the possibility of opening up a space for our future anterior.

The rhetorical tradition has been founded—from Plato to Haber- mas—on the systematic exclusion of sophistry. Rhetoric, as Aristotle claimed long ago, is and continues to be a counterpart to dialectic, a hand- maiden to the pursuit of truth—even if that truth is merely probable. This search for truth continues in current rhetoric and composition studies, manifesting itself in the discipline's assumptions that language is primarily communicative (that is, that it can represent truth more or less faithfully) and that rhetorical agents are primarily communicative (that is, that they can channel more or less faithfully). Why are we so invested in the notion of truth, in the notion that language represents truth, and in the notion that the speaking/writing subject has some es- sential relation to truth (or should have such a relation)? What is our desire to retain these notions even as our so-called new rhetorics vocif- erously argue contrariwise, even as our social-epistemic rhetorics pro- claim that we no longer posit a foundational self or truth? Gorgias, Nietzsche, Baudrillard, and the Woman with the rhetorical figure have some provocative prompts to these questions. Whether we will have been seduced remains questionable.

Notes

Bibliography

Index

Notes

Introduction: A Pre/Script Regarding the Subject of Woman, A Pre/Face Regarding the Figure of Woman

1. For excellent readings regarding Dora, see Charles Bernheimer and Claire Kahane, eds., *In Dora's Case: Freud-Hysteria-Feminism;* and Hélène Cixous's "Portrait of Dora."

2. See Freud's "Female Sexuality," "Femininity," and "Three Essays on Sexuality." There exists, of course, a plethora of illuminations, interpretations, and extrapolations concerning Freud's infamous question. See, for example, Teresa Brennan's *Interpretation of the Flesh: Freud and Femininity,* as well as my review of the same in *Studies in Psychoanalytic Theory;* also Michèle Montrelay's "Inquiry into Femininity"; Shoshana Felman's "Rereading Femininity"; Sarah Kofman's *Enigma of Woman* and "The Narcissistic Woman: Freud and Girard."

3. Throughout, I have capitalized the term "Woman" as well as "Man" to call attention to their abstract quality, to the fact that these are symbolic representations of an ideal, and to distinguish this representation from individual human beings.

4. Such calls include Sally Gearhart's "The Womanization of Rhetoric"; Susan Miller's "The Feminization of Composition"; and Catherine Lamb's "Beyond Argument in Feminist Composition."

5. The nomenclature "French feminist" includes continental women theorists such as Hélène Cixous, Julia Kristeva, Luce Irigaray, Monique Witting, and Marguerite Duras, among others.

6. Of course, this raises the spectre of essentialism. See Diana J. Fuss, *Essentially Speaking.* Also, for a critique of "strategic essentialism," see Drucilla Cornell, *Beyond Accommodation* 179–83.

7. This impossibility is perhaps most pointedly expressed by Lacan: "For what is love other than banging one's head against a wall" (*Feminine Sexuality* 170).

8. I use the gender-specific "his" to differentiate male subjectivity from female subjectivity or, more precisely, from the *lack* thereof.

9. *Fort* is German for "gone" and "far away," and *da* is German for "there." "Fort/da" refers to a game played with a wooden spool by Freud's grandson. Freud writes:

> One day I made an observation which confirmed my view. The
> child had a wooden spool with a piece of string tied round it. . . .
> [H]e held the spool by the string and with great address threw it
> over the edge of his little curtained bed, so that it disappeared into
> it . . . [H]e then pulled the spool out of the bed again by the string
> and hailed its appearance with a joyful *"Da."* This, then, was the
> complete game—disappearance and return. (*Beyond the Pleasure
> Principle* 13)

According to Freud, this "game" of reciprocal absence and presence was the
child's way of representing the presence and absence of his mother. For a discussion of Freud's theory as representative of the philosophic insistence on controlling presence, see Jacques Derrida, "Freud's Legacy," *Post Card.*

10. For a further discussion of this, see my "What Is It That the Audience
Wants?"

11. For a discussion of the possibilities of laughter, see D. Diane Davis,
Breaking Up [at] Totality.

1. The Business of "Isness": Philosophy Contra Sophistry, Woman, and Other Faithless Phenomena

1. Others include the work of Steve Whitson; John Poulakos's "Hegel's
Reception of the Sophists" and "Toward a Sophistic Definition of Rhetoric";
Vasile Florescu, "Rhetoric and Its Rehabilitation in Contemporary Philoso-
phy"; Roger Moss, "The Case for Sophistry"; and Brian Vickers, *In Defence of
Rhetoric.*

2. This debate is articulated in Calvin Schrag, "Rhetoric Resituated at
the End of Philosophy"; Jane Sutton, "The Death of Rhetoric and Its Rebirth
in Philosophy"; Ernesto Grassi, "Rhetoric and Philosophy"; and Brian Vickers,
"Territorial Disputes: Philosophy *versus* Rhetoric."

3. This argument is certainly not new to rhetorical studies. See, for ex-
ample, Eric A. Havelock, *The Muse Learns to Write;* Paul E. Corcoran, *Political
Language and Rhetoric* (particularly chapters 2 and 3); June Rachuy Brindel,
Ariadne; David Olson, "Cognitive Consequences of Literacy"; Robert J. Conners, "Greek Rhetoric and the Transition from Orality"; Susan C. Jarratt, "The
Role of the Sophists in Histories of Consciousness"; Shirley Brice Heath, "Protean Shapes in Literacy Events"; Tony Lentz, *Orality and Literacy in Hellenic
Greece;* C. Jan Swearingen, "Literate Rhetors and Their Illiterate Audiences";
and Vincent Farenga, "Periphrasis on the Origin of Rhetoric."

4. For further discussion of Parmenides' metaphysics, see David J. Furley's "Notes on Parmenides" and Alexander P. D. Mourelatos's "Heraclitus,
Parmenides, and the Naive Metaphysics of Things," both in *Exegesis and Argument,* ed. E. N. Lee, A. P. D. Mourelatos, and R. M. Rorty.

5. I discuss this further in "Reproducing Desire."

6. To Dionysus [of Halicarnassus], writing in the first century BCE, a new
rhetoric from some "Asiatic death-hold" has sprung up and replaced the old
Attic philosophical rhetoric. It is just like what happens in "the houses of the
profligate and abandoned: there sits the lawful wife, freeborn and chaste, but

with no authority over her domain, while an insensate harlot, bent on destroying her livelihood, claims control of the whole estate" (quoted in Moss 207).

7. It is interesting to note that Gorgias's student Lycophron avoided the use of the verb "to be" altogether, even as a copula (Gomperz 493).

8. As is suggested by the word "autonomous"—a defining characteristic of the "individual." The Greek verb *autonomeomai* is translated as "to govern oneself."

9. On the sexual practices and beliefs of this period, consult K. J. Dover, "Classical Greek Attitudes to Sexual Behavior"; John J. Winkler, *The Constraints of Desire*; David M. Halperin, John J. Winkler, and Froma I. Zeitlin, eds., *Before Sexuality: The Construction of Erotic Experience in the Ancient Greek World;* David M. Halperin, *One Hundred Years of Homosexuality,* "Platonic *Eros* and What Men Call Love," and "Plato and Erotic Reciprocity"; Thomas Laqueur's *Making Sex;* and *Fragments for a History of the Human Body,* ed. Michel Feher.

10. As I have argued in "Re/Dressing Histories."

2. Seduction and Sacrificial Gestures: Gorgias, Helen, and Nothing

1. Although the "original" text of Gorgias's argument, "On Nature," is not available, two ancient authors have articulated the argument: Sextus Empiricus, *Against the Logicians* 2.1.65–87; and [Pseudo] Aristotle, "On Gorgias" 979a.12–980b.22.

2. Guthrie, for example, writes, "It is all, of course, engaging nonsense" (*History of Greek Philosophy* 3.197 n. 2). See Kerferd's comments tracing the historical reception of Gorgias's arguments (*Sophistic Movement* 93–96).

3. There are several resourceful materials regarding women's social and political situations in antiquity. For example, Skinner, ed., *Rescuing Creusa: New Methodological Approaches to Women in Antiquity,* a special issue of *Helios* 13.2 (fall 1986); Eva Cantarella, *Pandora's Daughters;* John Peradotto and J. P. Sullivan, eds., *Women in the Ancient World;* Eva Keuls, *The Reign of the Phallus;* Elaine Fantham's annotated bibliography "Women in Antiquity"; and Leanna Goodwater's annotated bibliography "Women in Antiquity."

4. See the work of Victor J. Vitanza, particularly "Three Countertheses: Or, A Critical In(ter)vention into Composition Theories and Pedagogies" and "'Some More' Notes."

5. For biographical detail regarding Gorgias, see Guthrie, *Sophists* (269–73); Kerferd, *Sophistic Movement* (44–45); and Untersteiner, *Sophists* (92–100).

6. For example, Edward Schiappa, "An Examination and Exculpation of the Composition Style of Gorgias of Leontini"; Scott Consigny, "The Style of Gorgias"; and Bromley Smith, "Gorgias: A Study of Oratorical Style."

7. Bromley Smith catalogues the tradition's criticisms of Gorgias as such: "The main contentions of the critics were that Gorgianism was affected, pompous, and pretentious, that the ideas were superficial, the assonances tedious, that sense was sacrificed to sound, that the antitheses were verbal rather than real" (357).

8. The attributed works of Gorgias include, according to G. B. Kerferd, "On Nature,"

> said to have been written in the 84th Olympiad i.e. 444–441 B.C. (DK 82A10). Summaries or parts of references survive from speeches entitled *Funeral Oration, Olympian Oration, Pythian Oration, Encomium to the Eleans, Encomium to Helen, Apology of Palamedes.* It is probable that he also wrote a technical treatise on rhetoric, whether its title was simply *Art* or possibly *On the Right Moment in Time (Peri Kairou).* (45)

Kerferd also attributes *Onomastikon* to Gorgias (*Sophistic Movement* 45).

9. For detailed synopses of these three major arguments forwarded by Gorgias, there are excellent and thorough discussions to be found in Guthrie 192–200; Versényi 40–41; Smith 343; Enos 46–47; Cope 79; Gomperz 482; Grote 173; and of course, Untersteiner 145–58. See also Gaines's alternate reading.

10. See Eric Charles White's discussion of the "paradox" in his *Kaironomia* 11–43. Recall the "Paradox of the Liar": if I am a liar and I say "I am a liar," then I am not a liar; but anyone who is not a liar who says "I am a liar" is a liar.

11. Those who have written on Gorgias's epistemology also include Richard Engnell ("Implications for Communication of the Rhetorical Epistemology of Gorgias of Leontini") and Charles Segal ("Gorgias and the Psychology of the Logos").

12. It is interesting to note how difficult it is for even sympathetic readers of Gorgias to be seduced by this dissolution of the truth/deception binary. For example, Versényi writes:

> the question is not one of truth or deception, but whether or not the deception is of the right kind, i.e., whether or not it strikes through the veil, the mask, the deceptive layers of opinions and produces unobstructed vision. If it does that, then, for all its untruth, nothing could be more full of truth than the Gorgian *logos.* (*Socratic Humanism* 50)

13. Examples include Susan Biesecker's "Feminist Criticism of Classical Rhetorical Texts" and Mihoko Suzuki's *Metamorphoses of Helen.*

14. Betsy Wing, translator of Hélène Cixous and Catherine Clément's *The Newly Born Woman,* renders the French *propre* as "Selfsame" (167).

15. See Robin Osborne's "Women and Sacrifice in Classical Greece" for a resourceful interpretation of the relationship between gendered beings and sacrificial rites in ancient Greece.

16. See also Rebecca Comay, "Gifts Without Presents"; John Carlos Rowe, "Surplus Economies"; and Jean-Luc Nancy, "The Unsacrificeable."

17. Feminism, as a revolutionary strategy, will never escape—but will, rather, reinstate—the very conditions it opposes as long as it claims for itself the political goal of unity. Judith Butler comments,

> Despite the clearly democratizing impulse that motivates coalition building, the coalitional theorist can inadvertently reinsert herself

as sovereign of the process by trying to assert an ideal form for coalitional structures *in advance,* one that will effectively guarantee unity as the outcome. (*Gender Trouble* 14; emphasis hers)

18. In Homer's rendition of Helen's figuration, as in other accounts, Helen is characterized as a "weaver." In ancient Greece, there existed a relation between weaving and *poïēsis*—invention and composition. See Ann Bergren, "Helen's Web"; Linda Lee Clader, *Helen;* and George Kennedy, "Helen's Web Unraveled."

3. Nietzsche and the Other Woman: On Forgetting in an Extra-Moral Sense

1. Regarding Nietzsche and nihilism, see Ofelia Schutte, *Beyond Nihilism;* Gianni Vattimo, *The End of Modernity;* and Karen L. Carr, *The Banalization of Nihilism.*

2. See Dodds's *Greeks and the Irrational* for his discussion of the anthropological distinction made between guilt and shame cultures. As I have suggested in chapter 1, there is a relationship among the advent of literacy, the creation of subjectivity, and the development of guilt. Norman Austin writes,

My view is that literacy contributes significantly to increasing guilt and devaluing shame, since it moves the locus of judgment from the public arena to the private screen of the individual reader. Readers learn to internalize what in nonliterate cultures is played out on the highly public stage. (*Helen of Troy and Her Shameless Phantom* 29ff)

3. See Peter Sloterdijk's *Thinker on Stage* and Tracy B. Strong's *Friedrich Nietzsche and the Politics of Transfiguration* for a discussion of the "Dionysian" vis-à-vis the "Apollonian."

4. References to the First Woman include "women's love and sympathy— is there anything more egoistic?" (*Will to Power* 407);

One-half of mankind is weak, typically sick . . . —woman needs strength in order to cleave to it; she needs a religion of weakness that glorifies being weak, loving, and being humble as divine: or better, she makes the strong weak—she rules when she succeeds in overcoming the strong. Woman has always conspired with the types of decadence, the priests, against the "powerful," the "strong," the men—. Woman brings the children to the cult of piety, pity, love: the mother represents altruism convincingly. (*Will to Power* 460)

Other references include *Beyond Good and Evil* 219; *Gay Science* 98, 125–30, 319; *Will to Power* 56, 78; *Thus Spoke Zarathustra* 83.

5. References to the Second Woman include: *Beyond Good and Evil* 162–70; *Gay Science* 338; *Will to Power* 191.

6. Hélène Cixous uses the French verb *voler,* which has a double meaning: to steal but also to fly. She writes: "Flying is woman's gesture—flying in

language and making it fly. We have all learned the art of flying and its numerous techniques; for centuries we've been able to possess anything only by flying; we've lived in flight, stealing away" . . . ("The Laugh of the Medusa" 258). Cixous is alternately, as is Lou, the Second Woman and the Third Woman. Cf. Nietzsche's comment in *Beyond Good and Evil*: "Men have so far treated women like birds who had strayed to them from some height: as something more refined and vulnerable, wilder, stranger, sweeter, and more soulful—but as something one has to lock up lest it fly away" (166).

7. See chapter 2 concerning the triangle as the symbol of the dialectic, humanistic, and Oedipal epistemology.

8. For biographical information, see Walter Sorell, *Three Women: Lives of Sex and Genius;* Rudolph Binion, *Frau Lou;* and Biddy Martin, *Woman and Modernity;* as well as Margaret Morrison's review of the same in *Studies in Psychoanalytic Theory.* Also of note is Lou Andreas-Salomé's biography of Nietzsche.

9. The majority of men with whom Lou had romantic attachments eventually committed suicide following the severance of the relationship. It is rumored that one such man, Dr. Victor Tausk (one of Freud's most gifted disciples), castrated himself prior to killing himself (Peters, *My Sister, My Spouse* 281). The castrating impulse, according to Nietzsche, is engendered by Christianity. He writes: "The Church combats the passions with excision in every sense of the word: its practice, its 'cure' is *castration*" (*Twilight* 42; emphasis his).

10. References to the Third Woman include "*Vita femina*," *Gay Science* 271; *Will to Power* 94; *Thus Spoke Zarathustra* 68, 91–92, 131.

11. The issue is addressed also on 163–64.

12. See also Nietzsche, *Philosophy* 50–68.

13. For biographical information on Aspasia, see Cheryl Glenn, *Rhetoric Retold* and "sex, lies, and manuscript"; John D. Stone, "Classical Female Rhetoricians"; Mary R. Beard, *On Understanding Women* 77–176; Willis J. Abbot, *Notable Women in History;* Arthur Weigall, *Personalities of Antiquity* 135–43; Thucydides bk. 1; Plutarch, *Selected Lives;* and W. L. Courtney, *Old Saws and Modern Instances* 89–108.

4. *Après l'orgie:* Baudrillard and the Seduction of Truth

1. "There is an Indian story . . . about an Englishman who, having been told that the world rested on a platform which rested on the back of an elephant which rested in turn on the back of a turtle, asked . . . what did the turtle rest on? Another turtle. And that turtle? 'Ah, Sahib, after that it is turtles all the way down'" (Clifford Geertz, "Thick Description" 28–29).

2. Baudrillard's interest in the magical uses of language has led him to the study of anagrams. See also Derrida's essay on cryptology "*Fors:* The Anglish Words of Nicolas Abraham and Maria Torok," as well as Nicolas Abraham and Maria Torok's *The Wolf Man's Magic Word.*

3. Regarding the Sphinx as the figuration of ambiguity of language, see Charles Segal's "The Music of the Sphinx: The Problem of Language in Oedipus Tyrannus." Segal argues that

[t]he riddle, with its plural meanings for each signifier, undermines the denotative and differentiating function of language. It misuses, or perhaps overuses, language, by exploiting its ambiguity rather than its precision. It thereby projects a world whose meaning corresponds to the shifting, uncertain, "enigmatic" quality of language. (151)

See also Baudrillard, *Fatal Strategies* 141, 190.

4. On woman and artifice, see Joan Riviere, "Womanliness as a Masquerade"; and Stephen Heath, "Joan Riviere and the Masquerade."

5. "Homer's Contest" raises the distinction between, in James P. Carse's terminology, "finite" games and "infinite" games: "A finite game is played for the purpose of winning, an infinite game for the purpose of continuing the play" (3). See also Algirdas Julien Greimas, "About Games"; René Thom, "Remarks for the Polylogue on Play" and "At the Boundaries of Man's Power"; Donald Rice, "Catastrop(h)es"; and Lyotard, *Just Gaming*.

6. Baudrillard's conception of the fatal is largely influenced by "pataphysics," a way of thought created by Alfred Jarry (1873–1907). Jarry defines "pataphysics" as "the science of imaginary solutions, that symbolically attributes the properties of objects, described by their virtuality, to lineaments" (*Faustroll*, quoted in Stillman 19). Linda Klieger Stillman characterizes "pataphysics" as "[t]he science of the Possible, not the Probable, Pataphysics studies the aberrant and the absurd" (*Alfred Jarry* 19). See also Maurice Marc LaBelle, *Alfred Jarry*. Baudrillard's conception avoids the determined/aleatory binary, and therefore requires us to radically reconceive of "fate" and/or "chance." In this way, Baudrillard's thought could be read in relationship to "catastrophe theory" or "chaos theory." See James Gleick's *Chaos* and Ilya Prigogine's *Order out of Chaos*.

7. On this point, see Baudrillard, *Fatal Strategies* 25, 26, 44, 49, 56, 61, and 77; *Seduction* 155, 164; *Revenge of the Crystal* 28; *Cool Memories* 113; *Symbolic Exchange* 121, 122; *Forget* 53; and Gane, *Bestiary* 43, 80, 85, 131, 136, 137, 139.

8. Seduction thus offers an alternative to the totalizing theories of subjectivity, truth, and communication based on consensus, which Lyotard argues, "does violence to the heterogeneity of language games. And invention is always born of a dissension" (*Postmodern Condition* xxv).

5. Seduction and the "Third Sophistic": (Femme) Fatale Tactics Contra Fetal Pedagogies, Critical Practices, and Neopragmatic Politics

1. See, for example, Susan Miller, "The Feminization of Composition"; Catherine E. Lamb, "Beyond Argument in Feminist Composition"; Madeleine R. Grumet, "Pedagogy for Patriarchy"; Robert J. Bezucha, "Feminist Pedagogy as a Subversive Activity"; and Carmen Luke and Jennifer Gore's collection, entitled *Feminisms and Critical Pedagogy*.

2. "Rogerian rhetoric" is a rhetorical appropriation of Carl Rogers's communication theory, which is used mainly in the context of a patient-client

therapy. Usually contrasted with Aristotelian notions of rhetoric, Rogerian rhetoric rests on, according to Young, Becker, and Pike, "the assumption that man holds to his beliefs about who he is and what the world is like because other beliefs threaten his identity and integrity" (*Rhetoric: Discovery and Change* 7). Therefore, although Aristotle characterized the subject as essentially rational and thus moved by logical appeals, Rogerian rhetoric suggests that no amount of reasoning will *necessarily* convince one of anything. For discussions of Aristotelian vs. Rogerian rhetoric, see Paul Bator's "Aristotelian and Rogerian Rhetoric" and Andrea A. Lunsford's "Aristotelian vs. Rogerian Argument." Also, for a feminist rejection, see Phyllis Lassner's "Feminist Responses to Rogerian Argument."

3. Gilligan is perhaps best known for her study of the moral development of women entitled *In a Different Voice.* She argues that the ethical decisions that women make are based on complex, contextualized variables which seek to sustain connectedness and harmony. In contrast, she identifies the decision-making process of men as based on the "logic of justice," where unnegotiable rules govern judgment.

4. *Women's Ways of Knowing,* by Mary Field Belenky, Blythe McVicker Clinchy, Nancy Rule Goldberger, and Jill Mattuck Tarule, attempts to demonstrate how women come to know through a principle of connectedness.

5. It is interesting to note that the criticisms leveled against Lamb's article after it appeared were focused almost exclusively on her failure to properly acknowledge where such notions of collaboration and dialogic originated. That is, she was criticized for not properly charting her ideas' lineage and paternity—for not legitimating her argument with the names of the fathers: Booth, Burke, Perelman (see Farrar, Musgrove, Stewart, and Cosby, "Responses to Catherine E. Lamb").

6. See James V. Catano, "The Rhetoric of Masculinity"; and Miriam Brody, *Manly Writing* for examples of how masculine ideals are alive and well in composition studies.

7. See Benjamin for a discussion of "recognition" in terms of "The First Bond," the mother-child dyad (11–84).

8. See also Badinter's *Mother Love,* in which she discusses the modern history of the "maternal instinct" and demonstrates how maternal *indifference* has, historically, been the normal behavior of mothers. Naomi Wolf reports figures demonstrating that

> Females account for 49.5 percent of all physical abuse of children, including 56.8 percent of major physical abuse, 48.5 percent of minor physical abuse, 17.6 percent of sexual abuse or exploitation, 69.7 percent of abuse by neglect, 52.2 percent of "emotional maltreatment," and 65.5 percent of "other maltreatment." (221)

9. See Silverman's reading of Julia Kristeva, "The Fantasy of the Maternal Voice," (*Acoustic* 101–40) for a compelling argument suggesting that Kristeva's "maternal" is, ultimately, unhelpful as a subversive agent.

10. Baudrillard explains:

nothing takes place in real time. Not even history. History in real time is CNN, instant news, which is the exact opposite of history. But this is precisely our fantasy of passing beyond the end, of emancipating ourselves from time. And the CNN presenter locked away in his studio at the virtual centre of the world is the homologue of his Bio 2 brothers and sisters. They have all passed over into real time, the one into the real time of events, the others into real-time survival. And, of course, into the same unreality. (*Illusion of the End* 90; emphasis his)

Bibliography

Abbot, Willis J. *Notable Women in History.* Philadelphia: Winston, 1913.

Abraham, Nicolas, and Maria Torok. *The Wolf Man's Magic Word.* Trans. Nicholas Rand. Minneapolis: U of Minnesota P, 1986.

Ackerman, Robert John. *Nietzsche: A Frenzied Look.* Amherst: U of Massachusetts P, 1990.

Adkins, A. W. H. *From the Many to the One.* Ithaca: Cornell UP, 1970.

Adorno, Theodor W. *Negative Dialectics.* Trans. E. B. Ashton. New York: Seabury, 1973.

Ainley, Alison. "The Ethics of Sexual Difference." *Abjection, Melancholia and Love: The Work of Julia Kristeva.* Ed. John Fletcher and Andrew Benjamin. London: Routledge, 1990. 53–62.

Alcoff, Linda. "Cultural Feminism Versus Post-Structuralism: The Identity Crisis in Feminist Theory." *Signs* 13.3 (1988): 405–36.

Allison, David, ed. *The New Nietzsche.* Cambridge: MIT P, 1985.

Althusser, Louis. *Essays in Self Criticism.* London: NLB, 1971.

———. "Freud and Lacan." *Lenin and Philosophy.* Trans. Ben Brewster. New York: Monthly Review, 1971. 189–219.

———. "Ideology and Ideological State Apparatuses (Notes Towards an Investigation)." *Lenin and Philosophy.* Trans. Ben Brewster. New York: Monthly Review, 1971. 127–86.

———. *Lenin and Philosophy and Other Essays.* Trans. Ben Brewster. New York: Monthly Review, 1971.

———. "Marxism and Humanism." *For Marx.* Trans. Ben Brewster. London: Lane, 1969. 221–47.

Anonymous. *"Dissoi Logoi." The Older Sophists.* Ed. Rosamond Kent Sprague. Columbia: U of South Carolina P, 1972. 279–93.

Apollodorus. *The Library.* Trans. Sir James George Frazer. London: Heinemann, 1961.

Aristotle. *Ethics: The Nicomachean Ethics.* Trans. J. A. K. Thomson. New York: Penguin, 1988.

———. *On Rhetoric: A Theory of Civic Discourse.* Trans. George A. Kennedy. New York: Oxford UP, 1991.

———. *Poetics.* Trans. Ingram Bywater. New York: Modern Library, 1954, 1984.

———. *Rhetoric.* Trans. W. Rhys Roberts. New York: Modern Library, 1954, 1984.

[Pseudo] Aristotle. "On Gorgias." *Minor Works.* Trans. W. S. Hett. Cambridge: Harvard UP, 1955. 496–507.

Aronowitz, Stanley, and Henry A. Giroux. *Education Under Siege: The Conservative, Liberal, and Radical Debate over Schooling.* South Hadley: Bergin, 1985.

Ashton-Jones, Evelyn. "Collaboration, Conversation, and the Politics of Gender." *Feminine Principles and Women's Experience in American Composition and Rhetoric.* Ed. Louise Wetherbee Phelps and Janet Emig. Pittsburgh: U of Pittsburgh P, 1995. 5–26.

Atwill, Janet M. *Rhetoric Reclaimed: Aristotle and the Liberal Arts Tradition.* Ithaca: Cornell UP, 1998.

Augustine, Saint. *The City of God.* Trans. Marcus Dods. New York: Random, 1950.

——. *On Christian Doctrine.* Trans. D. W. Robertson, Jr. New York: Macmillan, 1986.

Austin, Norman. *Helen of Troy and Her Shameless Phantom.* Ithaca: Cornell UP, 1994.

Badinter, Elisabeth. *Mother Love: Myth and Reality.* New York: Macmillan, 1980.

——. *XY: On Masculine Identity.* Trans. Lydia Davis. New York: Columbia UP, 1995.

Ballif, Michelle. "Extricating Ethics from the Ego: Liminal Subjects and the Discourse of the Other." *Studies in Psychoanalytic Theory* 1.1 (spring 1992): 103–13.

——. "Mothers in the Classroom: Composing Masculinity via Fetal Pedagogies." *Pre/Text* 16.3–4 (fall–winter 1995): 288–314.

——. "Re/Dressing Histories; or, On Re/Covering Figures Who Have Been Laid Bare by Our Gaze." *Rhetoric Society Quarterly* 22.1 (winter 1992): 91–98.

——. "Reproducing Desire: Plato in the Family Way." Unpublished ms.

——. "Review of Teresa Brennan's *The Interpretation of the Flesh: Freud and Femininity.*" *Studies in Psychoanalytic Theory* 3.2 (fall 1994): 116–19.

——. "Seducing Composition: A Challenge to Identity-Disclosing Pedagogies." *Rhetoric Review* 16.1 (fall 1997): 76–91.

——. "What Is It That the Audience Wants? Or, Notes Toward a Listening with a Transgendered Ear for (Mis)Understanding." *JAC: A Journal of Composition Theory* 19.1 (winter 1999): 51–70.

——. "Writing the Third-Sophistic Cyborg: Periphrasis on an [In]Tense Rhetoric." *Rhetoric Society Quarterly* 28.4 (fall 1998): 51–72.

Balsamo, Anne. *Technologies of the Gendered Body: Reading Cyborg Women.* Durham: Duke UP, 1996.

Barrett, Harold. *The Sophists: Rhetoric, Democracy, and Plato's Idea of Sophistry.* Novato: Chandler, 1987.

Barthes, Roland. "The Death of the Author." *The Rustle of Language.* Trans. Richard Howard. New York: Hill, 1986. 49–55.

——. *A Lover's Discourse: Fragments.* Trans. Richard Howard. New York: Farrar, 1978.

Bartholomae, David. "Inventing the University." *Perspectives on Literacy.* Ed.

Eugene R. Kintgen, Barry M. Kroll, and Mike Rose. Carbondale: Southern Illinois UP, 1988. 134–65.

———. "A Reply to Stephen North." *Pre/Text* 11 (1990): 122–30.

Bataille, Georges. *The Accursed Share*. Vols. 2 and 3. Trans. Robert Hurley. New York: Zone, 1991.

———. "Hegel, Death, and Sacrifice." *Yale French Studies* 78 (1990): 9–43.

———. "Reflections on the Executioner and the Victim." *Yale French Studies* 79 (1991): 15–19.

Bator, Paul. "Aristotelian and Rogerian Rhetoric." *College Composition and Communication* 31.4 (Dec. 1980): 427–32.

Baudrillard, Jean. *America*. Trans. Chris Turner. New York: Verso, 1988.

———. "Beyond The Unconscious: The Symbolic." *Discourse* 3 (1981): 60–87.

———. "Consumer Society." *Selected Writings*. Ed. Mark Poster. Stanford: Stanford UP, 1988. 29–56.

———. *Cool Memories*. Trans. Chris Turner. New York: Verso, 1990.

———. *Cool Memories II, 1987–1990*. Trans. Chris Turner. Durham: Duke UP, 1996.

———. *The Evil Demon of Images*. Trans. Paul Patton and Paul Foss. Sydney: Power Institute of Fine Arts, 1987.

———. "Fatality or Reversible Imminence: Beyond the Uncertainty Principle." *Social Research* 49.2 (1981): 272–93.

———. *Fatal Strategies*. Trans. Philip Beitchman and W. G. J. Niesluchowski. New York: Semiotext(e): 1990.

———. *For a Critique of the Political Economy of the Sign*. Trans. Charles Levin. St. Louis: Telos, 1981.

———. *Forget Foucault and Forget Baudrillard: An Interview with Sylvère Lotringer*. New York: Semiotext(e), 1987.

———. *The Illusion of the End*. Trans. Chris Turner. Stanford: Stanford UP, 1994.

———. *In the Shadow of the Silent Majorities*. Trans. Paul Foss, Paul Patton, and John Johnston. New York: Semiotext(e), 1983.

———. "The Masses: The Implosion of the Social in the Media." *New Literary History* 16.3 (1985): 577–89.

———. *The Mirror of Production*. Trans. Mark Poster. St Louis: Telos, 1975.

———. "Modernity." *Canadian Journal of Political and Social Theory* 11.3 (1987): 63–72.

———. "On Seduction." *Selected Writings*. Ed. Mark Poster. Stanford: Stanford UP, 1988. 149–65.

———. *Revenge of the Crystal*. Ed. and trans. Paul Foss and Julian Pefanis. London: Pluto, 1990.

———. *Seduction*. Trans. Brian Singer. New York: St. Martin's, 1990.

———. *Selected Writings*. Ed. Mark Poster. Stanford: Stanford UP, 1988.

———. *Simulations*. Trans. Paul Foss, Paul Patton, and Philip Beitchman. New York: Semiotext(e), 1983.

———. "Symbolic Exchange and Death." *Selected Writings*. Ed. Mark Poster. Stanford: Stanford UP, 1988. 119–48.

———. "The System of Objects." *Selected Writings*. Ed. Mark Poster. Stanford: Stanford UP, 1988. 10–28.

———. *The Transparency of Evil: Essays on Extreme Phenomena.* Trans. James Benedict. London: Verso, 1993.

———. "Transpolitics, Transsexuality, Transaesthetics." *Jean Baudrillard: The Disappearance of Art and Politics.* Ed. William Sterns and William Chaloupka. New York: St. Martin's, 1992. 9–26.

———. "What Are You Doing after the Orgy?" *Artforum* 22 (Oct. 1983): 42–46.

Beard, Mary R. *On Understanding Women.* London: Longmans, 1931.

Belenky, Mary Field, et al. *Women's Ways of Knowing: The Development of Self, Voice, and Mind.* New York: Basic, 1986.

Belsey, Catherine. *Critical Practice.* London: Methuen, 1980.

Benjamin, Jessica. *The Bonds of Love: Psychoanalysis, Feminism, and the Problem of Domination.* New York: Pantheon, 1988.

Berg, Elizabeth. "The Third Woman." *Diacritics* 12 (summer 1982): 11–20.

Bergren, Ann. "Helen's Good 'Drug.' Odyssey iv. 1–305." *Contemporary Literary Hermeneutics and Interpretation of Classical Texts.* Ed. Stephanus Kresic. Ottawa: U of Ottawa P, 1981.

———. "Helen's Web: Time and Tableau in the *Iliad.*" *Helios* 7 (1969): 19–34.

———. "Language and the Female in Early Greek Thought." *Arethusa* 16 (1983): 69–95.

Berlin, James A. "Composition Studies and Cultural Studies: Collapsing Boundaries." *Into the Field: Sites of Composition Studies.* Ed. Anne Ruggles Gere. New York: MLA, 1993. 99–116.

———. "Contemporary Composition: The Major Pedagogical Theories." *College English* 44.8 (Dec. 1982): 765–77.

———. "James Berlin Responds." *College English* 51.7 (Nov. 1989): 770–77.

———. "Postmodernism, the College Curriculum, and Composition." *Composition in Context.* Ed. W. Ross Winterowd and Vincent Gillespie. Carbondale: Southern Illinois UP, 1994. 46–61.

———. "Rhetoric and Ideology in the Writing Class." *College English* 50.5 (Sept. 1988): 477–94.

———. *Rhetoric and Reality: Writing Instruction in American Colleges, 1900–1985.* Carbondale: Southern Illinois UP, 1987.

Berlin, James A., and Robert P. Inkster. "Current-Traditional Rhetoric: Paradigm and Practice." *Freshman English News* 8.3 (winter 1980): 1–14.

Bernard-Donals, Michael, and Richard R. Glejzer, eds. *Rhetoric in an Antifoundational World.* New Haven: Yale UP, 1998.

Bernheimer, Charles, and Claire Kahane, eds. *In Dora's Case: Freud-Hysteria-Feminism.* New York: Columbia UP, 1985.

Bernstein, Richard. "Serious Play: The Ethical-Political Horizon of Jacques Derrida." *The Journal of Speculative Philosophy* 1.2 (1987): 93–117.

Best, Steven, and Douglas Kellner. *Postmodern Theory: Critical Interrogations.* New York: Guilford, 1991.

Bezucha, Robert J. "Feminist Pedagogy as a Subversive Activity." *Gendered Subjects: The Dynamics of Feminist Teaching.* Ed. Margo Culley and Catherine Portuges. Boston: Routledge, 1985. 81–95.

Biesecker, Susan. "Feminist Criticism of Classical Rhetorical Texts: A Case Study of Gorgias' *Helen.*" *Realms of Rhetoric.* Ed. Victor J. Vitanza and Michelle Ballif. Arlington, TX: Rhetoric Soc. of America, 1990. 67–84.

Binion, Rudolph. *Frau Lou: Nietzsche's Wayward Disciple*. Princeton: Princeton UP, 1968.

Bitzer, Lloyd. "The Rhetorical Situation." *Philosophy and Rhetoric* 1.1 (Jan. 1968): 1–14.

Bizzell, Patricia. "Beyond Anti-Foundationalism to Rhetorical Authority: Problems Defining 'Cultural Literacy.'" *College English* 52.6 (Oct. 1990): 661–75.

———. "Cognition, Convention, and Certainty: What We Need to Know about Writing." *Pre/Text* 3 (fall 1982): 213–43.

———. "Fredric Jameson and Composition Studies." *JAC: A Journal of Composition Theory* 16.3 (spring 1996): 471–87.

———. "The Prospect of Rhetorical Agency." *Making and Unmaking the Prospects for Rhetoric*. Ed. Theresa Enos and Richard McNabb. Mahwah: Erlbaum, 1997. 37–42.

———. "Thomas Kuhn, Scientism, and English Studies." *College English* 40.7 (Mar. 1979): 764–71.

Bobzien, Susanne. "The Inadvertent Conception and Late Birth of the Free-Will Problem." *Phronesis* 63.2 (1998): 133–75.

Booth, Wayne C. *The Company We Keep: An Ethics of Fiction*. Berkeley: U of California P, 1988.

———. *Critical Understanding: The Powers and Limits of Pluralism*. Chicago: U of Chicago P, 1979.

———. *Modern Dogma and the Rhetoric of Assent*. Chicago: U of Chicago P, 1974.

———. "The Pleasures and Pitfalls of Irony: or, Why Don't You Say What You Mean?" *Rhetoric, Philosophy, and Literature: An Exploration*. Ed. Don M. Burks. West Lafayette: Purdue U, 1978. 1–13.

———. "The Rhetorical Stance." *College Composition and Communication* 14.3 (Oct. 1963): 139–45.

Braidotti, Rosi. *Nomadic Subjects: Embodiment and Sexual Difference in Contemporary Feminist Theory*. New York: Columbia UP, 1994.

———. *Patterns of Dissonance*. Trans. Elizabeth Guild. New York: Routledge, 1991.

Brennan, Teresa. *The Interpretation of the Flesh: Freud and Femininity*. London: Routledge, 1992.

Brindel, June Rachuy. *Ariadne: A Novel of Ancient Crete*. New York: St. Martin's, 1980.

Brockriede, Wayne. "Arguers as Lovers." *Philosophy and Rhetoric* 5.1 (winter 1972): 1–11.

Brody, Miriam. *Manly Writing: Gender, Rhetoric, and the Rise of Composition*. Carbondale: Southern Illinois UP, 1993.

Bruffee, Kenneth A. "Collaborative Learning and 'The Conversation of Mankind.'" *College English* 46.7 (Nov. 1984): 635–52.

———. "Liberal Education and the Social Justification of Belief." *Liberal Education* 68 (1982): 95–114.

———. "Social Construction, Language, and the Authority of Knowledge: A Bibliographical Essay." *College English* 48.8 (Dec. 1986): 773–90.

Buber, Martin. *Between Man and Man*. London: Routledge, 1947.

Burke, Carolyn. "Irigaray Through the Looking Glass." *Feminist Studies* 7.2 (1981): 288–306.

Burke, Kenneth. *A Grammar of Motives.* Berkeley: U of California P, 1969.

——. *Permanence and Change: An Anatomy of Purpose.* New York: New Republic, 1936.

——. *A Rhetoric of Motives.* Berkeley: U of California P, 1969.

——. *The Rhetoric of Religion: Studies in Logology.* 1961. Berkeley: U of California P, 1970.

Butler, Judith. *Bodies That Matter: On the Discursive Limits of "Sex."* New York: Routledge, 1993.

——. "The Body Politics of Julia Kristeva." *Ethics, Politics, and Difference in Julia Kristeva's Writing.* Ed. Kelly Oliver. New York: Routledge, 1993. 164–78.

——. "Contingent Foundations: Feminism and the Question of 'Postmodernism.'" *Feminists Theorize the Political.* Ed. Judith Butler and Joan W. Scott. New York: Routledge, 1992. 3–21.

——. *Excitable Speech.* New York: Routledge, 1997.

——. *Gender Trouble: Feminism and the Subversion of Identity.* New York: Routledge, 1990.

——. *Subjects of Desire: Hegelian Reflections in Twentieth-Century France.* New York: Columbia UP, 1987.

Calderonello, Donna Beth Nelson, and Sue Carter Simmons. "An Interview with Andrea Lunsford and Lisa Ede: Collaboration as a Subversive Activity." *Writing on the Edge* 2.2 (spring 1991): 7–18.

Cantarella, Eva. *Pandora's Daughters: The Role and Status of Women in Greek and Roman Antiquity.* Trans. Maureen B. Fant. Baltimore: Johns Hopkins UP, 1987.

Carr, Karen L. *The Banalization of Nihilism: Twentieth-Century Responses to Meaninglessness.* Albany: State U of New York P, 1992.

Carse, James P. *Finite and Infinite Games: A Vision of Life as Play and Possibility.* New York: Ballantine, 1986.

Carson, Anne. *Eros: The Bittersweet.* Princeton: Princeton UP, 1986.

——. "Putting Her in Her Place: Woman, Dirt, and Desire." *Before Sexuality: The Construction of Erotic Experience in the Ancient Greek World.* Ed. David M. Halperin, John J. Winkler, and Froma I. Zeitlin. Princeton: Princeton UP 1990. 135–70.

Catano, James V. "The Rhetoric of Masculinity: Origins, Institutions, and the Myth of the Self-Made Man." *College English* 52.4 (Apr. 1990): 421–36.

Chamberlain, Lori. "Bombs and Other Exciting Devices, or the Problem of Teaching Irony." *College English* 51.1 (Jan. 1989): 29–40.

Chanter, Tina. "Kristeva's Politics of Change: Tracking Essentialism with the Help of a Sex/Gender Map." *Ethics, Politics, and Difference in Julia Kristeva's Writing.* Ed. Kelly Oliver. New York: Routledge, 1993. 179–95.

Chodorow, Nancy. *The Reproduction of Mothering.* Berkeley: U of California P, 1978.

Christ, Carol. "Why Women Need the Goddess: Phenomenological, Psychological, and Political Reflections." *Womanspirit Rising: A Feminist Reader in Religion.* Ed. Carol Christ and Judith Plaskow. San Francisco: Harper, 1979. 273–87.

Cicero, Marcus Tullius. *De Finibus Bonorum et Malorum.* Trans. H. Rackham. London: Heinemann, 1931.

Cixous, Hélène. "Castration or Decapitation?" Trans. Annette Kuhn. *Signs: Journal of Women in Culture and Society* 7.1 (1981): 41–55.

——. "Laugh of the Medusa." Trans. Keith Cohen and Paula Cohen. *New French Femininisms.* Ed. Elaine Marks and Isabelle de Courtivron. New York: Schocken, 1980. 245–64.

——. "Portrait of Dora." *Diacritics* (spring 1983): 2–32.

——. "Sorties." Trans. Ann Liddle. *New French Femininisms.* Ed. Elaine Marks and Isabelle de Courtivron. New York: Schocken, 1980. 90–98.

Cixous, Hélène, and Catherine Clément. *The Newly Born Woman.* Trans. Betsy Wing. Minneapolis: U of Minnesota P, 1975.

Clader, Linda Lee. *Helen: The Evolution from Divine to Heroic in Greek Epic Tradition.* Leiden, NY: Brill, 1976.

Clark, Gregory. *Dialogue, Dialectic, and Conversation: A Social Perspective on the Function of Writing.* Carbondale: Southern Illinois UP, 1990.

Clark, Suzanne, and Lisa Ede. "Collaboration, Resistance, and the Teaching of Writing." *The Right to Literacy.* Ed. Andrea Lunsford, Helene Moglen, and James Slevin. New York: MLA, 1990. 276–85.

Clément, Catherine. "Enclave Esclave." *New French Feminisms.* Ed. Elaine Marks and Isabelle de Courtivron. New York: Schocken, 1981. 130–36.

Cohen, Tom. "The 'Genealogies' of Pragmatism." *Rhetoric, Sophistry, Pragmatism.* Ed. Steven Mailloux. Cambridge: Cambridge UP, 1995. 94–108.

Cole, Thomas. *The Origins of Rhetoric in Ancient Greece.* Baltimore: Johns Hopkins UP, 1991.

Coles, William E., Jr. *The Plural I: The Teaching of Writing.* New York: Holt, 1978.

Comay, Rebecca. "Gifts Without Presents: Economies of 'Experience' in Bataille and Heidegger." *Yale French Studies* 78 (1990): 66–89.

Con Davis, Robert, and Ronald Schleifer. *Contemporary Literary Criticism.* 3rd ed. White Plains: Longman, 1994.

Conners, Robert J. "Greek Rhetoric and the Transition from Orality." *Philosophy and Rhetoric* 19.1 (1986): 38–65.

Consigny, Scott. "Sophistic Freedom: Gorgias and the Subversion of *Logos.*" *Pre/Text* 12.3–4 (fall/winter 1991): 225–36.

——. "The Style of Gorgias." *Rhetoric Society Quarterly* 22.3 (summer 1992): 43–53.

Coontz, Stephanie. "Menaces to Society?" *Vogue* (Dec. 1994): 88–92.

——. *The Way We Never Were: American Families and the Nostalgia Trap.* New York: Basic, 1992.

Cope, E. M. "I: On the Sophistical Rhetoric." *Journal of Classical and Sacred Philology* 2 (May 1855): 129–69.

——. "II: On the Sophistical Rhetoric." *Journal of Classical and Sacred Philology* 3 (Mar. 1856): 34–80, 252–88.

Corcoran, Paul. *Political Language and Rhetoric.* Austin: U of Texas P, 1979.

Corder, Jim. "Argument as Emergence, Rhetoric as Love." *Rhetoric Review* 4.1. (1985): 16–32.

Cornell, Drucilla. *Beyond Accommodation: Ethical Feminism, Deconstruction, and the Law.* New York: Routledge, 1991.

Cose, Ellis. *A Man's World: How Real Is Male Privilege—and How High Is Its Price?* New York: Harper, 1995.

Courtney, W. L. *Old Saws and Modern Instances*. New York: Dutton, 1918.

Covino, William. "Grammars of Transgression: Golems, Cyborgs, and Mutants." *Rhetoric Review* 14.2 (spring 1996): 355–73.

Critchley, Simon. "Deconstruction and Pragmatism—Is Derrida a Private Ironist or a Public Liberal?" *Deconstruction and Pragmatism*. Ed. Chantal Mouffe. London: Routledge, 1996. 19–40.

Crowley, Sharon. *Composition in the University*. Pittsburgh: U of Pittsburgh P, 1998.

——. "A Plea for the Revival of Sophistry." *Rhetoric Review* 7.2 (1989): 318–34.

Culler, Jonathan. *Ferdinand de Saussure*. Ithaca: Cornell UP, 1986.

Culley, Margo, et al. "The Politics of Nurturance." *Gendered Subjects: The Dynamics of Feminist Teaching*. Boston: Routledge, 1985. 31–58.

Cushman, Ellen. "The Rhetorician as an Agent of Social Change." *College Composition and Communication* 47.1 (Feb. 1996): 7–28.

Davis, D. Diane. *Breaking Up [at] Totality: A Rhetoric of Laughter*. Carbondale: Southern Illinois UP, 2000.

Davis, Janet. "Translating Gorgias in [Aristotle] 98a10." *Philosophy and Rhetoric* 30.1 (1997): 31–37.

de Beauvoir, Simone. *The Second Sex*. Trans. H. M. Parshley. New York: Bantam, 1952.

de Certeau, Michel. *The Practice of Everyday Life*. Trans. Steven F. Rendall. Berkeley: U of California P, 1984.

de Kerckhove, Derrick. "A Theory of Greek Tragedy." *Sub-stance* 29 (1981): 23–36.

de Lauretis, Teresa. *Alice Doesn't: Feminism, Semiotics, Cinema*. Bloomington: Indiana UP, 1984.

——. "Feminism and Its Differences." *Pacific Coast Philology* 25.1–2 (1990): 24–30.

——. *Technologies of Gender*. Bloomington: Indiana UP, 1987.

Deleuze, Gilles. *Masochism: Coldness and Cruelty*. New York: Zone, 1989.

——. *Nietzsche and Philosophy*. Trans. Hugh Tomlinson. Columbia UP, 1983.

Deleuze, Gilles, and Félix Guattari. *Anti-Oedipus: Capitalism and Schizophrenia*. Trans. Robert Hurley, Mark Seem, and Helen R. Lane. Minneapolis: U of Minnesota P, 1983.

——. *A Thousand Plateaus: Capitalism and Schizophrenia*. Trans. Brian Massumi. Minneapolis: U of Minnesota P, 1987.

de Man, Paul. *Allegories of Reading: Figural Language in Rousseau, Nietzsche, Rilke, and Proust*. New Haven: Yale UP, 1979.

——. *Blindness and Insight*. Minneapolis: U of Minnesota P, 1971. 1983.

Denyer, Nicholas. *Language, Thought, and Falsehood in Ancient Greek Philosophy*. London: Routledge, 1991.

de Romilly, Jacqueline. *Magic and Rhetoric in Ancient Greece*. Cambridge: Harvard UP, 1975.

Derrida, Jacques. *Aporias*. Trans. Thomas Dutoit. Stanford: Stanford UP, 1993.

——. "Choreographies." Trans. Christie McDonald. *The Ear of the Other*. Ed. Christie V. McDonald. Trans. Peggy Kamuf. Lincoln: U of Nebraska P, 1985. 163–85.

———. *Disseminations.* Trans. Barbara Johnson. Chicago: U of Chicago P, 1981.

———. *The Ear of the Other: Otobiography, Transference, Translation.* Ed. Christie V. McDonald. Trans. Peggy Kamuf. Lincoln: U of Nebraska P, 1985.

———. "Fors: The Anglish Words of Nicolas Abraham and Maria Torok." Trans. Barbara Johnson. *The Wolf Man's Magic Word.* By Nicolas Abraham and Maria Torok. Trans. Nicholas Rand. Minneapolis: U of Minnesota P, 1986. xi–xlviii.

———. "Living On • Border Lines." *Deconstruction and Criticism.* By Harold Bloom, Paul de Man, Jacques Derrida, Geoffrey H. Hartman, and J. Hillis Miller. New York: Seabury, 1979. 75–176.

———. *Of Grammatology.* Trans. Gayatri Chakravorty Spivak. Baltimore: Johns Hopkins UP, 1976.

———. *The Post Card: From Socrates to Freud and Beyond.* Trans. Alan Bass. Chicago: U of Chicago P, 1987.

———. "Remarks on Deconstruction and Pragmatism." *Deconstruction and Pragmatism.* Ed. Chantal Mouffe. London: Routledge, 1996. 77–88.

———. *Speech and Phenomena and Other Essays on Husserl's Theory of Signs.* Trans. David B. Allison. Evanston: Northwestern UP, 1973.

———. *Spurs: Nietzsche's Styles.* Trans. Barbara Harlow. Chicago: U of Chicago P, 1978.

———. "Structure, Sign, and Play in the Discourse of the Human Sciences." *Writing and Difference.* Trans. Alan Bass. Chicago: U of Chicago P, 1978. 278–93.

de Saussure, Ferdinand. *Course in General Linguistics.* Trans. Roy Harris. La Salle: Open Court, 1983.

Detienne, Marcel. *The Masters of Truth in Archaic Greece.* Trans. Janet Lloyd. New York: Zone, 1996.

Detienne, Marcel, and Jean-Pierre Vernant. *Cunning Intelligence in Greek Culture and Society.* Trans. Janet Lloyd. Sussex: Harvester, 1978.

Dews, Peter. *Logics of Disintegration.* London: Verso, 1987.

Dinnerstein, Dorothy. *The Mermaid and the Minotaur.* New York: Harper, 1977.

Doan, Laura, ed. *The Lesbian Postmodern.* New York: Columbia UP, 1994.

Dodds, E. R. *The Greeks and the Irrational.* Boston: Beacon, 1957.

Doueihi, Milad, ed. *The Métis of the Greeks. Diacritics* 16.2 (summer 1986).

Douglas, Ann. *The Feminization of American Culture.* New York: Knopf, 1977.

Dover, K. J. "Classical Greek Attitudes to Sexual Behavior." *Arethusa* 6 (1973): 143–57.

———. *Greek Homosexuality.* 1978. Cambridge: Harvard UP, 1989.

Dreyfus, Hubert L., and Paul Rabinow. *Michel Foucault: Beyond Structuralism and Hermeneutics.* 2nd ed. Chicago: U of Chicago P, 1983.

———. "What Is Maturity?" *Foucault: A Critical Reader.* Ed. David Couzens Hoy. New York: Blackwell, 1986. 109–21.

duBois, Page. *Centaurs and Amazons: Women and the Pre-History of the Great Chain of Being.* Ann Arbor: U of Michigan P, 1982.

———. *Sowing the Body: Psychoanalysis and Ancient Representations of Women.* Chicago: U of Chicago P, 1988.

Dworkin, Andrea. *Intercourse*. New York: Free, 1987.

Eagleton, Terry. "Capitalism, Modernism and Postmodernism." *New Left Review* 152 (1985): 60–73.

Ebert, Teresa L. *Ludic Feminism and After: Postmodernism, Desire, and Labor in Late Capitalism*. Ann Arbor: U of Michigan P, 1996.

Edelstein, Marilyn. "Toward a Feminist Postmodern *Poléthique*: Kristeva on Ethics and Politics." *Ethics, Politics, and Difference in Julia Kristeva's Writing*. Ed. Kelly Oliver. New York: Routledge, 1993.

Eichhorn, Jill, Sara Farris, Karen Hayes, et. al. "A Symposium on Feminist Experiences in the Composition Classroom." *College Composition and Communication* 43.3 (1992): 297–322.

Eisler, Riane. *The Chalice and the Blade: Our History, Our Future*. San Francisco: Harper, 1987.

Elbow, Peter. *Embracing Contraries: Explorations in Learning and Teaching*. New York: Oxford UP, 1986.

———. *Writing Without Teachers*. New York: Oxford UP, 1973.

———. *Writing with Power*. New York: Oxford UP, 1981.

Elshtain, Jean Bethke. "Feminist Discourse and Its Discontents: Language, Power, and Meaning." *Signs* 7.3 (1982): 603–21.

———. *Public Man, Private Woman: Women in Social and Political Thought*. Princeton: Princeton UP, 1981.

Engnell, Richard A. "Implications for Communication of the Rhetorical Epistemology of Gorgias of Leontini." *Western Speech* 37.3 (summer 1973): 175–84.

Enos, Richard L. "The Epistemology of Gorgias' Rhetoric: A Re-examination." *Southern Speech Communication Journal* 42 (fall 1976): 35–51.

Epstein, Julia, and Kristina Straub. "Introduction: The Guarded Body." *Body Guards: The Cultural Politics of Gender Ambiguity*. Ed. Julia Epstein and Kristina Straub. New York: Routledge, 1991. 1–28.

Erwin, Elizabeth. "Encouraging Civic Participation among First-Year Writing Students." *Rhetoric Review* 15 (1997): 382–99.

Faigley, Lester. "Competing Theories of Process: A Critique and a Proposal." *College English* 48.6 (Oct. 1986): 527–42.

———. *Fragments of Rationality: Postmodernity and the Subject of Composition*. Pittsburgh: U of Pittsburgh P, 1992.

Faludi, Susan. *Backlash: The Undeclared War Against American Women*. New York: Crown, 1991.

Fantham, Elaine. "Women in Antiquity: a Selective (and Subjective) Survey 1979–84." *Echos du Monde Classique/Classical Views* 1 (1986): 1–24.

Farenga, Vincent. "Periphrasis on the Origin of Rhetoric." *MLN* (1979): 1033–55.

Fausto-Sterling, Anne. "The Five Sexes: Why Male and Female Are Not Enough." *Sciences* (Mar./Apr. 1993): 20–25.

Feher, Michel, ed. *Fragments for a History of the Human Body*. 3 vols. New York: Zone, 1989.

Felman, Shoshana. "Rereading Femininity." *Yale French Studies* 62: 19–44.

———. "Women and Madness: The Critical Phallacy." *Diacritics* 5 (winter 1975): 2–10.

Feyerabend, Paul. *Against Method*. London: Verso, 1988.

Fineman, Martha Albertson. *The Neutered Mother, the Sexual Family and Other Twentieth Century Tragedies*. New York: Routledge, 1995.

Finke, Laurie. "Knowledge as Bait: Feminism, Voice, and the Pedagogical Unconscious." *College English* 55.1 (Jan. 1993): 7–27.

Finley, Moses. *The World of Odysseus*. New York: Viking, 1978.

Fish, Stanley. "Consequences." *Against Theory: Literary Studies and the New Pragmatism*. Ed. W. J. T. Mitchell. Chicago: U of Chicago P, 1985. 106–31.

———. *Is There a Text in This Class? The Authority of Interpretive Communities*. Cambridge: Harvard UP, 1980.

Flacelière, Robert. *Love in Ancient Greece*. Trans. James Cleugh. Westport: Greenwood, 1962.

Flannery, Kathryn T. "Review: Composing and the Question of Agency." *College English* 53.6 (Oct. 1991): 701–13.

Flax, Jane. "Postmodernism and Gender Relations in Feminist Theory." *Feminism/Postmodernism*. Ed. Linda J. Nicholson. New York: Routledge, 1990. 39–62.

Florescu, Vasile. "Rhetoric and Its Rehabilitation in Contemporary Philosophy." *Philosophy and Rhetoric* 3.4 (fall 1970): 193–223.

Flower, Linda. "Comment on 'Rhetoric and Ideology in the Writing Class'" *College English* 51.7 (Nov. 1989): 765–69.

———. "Literate Action." *Composition in the Twenty-First Century: Crisis and Change*. Ed. Lynn Z. Bloom, Donald A. Daiker, and Edward M. White. Carbondale: Southern Illinois UP, 1996. 249–60.

———. *Problem-Solving Strategies for Writing*. New York: Harcourt, 1981.

Flower, Linda, and John R. Hayes. "The Cognition of Discovery: Defining a Rhetorical Problem." *College Composition and Communication* 31 (Feb. 1980): 92–102.

———. "A Cognitive Process Theory of Writing." *College Composition and Communication* 32 (Dec. 1981): 365–87.

———. "The Dynamics of Composing: Making Plans and Juggling Constraints." *Cognitive Processes in Writing: An Interdisciplinary Approach*. Ed. Lee Gregg and Erwin Steinberg. Hillsdale: Erlbaum, 1980. 31–50.

———. "Identifying the Organization of Writing Processes." *Cognitive Processes in Writing: An Interdisciplinary Approach*. Ed. Lee Gregg and Erwin Steinberg. Hillsdale: Erlbaum, 1980. 3–30.

Flynn, Elizabeth A. "Composing as a Woman." *College Composition and Communication* 39.4 (Dec. 1988): 423–35.

Foucault, Michel. *The Archaeology of Knowledge and The Discourse on Language*. Trans. A. M. Sheridan Smith. New York: Pantheon, 1972.

———. *The Care of the Self*. New York: Vintage, 1986. Vol. 3 of *The History of Sexuality*.

———. *Discipline and Punish: The Birth of the Prison*. New York: Vintage, 1979.

———. *The History of Sexuality*. Trans. Robert Hurley. New York: Vintage, 1980.

———. "Nietzsche, Genealogy, History." *Language, Counter-Memory, Practice*. Trans. Donald F. Bouchard and Sherry Simon. Ithaca: Cornell UP, 1977.

———. *The Order of Things: An Archaeology of the Human Sciences*. New York: Vintage, 1970.

——. Preface. *Anti-Oedipus: Capitalism and Schizophrenia*. By Gilles Deleuze and Félix Guattari. Trans. Robert Hurley, Mark Seem, and Helen R. Lane. Minneapolis: U of Minnesota P, 1983. xi–xxiv.

——. *The Use of Pleasure*. Trans. Robert Hurley. New York: Vintage, 1986. Vol. 2 of *The History of Sexuality*.

——. "What Is Enlightenment?" *The Foucault Reader*. Ed. Paul Rabinow. New York: Pantheon, 1984. 32–50.

Fox-Genovese, Elizabeth. *Feminism Is Not the Story of My Life: How Today's Feminist Elite Has Lost Touch with the Real Concerns of Women*. New York: Doubleday, 1996.

——. "Placing Women's History in History." *New Left Review* 133 (1982): 5–29.

Francesconi, Robert. "The Implications of Habermas's Theory of Legitimation for Rhetorical Criticism." *Communication Monographs* 53 (Mar. 1986): 16–35.

Frankovits, André, ed. *Seduced and Abandoned: The Baudrillard Scene*. Australia: Stonemoss, 1984.

Freeman, Kathleen. *Ancilla to the Pre-Socratic Philosophers*. 1948. Cambridge: Harvard UP, 1983.

Freire, Paulo. *Pedagogy of the Oppressed*. Trans. Myra Bergman Ramos. New York: Continuum, 1989.

Freud, Sigmund. *Beyond the Pleasure Principle. The Standard Edition*. Vol. 18. London: Hogarth, 1955.

——. *Dora: An Analysis of a Case of Hysteria*. New York: Macmillan, 1963.

——. "Female Sexuality." *The Standard Edition*. Vol. 21. London: Hogarth, 1962. 225–43.

——. "Femininity." *The Standard Edition*. Vol. 22. London: Hogarth, 1964. 112–35.

——. "Some Psychical Consequences of the Anatomical Distinction Between the Sexes." *The Standard Edition*. Vol 19. London: Hogarth, 1961. 248–58.

——. "Three Essays on Sexuality." *The Standard Edition*. Vol. 7. London: Hogarth, 1953. 125–245.

Friedan, Betty. *The Feminine Mystique*. New York: Norton, 1963.

Friedman, Susan Stanford. "Post/Poststructuralist Feminist Criticism: The Politics of Recuperation and Negotiation." *New Literary History* 22 (1991): 465–90.

Frye, Marilyn. "On Being White: Toward a Feminist Understanding of Race and Race Supremacy." *The Politics of Reality: Essays in Feminist Theory*. Freedom: Crossing, 1983. 110–27.

——. *The Politics of Reality: Essays in Feminist Theory*. Freedom: Crossing, 1983.

Furley, David J. "Notes on Parmenides." *Exegesis and Argument*. Ed. E. N. Lee, A. P. D. Mourelatos, and R. M. Rorty. Assen, Netherlands: Van Gorcum, 1973. 1–15.

Fuss, Diana J. *Essentially Speaking: Feminism, Nature, and Difference*. New York: Routledge, 1989.

Gabilondo, Joseba. "Postcolonial Cyborgs." *The Cyborg Handbook*. Ed. Chris Hables Gray. New York: Routledge, 1995. 423–32.

Gadon, Elinor W. *The Once and Future Goddess: A Symbol for Our Time*. New York: Harper and Row, 1989.

Gaines, Robert N. "Knowledge and Discourse in Gorgias's On the Non-Existent or On Nature." *Philosophy and Rhetoric* 30.1 (1997): 1–12.

Gallop, Jane. *The Daughter's Seduction: Feminism and Psychoanalysis*. Ithaca: Cornell UP, 1982.

———. "French Theory and the Seduction of Feminism." *Men in Feminism*. Ed. Alice Jardine and Paul Smith. New York: Methuen, 1987. 111–15.

———. "Immoral Teachers." *Yale French Studies* 63 (1982): 117–28.

———. *Thinking Through the Body*. New York: Columbia UP, 1988.

Gane, Mike. *Baudrillard: Critical and Fatal Theory*. London: Routledge, 1991.

———. *Baudrillard's Bestiary: Baudrillard and Culture*. London: Routledge, 1991.

Gearhart, Sally Miller. "The Womanization of Rhetoric." *Women's Studies International Quarterly* 2 (1979): 195–201.

Geertz, Clifford. "Thick Description." *The Interpretation of Cultures: Selected Essays*. New York: Basic, 1973. 3–30.

Genosko, Gary. *Baudrillard and Signs: Signification Ablaze*. London: Routledge, 1994.

Gibson, James William. *Warrior Dreams: Violence and Manhood in Post-Vietnam America*. New York: Hill, 1994.

Gilligan, Carol. *In a Different Voice*. Cambridge: Harvard UP, 1982.

Girard, René. *Violence and the Sacred*. Baltimore: Johns Hopkins UP, 1977.

Giroux, Henry A. *Schooling for Democracy: Critical Pedagogy in the Modern Age*. London: Routledge, 1989.

Gleason, Maud W. *Making Men: Sophists and Self-Presentation in Ancient Rome*. Princeton: Princeton UP, 1995.

Gleick, James. *Chaos: Making a New Science*. New York: Penguin, 1987.

Glenn, Cheryl. *Rhetoric Retold: Regendering the Tradition from Antiquity through the Renaissance*. Carbondale: Southern Illinois UP, 1997.

———. "sex, lies, and manuscript: Refiguring Aspasia in the History of Rhetoric." *College Composition and Communication* 45.2 (May 1994): 180–99.

Gomperz, Theodor. *Greek Thinkers: A History of Ancient Philosophy*. Vol. 1. Trans. Laurie Magnus. 1901. London: Clowes, 1955.

Goodwater, Leanna. *Women in Antiquity: An Annotated Bibliography*. Metuchen: Scarecrow, 1975.

Gore, Jennifer M. *The Struggle for Pedagogies: Critical and Feminist Discourses as Regimes of Truth*. New York: Routledge, 1993.

Gorgias. "Encomium of Helen." *The Older Sophists*. Ed. Rosamond Kent Sprague. Columbia: U of South Carolina P, 1972. 50–54.

———. "On Nature." *The Older Sophists*. Ed. Rosamond Kent Sprague. Columbia: U of South Carolina P, 1972. 42–46.

Goshorn, A. Keith. "Jean Baudrillard's Radical Enigma." *Jean Baudrillard: The Disappearance of Art and Politics*. Ed. William Sterns and William Chaloupka. New York: St. Martin's, 1992. 209–32.

Grassi, Ernesto. "Rhetoric and Philosophy." *Philosophy and Rhetoric* 9.4 (1976): 200–16.

Gray, Chris Hables, Steven Mentor, and Heidi J. Figueroa-Sarriera. "Cyborgology: Constructing the Knowledge of Cybernetic Organisms." *The Cyborg Handbook*. Ed. Chris Hables Gray. New York: Routledge, 1995. 1–16.

Graybeal, Jean. *Language and "The Feminine" in Nietzsche and Heidegger*. Bloomington: Indiana UP, 1990.

Greimas, Algirdas Julien. "About Games." *Sub-stance* 25 (1980): 31–35.

Gronbeck, Bruce E. "Gorgias on Rhetoric and Poetic: A Rehabilitation." *Southern Speech Communication Journal* 38 (fall 1972): 27–38.

Gross, Nicolas P. *Amatory Persuasion in Antiquity*. Newark: U of Delaware P, 1985.

Grote, George. *A History of Greece*. Vol. 13. London: Murray, 1869.

Grumet, Madeleine. "Pedagogy for Patriarchy: The Feminization of Teaching." *Bitter Milk: Women and Teaching*. Amherst: U of Massachusetts P, 1988. 31–58.

Gubar, Susan. "This Is My Rifle, This is My Gun: World War II and the Blitz on Women." *Behind the Lines: Gender and the Two World Wars*. Ed. Margaret Randolph Higonnet et al. New Haven: Yale UP, 1983. 227–59.

Guthrie, W. K. C. *History of Greek Philosophy*. 6 vols. Cambridge: Cambridge UP, 1962–1981.

———. *The Sophists*. Cambridge: Cambridge UP, 1971.

Habermas, Jürgen. *Communication and the Evolution of Society*. Trans. Thomas McCarthy. Boston: Beacon, 1979.

———. *Legitimation Crisis*. Trans. Thomas McCarthy. Boston: Beacon, 1973.

———. "Modernity Versus Postmodernity." *New German Critique* 22 (winter 1981): 8–14.

———. *The Philosophical Discourse of Modernity: Twelve Lectures*. Trans. Frederick Lawrence. Cambridge: MIT P, 1987.

———. "Taking Aim at the Heart of the Present." *Foucault: A Critical Reader*. Ed. David Couzens Hoy. London: Blackwell, 1986. 103–8.

Hairston, Maxine C. "Breaking Our Bonds and Reaffirming Our Connections." *College Composition and Communication* 36 (1985): 272–82.

Halberstam, Judith, and Ira Livingston. *Posthuman Bodies*. Bloomington: Indiana UP, 1995.

Halloran, S. Michael. "Rhetoric in the American College Curriculum." *Pre/Text: The First Decade*. Ed. Victor J. Vitanza. Pittsburgh: U of Pittsburgh P, 1993. 93–116.

Halperin, David M. *One Hundred Years of Homosexuality and Other Essays on Greek Love*. New York: Routledge, 1990.

———. "Plato and Erotic Reciprocity." *CA* 5 (1986): 60–80.

———. "Platonic Eros and What Men Call Love." *Ancient Philosophy* 5 (1985): 161–204.

Halperin, David M., John J. Winkler, and Froma I. Zeitlin, eds. *Before Sexuality: The Construction of Erotic Experience in the Ancient Greek World*. Princeton: Princeton UP, 1989.

Haraway, Donna. "Ecce Homo, Ain't (Ar'n't) I a Woman, and Inappropriate/d Others: The Human in a Post-Humanist Landscape." *Feminists Theorize the Political*. Ed. Judith Butler and Joan W. Scott. New York: Routledge, 1992. 86–100.

———. "A Manifesto for Cyborgs: Science, Technology, and Socialist Feminism in the 1980s." *Feminism/Postmodernism.* Ed. Linda J. Nicholson. New York: Routledge, 1990. 190–233.

——. *Modest__Witness@Second__Millennium. FemaleMan©__Meets__Onco-Mouse.* New York: Routledge, 1997.

——. "Situated Knowledges: The Science Question in Feminism and the Privilege of Partial Perspective." *Feminist Studies* 14.3 (fall 1988): 575–99.

Harkin, Patricia, and John Schilb, eds. *Contending with Words: Composition and Rhetoric in a Postmodern Age.* New York: MLA, 1991.

Harpold, Terence. "The Contingencies of the Hypertext Link." *Writing on the Edge* 2.2 (spring 1991): 126–38.

Hartmann, Heidi. "The Unhappy Marriage of Marxism and Feminism: Towards a More Progressive Union." *Women and Revolution.* Ed. Lydia Sargent. Boston: Southend, 1981. 1–41.

Hartsock, Nancy. "The Feminist Standpoint: Developing the Ground for a Specifically Feminist Historical Materialism." *Discovering Reality.* Ed. Sandra Harding and Merrill B. Hintikka. Boston: Reidel, 1983. 283–310.

——. *Money, Sex, and Power: Toward a Feminist Historical Materialism.* Boston: Northeastern UP, 1985.

Havelock, Eric A. "The Linguistic Task of the Presocratics." *Language and Thought in Early Greek Philosophy.* Ed. Kevin Robb. LaSalle: Monist, 1983.

——. *The Muse Learns to Write: Reflections on Orality and Literacy from Antiquity to the Present.* New Haven: Yale UP, 1986.

——. *Preface to Plato.* Cambridge: Harvard UP, 1963.

Hays, Janice. "Intellectual Parenting and a Developmental Feminist Pedagogy of Writing." Ed. Louise Wetherbee Phelps and Janet Emig. *Feminine Principles and Women's Experience in American Composition and Rhetoric.* Pittsburgh: U of Pittsburgh P, 1995. 153–90.

Heath, Shirley Brice. "Protean Shapes in Literacy Events: Ever-shifting Oral and Literate Traditions." *Spoken and Written Language: Exploring Orality and Literacy.* Norwood: Ablex, 1982. 91–117.

Heath, Stephen. "Difference." *Screen* 19 (fall 1978): 51–112.

——. "Joan Riviere and the Masquerade." *Formations of Fantasy.* Ed. Victor Burgin, James Donald, and Cora Kaplan. London: Methuen, 1986. 45–61.

Hegel, G. W. F. *The History of Philosophy.* Trans. E. S. Haldane and Frances H. Simson. Vol. 1. 1940. London: Routledge, 1974.

——. *Phenomenology of Spirit.* Trans. A. V. Miller. Oxford: Clarendon, 1977.

Heidegger, Martin. *Early Greek Thinking.* Trans. David Farrell Krell and Frank A. Capuzzi. San Francisco: Harper, 1984.

——. "A Letter on Humanism." 1947. Trans. Frank A. Capuzzi and J. Glenn Gray. *Basic Writings.* Ed. D. F. Krell. London: Routledge, 1993.

——. *Nietzsche Volume 1: The Will to Power as Art.* Trans. David Farrell Krell. San Francisco: Harper, 1979.

——. *Nietzsche Volume 2: The Eternal Recurrence of the Same.* Trans. David Farrell Krell. San Francisco: Harper, 1984.

——. *Nietzsche Volume 3: The Will to Power as Knowledge and as Metaphysics.* Trans. Joan Stambaugh, David Farrell Krell, Frank A. Capuzzi. San Francisco: Harper, 1987.

——. *Nietzsche Volume 4: Nihilism.* Trans. Frank A. Capuzzi. San Francisco: Harper, 1982.

——. *On Time and Being.* Trans. Joan Stambaugh. New York: Harper, 1972.

——. *Parmenides.* Trans. Andre Schuwer and Richard Rojcewicz. Bloomington: Indiana UP, 1992.

——. "What Are Poets For?" *Poetry, Language, Thought.* New York: Harper, 1971.

Heim, Michael. *The Metaphysics of Virtual Reality.* New York: Oxford UP, 1993.

Hekman, Susan J. *Gender and Knowledge: Elements of a Postmodern Feminism.* Oxford: Polity, 1990.

——. "Reconstituting the Subject: Feminism, Modernism, and Postmodernism." *Hypatia* 6.2 (summer 1991): 44–63.

Hesiod. *Theogony.* Oxford: Clarendon, 1966.

Hohendahl, Peter U. "The Dialectic of Enlightenment." *New German Critique* 35 (spring–summer 1985): 3–26.

Holbrook, Sue Ellen. "Women's Work: The Feminizing of Composition." *Rhetoric Review* 9.2 (spring 1991): 201–29.

Holdcroft, David. "Irony as a Trope, and Irony as Discourse." *Poetics Today* 4.3 (1983): 493–511.

Hollis, Karyn L. "Feminism in Writing Workshops: A New Pedagogy." *College Composition and Communication* 43.3 (1992): 340–48.

Homer. *The Iliad.* Trans. E. V. Rieu. Harmondsworth, Eng.: Penguin, 1982.

hooks, bell. *Feminist Theory: From Margin to Center.* Boston: South End, 1984.

Houlgate, Stephen. *Hegel, Nietzsche and the Criticism of Metaphysics.* Cambridge: Cambridge UP, 1986.

Howard, Tharon. *A Rhetoric of Electronic Communities.* Greenwich: Ablex, 1997.

Hunt, Everett Lee. "Plato and Aristotle on Rhetoric and Rhetoricians." *Historical Studies of Rhetoric and Rhetoricians.* Ed. Raymond F. Howes. Ithaca: Cornell UP, 1961. 19–70.

Hunter, Dianne, ed. *Seduction and Theory.* Urbana: U of Illinois P, 1989.

Hunter, Susan. "A Woman's Place *Is* in the Composition Classroom." *Rhetoric Review* 9.2 (spring 1991): 230–45.

Hutcheon, Linda. *The Politics of Postmodernism.* London: Routledge, 1989.

Ijsseling, Samuel. *Rhetoric and Philosophy in Conflict.* The Hague: Martinus Nighoff, 1976.

Inwood, Michael. "Irony and Romanticism." *A Hegel Dictionary.* Oxford: Blackwell, 1992. 146–50.

Irigaray, Luce. *Marine Lover of Friedrich Nietzsche.* Trans. Gillian C. Gill. New York: Columbia UP, 1991.

——. *Speculum of the Other Woman.* Trans. Gillian C. Gill. Ithaca: Cornell UP, 1985.

——. *This Sex Which Is Not One.* Trans. Catherine Porter. Ithaca: Cornell UP, 1985.

Jaeger, Werner. *Paideia: The Ideals of Greek Culture.* 3 vols. Trans. Gilbert Highet. New York: Oxford UP, 1943–1945.

Jameson, Fredric. *Postmodernism, or, The Cultural Logic of Late Capitalism.* Durham: Duke UP, 1991.

——. "Postmodernism, or, The Cultural Logic of Late Capitalism." *New Left Review* 146 (July–Aug. 1984): 59–62.

Jardine, Alice A. *Gynesis: Configurations of Woman and Modernity.* Ithaca: Cornell UP, 1985.

Jarratt, Susan C. "Feminism and Composition: The Case for Conflict." *Contending with Words: Composition and Rhetoric in a Postmodern Age.* New York: MLA, 1991. 105–23.

——. "In Excess: Radical Extensions of Neopragmatism." *Rhetoric, Sophistry, Pragmatism.* Ed. Steven Mailloux. Cambridge: Cambridge UP, 1995. 206–27.

——. *Rereading the Sophists: Classical Rhetoric Refigured.* Carbondale: Southern Illinois UP, 1991.

——. "The Role of the Sophists in Histories of Consciousness." *Philosophy and Rhetoric* 23.2 (1990): 85–95.

Jarratt, Susan C., and Nedra C. Reynolds. "The Splitting Image: Contemporary Feminisms and the Ethics of *Ethos*." *Ethos: New Essays in Rhetorical and Critical Theory.* Ed. James S. Baumlin and Tita French Baumlin. Dallas: Southern Methodist UP, 1994. 37–63.

Jarratt, Susan C., and Lynn Worsham, eds. *Feminism and Composition Studies: In Other Words.* New York: MLA, 1998.

Jed, Stephanie H. *Chaste Thinking: The Rape of Lucretia and the Birth of Humanism.* Bloomington: Indiana UP, 1989.

Jeffords, Susan. *The Remasculinization of America: Gender and the Vietnam War.* Bloomington: Indiana UP, 1989.

Johnson, Barbara. "My Monster/My Self." *Diacritics* 12 (1982): 2–10.

Johnson, Buffie, and Tracy Boyd. "The Eternal Weaver." *Heresies* 2.1: 64–69.

Johnson-Eilola, Johndan. "Control and the Cyborg: Writing and Being Written in Hypertext." *JAC: A Journal of Composition Theory* 13.2 (1993): 381–400.

——. *Nostalgic Angels: Rearticulating Hypertext Writing.* Norwood: Ablex, 1997.

——. " 'Trying to See the Garden': Interdisciplinary Perspectives on Hypertext Use in Composition Instruction." *Writing on the Edge* 2.2 (spring 1991): 92–11.

Jones, Ann Rosalind. "Inscribing Femininity: French Theories of the Feminine." *Making a Difference: Feminist Literary Criticism.* Ed. Gayle Greene and Coppélia Kahn. London: Routledge, 1985. 80–112.

Kant, Immanuel. *Critique of Pure Reason.* Trans. and ed. Paul Guyer and Allen W. Wood. Cambridge: Cambridge UP, 1998.

——. "What is Enlightenment?" *Philosophical Writings.* Ed. Ernst Behler. New York: Continuum, 1986. 263–69.

Kaufmann, Angelica [Luanne T. Frank]. "Uncovering the Exhibitionist Goddesses I: 'The Metamorphoses of Baubo'" *Realms of Rhetoric.* Ed. Victor J. Vitanza and Michelle Ballif. Arlington: Rhetoric Society of America, 1990. 243–70.

Kellner, Douglas. *Jean Baudrillard: From Marxism to Postmodernism and Beyond.* Stanford: Stanford UP, 1989.

Kennedy, George A. *The Art of Persuasion in Greece.* Princeton: Princeton UP, 1963.

———. *Classical Rhetoric and Its Christian and Secular Tradition from Ancient to Modern Times.* Chapel Hill: U of North Carolina P, 1980.

———. "Helen's Web Unraveled." *Arethusa* 19.1 (1986): 5–14.

Kerferd, G. B. "Gorgias on Nature or That Which Is Not." *Phronesis* 1 (1955): 3–25.

———. *The Sophistic Movement.* Cambridge: Cambridge UP, 1981.

Keuls, Eva. *The Reign of the Phallus: Sexual Politics in Ancient Athens.* New York: Harper, 1985.

Kimbrell, Andrew. *The Masculine Mystique: The Politics of Masculinity.* New York: Ballantine, 1995.

Kinneavy, James L. *A Theory of Discourse.* Englewood Cliffs: Prentice, 1971.

Klein, Melanie. *Love, Guilt, and Reparation and Other Works, 1921–1945.* New York: Dell, 1975.

Klumpp, James F. "The Rhetoric of Community at Century's End." *Making and Unmaking the Prospects for Rhetoric.* Ed. Theresa Enos. Mahwah: Erlbaum, 1997. 75–82.

Koelb, Clayton, ed. *Nietzsche as Postmodernist.* New York: State U of New York P, 1990.

Kofman, Sarah. "Baubo: Theological Perversion and Fetishism." *Nietzsche's New Seas.* Ed. Michael Allen Gillespie and Tracy B. Strong. Chicago: U of Chicago P, 1988. 175–202.

———. *The Enigma of Woman: Woman in Freud's Writings.* Trans. Catherine Porter. Ithaca: Cornell UP, 1985.

———. "Metaphor, Symbol, Metamorphosis." *The New Nietzsche: Contemporary Styles of Interpretation.* Ed. David B. Allison. Cambridge: MIT P, 1985. 201–14.

———. "The Narcissistic Woman: Freud and Girard." *Diacritics* (Sept. 1980): 36–45.

———. "Nietzsche and the Obscurity of Heraclitus." *Diacritics* (fall 1987): 39–55.

Krell, David Farrell. *Postponements: Woman, Sensuality, and Death in Nietzsche.* Bloomington: Indiana UP, 1986.

Kristeva, Julia. *Black Sun: Depression and Melancholia.* New York: Columbia UP, 1989.

———. *Desire in Language.* Ed. Leon S. Roudiez. Trans. Thomas Gora, Alice Jardine, and Leon S. Roudiez. New York: Columbia UP, 1980.

———. "Oscillation Between Power and Denial." *New French Feminisms.* Ed. Elaine Marks and Isabelle de Courtivron. New York: Schocken, 1980. 165–67.

———. "Talking about Polylogue." Trans. Sean Hand. *French Feminist Thought: A Reader.* Ed. Toril Moi. New York: Blackwell, 1987.

———. "Woman Can Never Be Defined." *New French Feminisms.* Ed. Elaine Marks and Isabelle de Courtivron. New York: Schocken, 1980. 137–41.

———. "Women's Time." *Signs: Journal of Women in Culture and Society* 7 (1981): 13–35.

Kroker, Arthur, and David Cook. *The Postmodern Scene.* New York: St. Martin's, 1986.

Kroker, Arthur, and Marilouise Kroker, eds. *The Last Sex: Feminism and Outlaw Bodies.* New York: St. Martin's, 1993.

Kroker, Arthur, Marilouise Kroker, and David Cook. *Panic Encyclopedia: The Definitive Guide to the Postmodern Scene.* New York: St. Martin's, 1989.

Kroker, Arthur, and Michael Weinstein. *Data Trash: A Theory of the Virtual Class.* New York: St. Martin's, 1994.

Kuhn, Thomas S. *The Structure of Scientific Revolutions.* 2nd ed. Chicago: U of Chicago P, 1970.

Kundera, Milan. *The Joke.* 1967. New York: Harper, 1992.

Kustas, George L. "Before Discourse." *Colloquy 50.* Berkeley: Center for Hermeneutical Studies in Hellenistic and Modern Culture, 1986.

LaBelle, Maurice Marc. *Alfred Jarry: Nihilism and the Theater of the Absurd.* New York: New York UP, 1980.

Lacan, Jacques. *Écrits: A Selection.* Trans. Alan Sheridan. New York: Norton, 1977.

———. *The Four Fundamental Concepts of Psycho-Analysis.* Ed. Jacques-Alain Miller. Trans. Alan Sheridan. New York: Norton, 1981.

———. "The Signification of the Phallus." *Écrits: A Selection.* Trans. Alan Sheridan. New York: Norton, 1977. 281–91.

Lacan, Jacques, and the *école freudienne. Feminine Sexuality.* Ed. Juliet Mitchell and Jacqueline Rose. Trans. Jacqueline Rose. New York: Norton, 1982.

Lamb, Catherine E. "Beyond Argument in Feminist Composition." *College Composition and Communication* 42 (Feb. 1991): 11–24.

Lanham, Richard. *The Motives of Eloquence.* New Haven: Yale UP, 1976.

———. "The Rhetorical Paideia: The Curriculum as Work of Art." *College English* 48 (1986): 132–41.

Laqueur, Thomas. *Making Sex: Body and Gender from the Greeks to Freud.* Cambridge: Harvard UP, 1990.

Lassner, Phyllis. "Feminist Responses to Rogerian Argument." *Rhetoric Review* 8 (spring 1990): 220–32.

Lauer, Janice M. "The Feminization of Rhetoric and Composition Studies?" *Rhetoric Review* 13.2 (spring 1995): 276–85.

Lee, E. N., A. P. D. Mourelatos, and R. M. Rorty. *Exegesis and Argument.* Assen, Netherlands: Van Gorcum, 1973.

LeFevre, Karen Burke. *Invention as a Social Act.* Carbondale: Southern Illinois UP, 1987.

Lentricchia, Frank. *Criticism and Social Change.* Chicago: U of Chicago P, 1983.

Lentz, Tony. *Orality and Literacy in Hellenic Greece.* Carbondale: Southern Illinois UP, 1989.

Levin, Charles. *Jean Baudrillard: A Study in Cultural Metaphysics.* London: Prentice, 1996.

Lévi-Strauss, Claude. *The Elementary Structures of Kinship.* Trans. James Harle Bell and John Richard Von Sturmer. Boston: Beacon, 1969.

Liddell, Henry George, and Robert Scott. *A Greek-English Lexicon.* New York: Harper, 1852.

Limerick, Patricia Nelson. "Empire of Innocence." *The Legacy of Conquest: The Unbroken Past of the American West.* New York: Norton, 1987.

Lockard, Joseph. "Progressive Politics, Electronic Individualism and the Myth of Virtual Community." *Internet Culture.* Ed. David Porter. New York: Routledge, 1997. 219–32.

Loenen, J. H. M. M. *Parmenides, Melissus, Gorgias: A Reinterpretation of Eleatic Philosophy.* Assen, Netherlands: Van Gorcum, 1959.

Looser, Devoney. "Composing as an 'Essentialist'?: New Directions for Feminist Composition Theories." *Rhetoric Review* 12.1 (fall 1993): 54–69.

Loraux, Nicole. *The Experiences of Tiresias: The Feminine and the Greek Man.* Trans. Paula Wissing. Princeton: Princeton UP, 1995.

Lovejoy, Arthur O. *The Great Chain of Being: A Study of the History of an Idea.* Cambridge: Harvard UP, 1964.

Luke, Carmen, and Jennifer Gore, ed. *Feminisms and Critical Pedagogy.* New York: Routledge, 1992.

Lunsford, Andrea. "Aristotelian vs. Rogerian Argument: A Reassessment." *College Composition and Communication* 30.2 (May 1979): 146–51.

———. "Introduction." *Reclaiming Rhetorica: Women in the Rhetorical Tradition.* Ed. Andrea Lunsford. Pittsburgh: U of Pittsburgh P, 1995. 3–8.

Lunsford, Andrea, and Lisa Ede. "Why Write . . . Together: A Research Update." *Rhetoric Review* 5.1 (fall 1986): 71–77.

Lyotard, Jean-François. *The Differend: Phrases in Dispute.* 1983. Trans. Georges Van Den Abbeele. Minneapolis: U of Minnesota P, 1988.

———. *The Inhuman: Reflections on Time.* Trans. Geoffrey Bennington and Rachel Bowlby. Stanford: Stanford UP, 1991.

———. "One of the Things at Stake in Women's Struggles." *The Lyotard Reader.* Ed. Andrew Benjamin. Oxford: Blackwell, 1989. 111–21.

———. *The Postmodern Condition: A Report on Knowledge.* Trans. Geoff Bennington and Brian Massumi. Minneapolis: U of Minnesota P, 1988.

Lyotard, Jean-François, and Jean-Loup Thébaud. *Just Gaming.* Trans. Wlad Godzich. Minneapolis: U of Minnesota P, 1985.

Macauley, William R., and Angel J. Gordo-Lopez. "From Cognitive Psychologies to Mythologies." *The Cyborg Handbook.* Ed. Chris Hables Gray. New York: Routledge, 1995. 433–44.

MacDowell, D. M. *Gorgias: Encomium of Helen.* Bristol, Eng.: Bristol, 1982.

MacKinnon, Catharine A. *Feminism Unmodified: Discourses on Life and Law.* Cambridge: Harvard UP, 1987.

Macrorie, Ken. *Telling Writing.* Rochelle Park: Hayden, 1970.

Magnus, Bernd, Stanley Stewart, and Jean-Pierre Mileur. *Nietzsche's Case: Philosophy as/and Literature.* New York: Routledge, 1993.

Mailloux, Steven. "Afterword: A Pretext for Rhetoric: Dancing 'Round the Revolution." *Pre/Text: The First Decade.* Ed. Victor J. Vitanza. Pittsburgh: U of Pittsburgh P, 1993. 299–314.

———. *Reception Histories: Rhetoric, Pragmatism, and American Cultural Politics.* Ithaca: Cornell UP, 1998.

———. *Rhetorical Power.* Ithaca: Cornell UP, 1989.

———. "Rhetoric 2000: The New Prospects." *Making and Unmaking the Prospects for Rhetoric.* Ed. Theresa Enos. Mahwah: Erlbaum, 1997. 49–54.

———. "Sophistry and Rhetorical Pragmatism." *Rhetoric, Sophistry, Pragmatism.* Ed. Steven Mailloux. Cambridge: Cambridge UP, 1995. 1–31.

Marks, Elaine, and Isabelle de Courtivron. *New French Feminisms.* New York: Schocken, 1980.

Martin, Biddy. *Woman and Modernity: The (Life)styles of Lou Andreas-Salomé.* Ithaca: Cornell UP, 1991.

Masson, Jeffrey Moussaieff. *The Assault on Truth: Freud's Suppression of the Seduction Theory.* New York: Farrar, 1984.

———. *A Dark Science: Women, Sexuality and Psychiatry in the Nineteenth Century.* New York: Farrar, 1986.

Mauss, Marcel. *The Gift: Forms and Functions of Exchange in Archaic Societies.* Trans. Ian Cunnison. Glencoe: Free, 1954.

McComiskey, Bruce. "Gorgias and the Art of Rhetoric: Toward a Holistic Reading of the Extant Gorgianic Fragments." *Rhetoric Society Quarterly* 27.4 (fall 1997): 5–24.

McLaren, Peter. *Revolutionary Multiculturalism: Pedagogies of Dissent for the New Millennium.* Boulder: Westview, 1997.

Miller, Susan. "The Feminization of Composition." *Politics of Writing Instruction: Postsecondary.* Ed. Richard Bullock and John Trimbur. Portsmouth, NH: Boynton, 1991. 39–53.

———. *Rescuing the Subject: A Critical Introduction to Rhetoric and the Writer.* Carbondale: Southern Illinois UP, 1989.

———. "What Does It Mean to Be Able to Write? The Question of Writing in the Discourses of Literature and Composition." *College English* 45 (Mar. 1983): 219–35.

Mitchell, Juliet. "Introduction—I." *Feminine Sexuality.* By Jacques Lacan and the *école freudienne.* Ed. Juliet Mitchell and Jacqueline Rose. Trans. Jacqueline Rose. New York: Norton, 1982. 1–26.

Modleski, Tania. *Feminism Without Women: Culture and Criticism in a "Postfeminist" Age.* New York: Routledge, 1991.

Montrelay, Michèle. "Inquiry into Femininity." *m/f* 1 (1978): 83–101.

Moore, Suzanne. "Getting a Bit of the Other—the Pimps of Postmodernism." *Male Order: Unwrapping Masculinity.* London: Lawrence, 1988. 165–92.

Morgan, Thais E. "A Whip of One's Own: Dominatrix Pornography and the Construction of a Post-Modern (Female) Subjectivity." *American Journal of Semiotics* 6.4 (1989): 109–36.

Morris, Meaghan. *The Pirate's Fiancée.* London: Verso, 1988.

Morrison, Margaret. "Review of *Woman and Modernity: The (Life)styles of Lou Andreas-Salomé* by Biddy Martin." *Studies in Psychoanalytic Theory* 1.2 (fall 1992): 120–25.

Moss, Roger. "The Case for Sophistry." *Rhetoric Revealed.* Ed. Brian Vickers. Binghamton: Center for Medieval and Early Renaissance Studies, 1982. 207–24.

Mouffe, Chantal. "Feminism, Citizenship and Radical Democratic Politics." *Feminists Theorize the Political.* Ed. Judith Butler and Joan W. Scott. New York: Routledge, 1992. 369–83.

———. *The Return of the Political.* London: Verso, 1993.

———, ed. *Deconstruction and Pragmatism.* London: Routledge, 1996.

Moulthrop, Stuart. "In the Zones: Hypertext and the Politics of Interpretation." *Writing on the Edge* 1.1 (fall 1989): 18–27.

Mourelatos, Alexander P. D. "Heraclitus, Parmenides, and the Naive Metaphysics of Things." *Exegesis and Argument.* Ed. E. N. Lee, A. P. D. Mourelatos, and R. M. Rorty. Assen, Netherlands: Van Gorcum, 1973. 16–48.

Mukarovsky, Jan. *Aesthetic Function, Norm and Value as Social Facts.* Trans. Mark E. Suino. Ann Arbor: U of Michigan P, 1970.

Murray, Donald M. "Teaching the Other Self: The Writer's First Reader." *College Composition and Communication* 33.2 (May 1982): 140–47.

Myers, Greg. "Reality, Consensus, and Reform in the Rhetoric of Composition Teaching." *College English* 48.2 (Feb. 1986): 154–73.

Myers, Linnet. "U.S. Leads Other Nations in Rape Cases." *Atlanta Journal-Constitution.* Dec. 3, 1995. C13.

Nancy, Jean-Luc. "Shattered Love." *The Inoperative Community.* Trans. Peter Connor, Lisa Garbus, Michael Holland, and Simona Sawhney. Minneapolis: U of Minnesota P, 1991. 82–109.

——. "The Unsacrificeable." *Yale French Studies* 79 (1991): 20–38.

Neel, Jasper. *Aristotle's Voice: Rhetoric, Theory, and Writing in America.* Carbondale: Southern Illinois UP, 1994.

——. *Plato, Derrida, and Writing.* Carbondale: Southern Illinois UP, 1988.

Nelson, Mariah Burton. *The Stronger Women Get, the More Men Love Football: Sexism and the American Culture of Sports.* New York: Harcourt, 1994.

Nicholson, Linda J., ed. *Feminism/Postmodernism.* New York: Routledge, 1990.

Nietzsche, Friedrich. *Beyond Good and Evil.* Trans. Walter Kaufmann. New York: Vintage, 1966.

——. *The Birth of Tragedy and the Case of Wagner.* Trans. Walter Kaufmann. New York: Vintage, 1967.

——. *Ecce Homo.* Trans. Walter Kaufmann. New York: Vintage, 1969.

——. *Friedrich Nietzsche on Rhetoric and Language.* Ed., trans., and intro. Sander L. Gilman, Carole Blair, and David J. Parent. New York: Oxford UP, 1989.

——. *The Gay Science.* Trans. Walter Kaufmann. New York: Vintage, 1974.

——. "The Greek Woman." *The World's Best Essays.* Ed. F. H. Pritchard. New York: Boni, 1929. 576–79.

——. "Homer's Contest." *The Portable Nietzsche.* Trans. Walter Kaufmann. New York: Viking, 1954. 32–39.

——. *Human, All Too Human.* Trans. R. J. Hollingdale. Cambridge: Cambridge UP, 1986.

——. *My Sister and I.* Trans. Oscar Levy. 1951. Los Angeles: Amok, 1990.

——. *On the Genealogy of Morals.* Trans. Walter Kaufmann. New York: Vintage, 1969.

——. "On Truth and Lying in an Extra-Moral Sense." *Friedrich Nietzsche on Rhetoric and Language.* Ed., trans., and intro. Sander L. Gilman, Carole Blair, and David J. Parent. New York: Oxford UP, 1989. 246–57.

——. *Philosophy in the Tragic Age of the Greeks.* Trans. Marianne Cowan. Chicago: Regnery, 1962.

——. *Thus Spoke Zarathustra.* Trans. R. J. Hollingdale. London: Penguin, 1961.

——. *Twilight of the Idols and The Anti-Christ.* London: Penguin, 1968.

——. *Untimely Meditations.* Trans. R. J. Hollingdale. Cambridge: Cambridge UP, 1983.

——. *The Will to Power.* Trans. Walter Kaufmann and R. J. Hollingdale. Ed. Walter Kaufmann. New York: Vintage, 1967.

Nussbaum, Martha C. *The Fragility of Goodness: Luck and Ethics in Greek Tragedy and Philosophy.* Cambridge: Cambridge UP, 1986.

Nye, Andrea. *Words of Power: A Feminist Reading of the History of Logic.* New York: Routledge, 1990.

Oakeshott, Michael. *Rationalism in Politics.* New York: Basic, 1962.

Oliver, Kelly, ed. *Ethics, Politics, and Difference in Julia Kristeva's Writing.* New York: Routledge, 1993.

——. *Womanizing Nietzsche: Philosophy's Relation to the "Feminine."* New York: Routledge, 1995.

Olivier, Christiane. *Jocasta's Children: The Imprint of the Mother.* Trans. George Craig. New York: Routledge, 1989.

Olson, David R. "Cognitive Consequences of Literacy." *Canadian Psychology* 27.2 (1986): 109–21.

Olson, Gary A. "Social Construction and Composition Theory: A Conversation with Richard Rorty." *Journal of Advanced Composition.* 9.1 and 2 (1989): 1–9.

——. "Writing, Literacy and Technology: Toward a Cyborg Writing." *JAC: A Journal of Composition Theory* 16.1 (winter 1996): 1–26.

Ong, Walter J., S.J. *Orality and Literacy.* New York: Methuen, 1982.

——. *Ramus: Method and the Decay of Dialogue.* 1958. Cambridge: Harvard UP, 1983.

Osborne, Robin. "Women and Sacrifice in Classical Greece." *Classical Quarterly* 43.2 (1993): 392–405.

Padel, Ruth. "Women: Model for Possession by Greek Daemons." *Images of Women in Antiquity.* Ed. Averil Cameron and Amelie Kuhrt. London: Helm, 1983. 3–19.

Paglia, Camille. *Sexual Personae: Art and Decadence from Nefertiti to Emily Dickinson.* New York: Vintage, 1990.

Palmer, Richard. *Hermeneutics.* Evanston: Northwestern UP, 1969.

Parmenides. *Ancilla to the Pre-Socratic Philosophers.* Kathleen Freeman. Cambridge: Harvard UP, 1983. 41–46.

Patton, Paul., ed. *Nietzsche, Feminism and Political Theory.* London: Routledge, 1993.

Pecora, Vincent P. "Ethics, Politics, and the Middle Voice." *Yale French Studies* 79 (1991): 203–30.

——. "Nietzsche, Genealogy, Critical Theory." *New German Critique* 53 (spring/summer 1991): 104–30.

Pefanis, Julian. *Heterology and the Postmodern: Bataille, Baudrillard, and Lyotard.* Durham: Duke UP, 1991.

Peradotto, John, and J. P. Sullivan, eds. *Women in the Ancient World: The Arethusa Papers.* Albany: State U of New York P, 1984.

Perelman, Chaim, and Madame Olbrechts-Tyteca. *The New Rhetoric: A Treatise on Argumentation.* Trans. John Wilkinson and Purcell Weaver. 1958. Notre Dame: U of Notre Dame P, 1969.

Perez, Rolando. *On An(archy) and Schizoanalysis.* New York: Autonomedia, 1990.

Perniola, Mario. "Logique de la seduction." *Traverses* 18 (Feb. 1980): 2–9.

Peters, H. F. *My Sister, My Spouse: A Biography of Lou Andreas-Salomé.* New York: Norton, 1962.

——. *Zarathustra's Sister.* New York: Wiener, 1977.

Phelps, Louise Wetherbee. "Becoming a Warrior: Lessons of the Feminist Workplace." *Feminine Principles and Women's Experience in American Composition and Rhetoric.* Ed. Louise Wetherbee Phelps and Janet Emig. Pittsburgh: U of Pittsburgh P, 1995. 289–339.

Phelps, Louise Wetherbee, and Janet Emig, eds. *Feminine Principles and Women's Experience in American Composition and Rhetoric.* Pittsburgh: U of Pittsburgh P, 1995.

Plato. *Cratylus. The Collected Dialogues of Plato.* Ed. Edith Hamilton and Huntington Cairns. Princeton: Princeton UP, 1961.

———. *Gorgias.* Trans. W. C. Helmbold. New York: Macmillan, 1952.

———. *Menexenus.* Trans. R. G. Bury. Cambridge: Harvard UP, 1966.

———. *Meno. Plato: Five Dialogues.* Trans. G. M. A. Grube. Indianapolis: Hackett, 1981.

———. *Phaedo. Great Dialogues of Plato.* Trans. W. H. D. Rouse. New York: New American, 1956.

———. *Phaedrus.* Trans. W. C. Helmbold and W. G. Rabinowitz. Indianapolis: Bobbs, 1956.

———. *Protagoras. The Collected Dialogues of Plato.* Ed. Edith Hamilton and Huntington Cairns. Princeton: Princeton UP, 1961.

———. *Republic.* Trans. Desmond Lee. Harmondsworth, Eng.: Penguin, 1987.

———. *The Sophist.* Trans. Harold North Fowler. Cambridge: Harvard UP, 1952.

———. *Symposium. Great Dialogues of Plato.* Trans. W. H. D. Rouse. New York: New American, 1956.

———. *Theaetetus. The Collected Dialogues of Plato.* Ed. Edith Hamilton and Huntington Cairns. Princeton: Princeton UP, 1961.

———. *Timaeus. The Collected Dialogues of Plato.* Ed. Edith Hamilton and Huntington Cairns. Princeton: Princeton UP, 1961.

Plutarch. *Selected Lives.* Franklin Center: Franklin, 1982.

Podach, E. F. *The Madness of Nietzsche.* Trans. F. A. Voight. London: Putnam, 1931.

Porter, James L. "The Seductions of Gorgias." *Classical Antiquity* 12.2 (Oct. 1993): 267–99.

Poster, Mark. "Cyberdemocracy: Internet and the Public Sphere." *Internet Culture.* Ed. David Porter. New York: Routledge, 1997. 201–18.

Poulakos, John. "Gorgias' *Encomium to Helen* and the Defense of Rhetoric." *Rhetorica* 1.2 (autumn 1983): 1–16.

———. "Hegel's Reception of the Sophists." *Western Journal of Speech Communication* 54 (spring 1990): 160–71.

———. "Interpreting Sophistical Rhetoric: A Response to Schiappa." *Philosophy and Rhetoric* 23.3 (1990): 218–28.

———. "Kairos in Gorgias' Rhetorical Compositions." *Rhetoric and Kairos: Essays in History, Theory, and Praxis.* Ed. Phillip Sipiora and James S. Baumlin. Albany: State U of New York P, forthcoming.

———. "Nietzsche and Histories of Rhetoric." *Writing Histories of Rhetoric.* Ed. Victor J. Vitanza. Carbondale: Southern Illinois UP, 1994. 81–97.

———. "Rhetoric, the Sophists, and the Possible." *Communication Monographs* 51 (Sept. 1984): 215–26.

——. *Sophistical Rhetoric in Classical Greece.* Columbia: U of South Carolina P, 1995.

——. "Toward a Sophistic Definition of Rhetoric." *Philosophy and Rhetoric* 16 (1983): 35–48.

Poulakos, Takis. "Human Agency in the History of Rhetoric: Gorgias' *Encomium of Helen.*" *Writing Histories of Rhetoric.* Ed. Victor J. Vitanza. Carbondale: Southern Illinois UP, 1994. 59–80.

Prigogine, Ilya, and Isabelle Stengers. *Order out of Chaos: Man's New Dialogue with Nature.* Toronto: Bantam, 1984.

Rankin, H. D. *The Sophists, Socratics, and Cynics.* Totowa: Barnes, 1983.

Ratcliffe, Krista. *Anglo-American Feminist Challenges to the Rhetorical Traditions: Virginia Woolf, Mary Daly, and Adrienne Rich.* Carbondale: Southern Illinois UP, 1995.

Reddy, Michael. "The Conduit Metaphor." *Metaphor and Thought.* Ed. Andrew Ortony. London: Cambridge UP, 1979. 284–324.

Reichert, Pegeen. "A Contributing Listener and Other Composition Wives: Reading and Writing the Feminine Metaphors in Composition Studies." *JAC: A Journal of Composition Theory* 16.1 (1996): 141–58.

Reynolds, Nedra, et al. "Fragments in Response: An Electronic Discussion of Lester *Faigley's Fragments of Rationality.*" *College Composition and Communication* 45.2 (May 1994): 264–73.

Rice, Donald. "Catastrop(h)es: The Morphogenesis of Metaphor, Metonymy, Synecdoche, and Irony." *Sub-stance* 26 (1980): 3–18.

Rich, Adrienne. *Blood, Bread, and Poetry.* New York: Norton, 1986.

——. *Of Woman Born: Motherhood as Experience and Institution.* New York: Bantam, 1976.

Rieff, Philip. Introduction. *Dora: An Analysis of a Case of Hysteria.* By Sigmund Freud. New York: Macmillan, 1963. 7–20.

Riley, Denise. *"Am I That Name?" Feminism and the Category of "Women" in History.* Minneapolis: U of Minnesota P, 1988.

Riviere, Joan. "Womanliness as a Masquerade." *Formations of Fantasy.* Ed. Victor Burgin, James Donald, and Cora Kaplan. London: Methuen, 1986. 35–44.

Ronell, Avital. "Support Our Tropes II (Or Why in Cyburbia There Are a Lot of Cowboys)." *Yale Journal of Criticism* 5.2 (spring 1992): 73–80.

Rorty, Richard. *Consequences of Pragmatism.* Minneapolis: U of Minnesota P, 1982.

——. *Contingency, Irony, and Solidarity.* Cambridge: Cambridge UP, 1989.

——. "Habermas and Lyotard on Postmodernity." *Habermas and Modernity.* Ed. Richard J. Bernstein. Cambridge: MIT P, 1985. 161–75.

——. *Philosophy and the Mirror of Nature.* Princeton: Princeton UP, 1979.

——. "Response to Simon Critchley." *Deconstruction and Pragmatism.* Ed. Chantal Mouffe. London: Routledge, 1996. 41–46.

Rose, Jacqueline. "Introduction—II." *Feminine Sexuality.* By Jacques Lacan and the *école freudienne.* Ed. Juliet Mitchell and Jacqueline Rose. Trans. Jacqueline Rose. New York: Norton, 1982. 27–57.

Rose, Mike. *Lives on the Boundary.* New York: Penguin, 1989.

Rosenmeyer, Thomas G. "Gorgias, Aeschylus, and Apate." *American Journal of Philology* 76.3 (1955): 225–60.

Rotundo, E. Anthony. *American Manhood: Transformations in Masculinity from the Revolution to the Modern Era.* New York: Basic, 1993.

Rowe, John Carlos. "Surplus Economies: Deconstruction, Ideology, and the Humanities." *The Aims of Representation: Subject/Text/History.* Ed. Murray Krieger. New York: Columbia UP, 1987. 131–58.

Royster, Jacqueline Jones. "When the First Voice You Hear Is Not Your Own." *College Composition and Communication* 47.1 (Feb. 1996): 29–40.

Ruddick, Sara. "Maternal Thinking." *Mothering: Essays in Feminist Theory.* Ed. Joyce Trebilcot. Totowa: Rowman, 1984. 213–30.

Russell, David. *Writing in the Academic Disciplines.* Carbondale: Southern Illinois UP, 1991.

Ryan, Michael. "Deconstruction and Radical Teaching." *Yale French Studies* 63 (1982): 45–58.

Salomé, Lou. *Nietzsche.* 1894. Redding Ridge: Black Swan, 1988.

Schiappa, Edward. "Did Plato Coin Rhetorike?" *American Journal of Philology* 111 (1990): 457–70.

———. "An Examination and Exculpation of the Composition Style of Gorgias of Leontini." *Pre/Text* 12.3–4 (fall/winter 1991): 237–57.

———. "Gorgias's Helen Revisited." *Quarterly Journal of Speech* 81 (1995): 310–24.

———. "Interpreting Gorgias's 'Being' in *On Not-Being or On Nature.*" *Philosophy and Rhetoric* 30.1 (1997): 13–30.

———. "Neo-Sophistic Rhetorical Criticism or the Historical Reconstruction of Sophistic Doctrines?" *Philosophy and Rhetoric* 23.3 (1990): 192–217.

———. *Protagoras and Logos.* Columbia: U of South Carolina P, 1991.

———. "Sophistic Rhetoric: Oasis or Mirage?" *Rhetoric Review* 10.1 (fall 1991): 5–18.

Schilb, John. "Cultural Studies, Postmodernism, and Composition." *Contending with Words.* Ed. Patricia Harkin and John Schilb. New York: MLA, 1991. 173–88.

Schneiderman, Stuart. *Jacques Lacan: The Death of an Intellectual Hero.* Cambridge: Harvard UP, 1983.

Schor, Naomi. "Dreaming Dissymetry: Barthes, Foucault, and Sexual Difference." *Men in Feminism.* Ed. Alice Jardine and Paul Smith. New York: Methuen, 1987. 98–110.

Schott, Robin May. *Cognition and Eros.* Boston: Beacon, 1988.

Schrag, Calvin O. "Rhetoric Resituated at the End of Philosophy." *Quarterly Journal of Speech* 71 (1985): 164–74.

Schutte, Ofelia. *Beyond Nihilism: Nietzsche Without Masks.* Chicago: U of Chicago P, 1984.

———. "Nietzsche on Gender Difference: A Critique." *Newsletter on Feminism and Philosophy* 88.3 (1989): 31–35.

Scott, Joan W. "Experience." *Feminists Theorize the Political.* Ed. Judith Butler and Joan W. Scott. New York: Routledge, 1992. 22–40.

———. *Gender and the Politics of History.* New York: Columbia, 1988.

Scott, Robert. "On Viewing Rhetoric as Epistemic." *Professing the New Rheto-*

rics. Ed. Theresa Enos and Stuart C. Brown. Englewood Cliffs: Blair, 1994. 307–18.

Segal, Charles P. "Gorgias and the Psychology of the Logos." *Harvard Studies in Classical Philology* 66 (1962): 99–155.

———. "The Music of the Sphinx: The Problem of Language in Oedipus Tyrannus." *Contemporary Literary Hermeneutics and Interpretation of Classical Texts.* Ed. Stephanus Kresic. Ottawa: Ottawa UP, 1981. 151–63.

Serres, Michel. *Hermes: Literature, Science, Philosophy.* Ed. Josué V. Harari and David F. Bell. Baltimore: Johns Hopkins UP, 1982.

———. "Noise." *Sub-stance* 40 (1983): 48–60.

Sextus Empiricus. *Against the Logicians.* 3 vols. Trans. R. G. Bury. Cambridge: Harvard UP, 1935, 1957, 1961.

Shapiro, Gary. *Alcyone: Nietzsche on Gifts, Noise, and Women.* New York: State U of New York P, 1991.

Shor, Ira. *Critical Teaching and Everyday Life.* Boston: South End, 1980.

Silverman, Kaja. *The Acoustic Mirror: The Female Voice in Psychoanalysis and Cinema.* Bloomington: Indiana UP, 1988.

———. *Male Subjectivity at the Margins.* New York: Routledge, 1992.

———. *The Subject of Semiotics.* New York: Oxford UP, 1983.

Simmel, Georg. *Schopenhauer and Nietzsche.* Amherst: U of Massachusetts P, 1986.

Simpson, Mark. *Male Impersonators: Men Performing Masculinity.* New York: Routledge, 1994.

Sipiora, Phillip. "The Ancient Concept of *Kairos.*" *Rhetoric and Kairos: Essays in History, Theory, and Praxis.* Ed. Phillip Sipiora and James Baumlin. Albany: State U of New York P, 2000.

Sipiora, Phillip, and Janet Atwill. "Rhetoric and Cultural Explanation: A Discussion with Gayatri Chakravorty Spivak." *Journal of Advanced Composition* 10.2 (fall 1990): 293–304.

Sirc, Geoffrey. "Writing Classroom as A and P Parking Lot." *Pre/Text* 14.1–2 (1993): 27–70.

Skinner, Marilyn, ed. *Rescuing Creusa: New Methodological Approaches to Women in Antiquity.* Special issue of *Helios* 13(2). Lubbock: Texas Tech UP, 1987.

Sloterdijk, Peter. *Thinker on Stage: Nietzsche's Materialism.* Trans. Jamie Owen Daniel. Minneapolis: U of Minnesota P, 1989.

Smith, Bromley. "Gorgias: A Study of Oratorical Style." *Quarterly Journal of Speech Education* 7.4 (Nov. 1921): 335–59.

Smith, Paul. *Discerning the Subject.* Minneapolis: U of Minnesota P, 1988.

Soper, Kate. *Humanism and Anti-Humanism.* La Salle: Open Court, 1986.

Sophocles. *Antigone. The Theban Plays.* Trans. E. F. Watling. London: Penguin, 1974.

Sorell, Walter. *Three Women: Lives of Sex and Genius.* Indianapolis: Bobbs, 1975.

Spelman, Elizabeth V. *Inessential Woman: Problems of Exclusion in Feminist Thought.* Boston: Beacon, 1988.

———. "Woman as Body: Ancient and Contemporary Views." *Feminist Studies* 8.1 (spring 1982): 109–31.

Spivak, Gayatri Chakravorty. "Can the Subaltern Speak?" *Marxism and the Interpretation of Culture.* Ed. Cary Nelson and Lawrence Grossberg. Urbana: U of Illinois P, 1988. 271–313.

——. "Displacement and the Discourse of Woman." *Displacement: Derrida and After.* Ed. Mark Krupnick. Bloomington: Indiana UP, 1983.

——. "Feminism and Deconstruction, Again: Negotiating with Unacknowledged Masculinism." *Between Feminism and Psychoanalysis.* Ed. Teresa Brennan. London: Routledge, 1989. 206–23.

——. "In a Word, Interview." *Differences: A Journal of Feminist Cultural Studies* 1 (summer 1989): 124–56.

——. *The Post-Colonial Critic: Interviews, Strategies, Dialogues.* Ed. Sarah Harasym. New York: Routledge, 1990.

Sprague, Rosamond Kent, ed. *The Older Sophists.* Columbia: U of South Carolina P, 1972.

Starhawk. "Feminist, Earth-based Spirituality and Ecofeminism." *Healing the Wounds: The Promise of Ecofeminism.* Ed. Judith Plant. Philadelphia: New Society, 1989.

Steele, Shelby. "I'm Black, You're White, Who's Innocent?" *The Content of Our Character: A New Vision of Race in America.* New York: St. Martin's, 1990.

Sterns, William, and William Chaloupka. *Jean Baudrillard: The Disappearance of Art and Politics.* New York: St. Martin's, 1992.

Stillman, Linda Klieger. *Alfred Jarry.* Boston: Twayne, 1983.

Stone, John D. "Classical Female Rhetoricians." Unpublished ms.

Stone, Merlin. *When God Was a Woman.* New York: Dorset, 1976.

Stone, Sandy. "Split Subjects, Not Atoms; or, How I Fell in Love with My Prosthesis." *The Cyborg Handbook.* Ed. Chris Hables Gray. New York: Routledge, 1995. 393–406.

Stratton, Jon. "Cyberspace and the Globalization of Culture." *Internet Culture.* Ed. David Porter. New York: Routledge, 1997. 253–76.

Strong, Tracy B. *Friedrich Nietzsche and the Politics of Transfiguration.* Berkeley: U of California P, 1975.

Suleiman, Susan Rubin. "Writing and Motherhood." *The (M)other Tongue: Essays in Feminist Psychoanalytic Interpretation.* Ed. Shirley Nelson Garner, Claire Kahane, and Madelon Sprengnether. Ithaca: Cornell UP, 1985. 352–77.

Sutton, Jane. "The Death of Rhetoric and Its Rebirth in Philosophy." *Rhetorica* 4.3 (summer 1986): 203–26.

——. "The Taming of *Polos/Polis:* Rhetoric as an Achievement Without Woman." *Southern Communication Journal* 57 (1992): 97–119.

Suzuki, Mihoko. *Metamorphoses of Helen: Authority, Difference, and the Epic.* Ithaca: Cornell UP, 1989.

Swearingen, C. Jan. "Literate Rhetors and Their Illiterate Audiences: The Orality of Early Literacy." *Pre/Text* 7.3–4 (fall/winter 1986): 145–64.

——. *Rhetoric and Irony: Western Literacy and Western Lies.* New York: Oxford UP, 1991.

Swearingen, C. Jan, and Diane Mowery. "Ecofeminist Poetics: A Dialogue on Keeping Body and Mind Together." *Composition in Context.* Ed. W. Ross

Winterowd and Vincent Gillespie. Carbondale: Southern Illinois UP, 1994. 219–34.

Tallen, Bette S. "How Inclusive Is Feminist Political Theory?" *Lesbian Philosophies and Cultures.* Ed. Jeffner Allen. Albany: State U of New York P, 1990. 241–57.

Tedesco, Janis. "Women's Ways of Knowing/Women's Ways of Composing." *Rhetoric Review* 9.2 (spring 1991): 246–57.

Theweleit, Klaus. *Male Fantasies, Volume 1: Women, Floods, Bodies, History.* Trans. Stephen Conway. Minneapolis: U of Minnesota P, 1987.

———. *Male Fantasies, Volume 2: Male Bodies—Psychoanalyzing the White Terror.* Trans. Erica Carter and Chris Turner. Minneapolis: U of Minnesota P, 1989.

Thiele, Leslie Paul. *Friedrich Nietzsche and the Politics of the Soul.* Princeton: Princeton UP, 1990.

Thom, René. "At the Boundaries of Man's Power: Play." *Sub-stance* 25 (1980): 11–19.

———. "Remarks for the Polylogue on Play." *Sub-stance* 25 (1980): 36–38.

Thornton, Bruce S. *Eros: The Myth of Ancient Greek Sexuality.* Boulder: Westview, 1997.

Thucydides. *Thucydides.* Vol. 1. Trans. Benjamin Jowett. Oxford: Clarendon, 1900.

Todorov, Tzvetan. *Theories of the Symbol.* Trans. Catherine Porter. Ithaca: Cornell UP, 1982.

Tomlinson, Hugh. Preface to the English translation. *Nietzsche and Philosophy.* By Gilles Deleuze. New York: Columbia UP, 1983. ix–xiv.

Trimbur, John. "Composition Studies: Postmodern or Popular?" *Into the Field: Sites of Composition Studies.* Ed. Anne Ruggles Gere. New York: MLA, 1993. 117–32.

———. "Consensus and Difference in Collaborative Learning." *College English* 51.6 (Oct. 1989): 602–16.

Turner, Victor, and Edward M. Bruner, ed. *The Anthropology of Experience.* Urbana: U of Illinois P, 1986.

Tyler, Stephen A. *The Unspeakable: Discourse, Dialogue, and Rhetoric in the Postmodern World.* Madison: U of Wisconsin P, 1987.

Ulmer, Gregory L. *Applied Grammatology: Post(e)-Pedagogy from Jacques Derrida to Joseph Beuys.* Baltimore: Johns Hopkins UP, 1985.

———. "The Post Age." *Diacritics* 11 (1981): 39–56.

———. *Teletheory: Grammatology in the Age of Video.* New York: Routledge, 1989.

Ungar, Steven. "The Professor of Desire." *Yale French Studies* 63 (1982): 80–97.

Untersteiner, Mario. *The Sophists.* Trans. Kathleen Freeman. Oxford: Blackwell, 1954.

Vattimo, Gianni. *The End of Modernity: Nihilism and Hermeneutics in Postmodern Culture.* Trans. Jon R. Snyder. Baltimore: Johns Hopkins UP, 1988.

Verdenius, W. J. "Gorgias' Doctrine of Deception." *The Legacy of the Sophists.* Ed. G. B. Kerferd. Wiesbaden: Steiner, 1981. 116–28.

Vernant, Jean-Pierre. *Myth and Thought among the Greeks.* 1965. London: Routledge, 1983.

——. "One . . . Two . . . Three: *Eros.*" *Before Sexuality: The Construction of Erotic Experience in the Ancient Greek World.* Ed. David M. Halperin, John J. Winkler, and Froma I. Zeitlin. Princeton: Princeton UP, 1989. 465–78.

——. *The Origins of Greek Thought.* New York: Cornell UP, 1982.

Versényi, Laszlo. *Socratic Humanism.* New Haven: Yale UP, 1963.

Vickers, Brian. *In Defence of Rhetoric.* Oxford: Clarendon, 1988.

Vitanza, Victor J. "Canonicity, Rape Narratives, and the History of Rhetoric." Unpublished ms.

——. "A Comment on 'Protocols, Retrospective Reports, and the Stream of Consciousness.'" *College English* 49.8 (Dec. 1987): 926–28.

——. "Concerning a Post-Classical *Ethos,* as a Para/Rhetorical Ethics, the 'Selphs,' and the Excluded Third." *Ethos: New Essays in Rhetorical and Cultural Theory.* Ed. James Baumlin and Tita Baumlin. Dallas: Southern Methodist UP, 1994. 389–431.

——. "Critical Sub/Versions of the History of Philosophical Rhetoric." *Rhetoric Review* 6.1 (fall 1987): 41–66.

——. "A Feminist Sophistic?" *JAC: A Journal of Composition Theory* 15.2 (1995): 321–49.

——. "Invention, Serendipity, Catastrophe, and a Unified, Ironic Theory of Change: The Two Master and Two Mistress Tropes, with Attendant Offspring." *Visions of Rhetoric: History, Theory and Criticism.* Ed. Charles W. Kneupper. Arlington: Rhetoric Soc. of America, 1987. 132–45.

——. *Negation, Subjectivity, and the History of Rhetoric.* Albany: State U of New York P, 1997.

——. "'Notes' Towards Historiographies of Rhetorics; or the Rhetorics of the Histories of Rhetorics: Traditional, Revisionary, and Sub/Versive." *Pre/Text* 8 (1987): 64–125.

——. "On Negation—and Yet Affirmation—in Dis/Respect to Critical Theory." Unpublished ms.

——. "'Some More' Notes, Toward a 'Third' Sophistic." *Argumentation* 5 (1991): 117–39.

——. "Teaching—Nothing." Unpublished ms.

——. "Three Countertheses: or, A Critical In(ter)vention into Composition Theories and Pedagogies." *Contending with Words: Composition and Rhetoric in a Postmodern Age.* Ed. Patricia Harkin and John Schilb. New York: MLA, 1991. 139–72.

——. "Threes." *Composition in Context.* Ed. W. Ross Winterowd and Vincent Gillespie. Carbondale: Southern Illinois UP, 1994. 196–218.

——, ed. *Writing Histories of Rhetoric.* Carbondale: Southern Illinois UP, 1994.

Walker, Jeffrey. "Aristotle and Democracy." Online posting. 15 Jan. 1998. H-RHETOR. <jswl@psu.edu>.

——. "The Body of Persuasion: A Theory of the Enthymeme." *College English* 56.1 (Jan. 1994): 46–60.

Warren, Mark. *Nietzsche and Political Thought.* Cambridge: MIT P, 1988.

Watson, Stephen. "Jürgen Habermas and Jean-François Lyotard: Post-modernism and the Crisis of Rationality." *Philosophy and Social Criticism* 10.2 (1984): 1–24.

Weber, Samuel. "The Debts of Deconstruction and Other, Related Assumptions." *Taking Chances: Derrida, Psychoanalysis, and Literature.* Ed. Joseph H. Smith and William Kerrigan. Baltimore: Johns Hopkins UP, 1984. 33–65.

Weedon, Chris. "Post-structuralist Feminist Practice." *Theory/Pedagogy/Politics: Texts for Change.* Ed. Donald Morton and Mas'ud Zavarzadeh. Urbana: U of Illinois P, 1991. 47–63.

Weigall, Arthur. *Personalities of Antiquity.* 1928. Freeport: Books for Libraries, 1969.

Welldon, Estela V. *Mother, Madonna, Whore: The Idealization and Denigration of Motherhood.* London: Free Association, 1988.

Wendell, Susan. "A (Qualified) Defense of Liberal Feminism." *Hypatia* 2.2 (summer 1987): 65–92.

White, Alan. *Within Nietzsche's Labyrinth.* New York: Routledge, 1990.

White, Eric Charles. *Kaironomia: On the Will-to-Invent.* Ithaca: Cornell UP, 1987.

Whitson, Steve. "Nietzsche, Deception, and the History of Rhetoric." Unpublished ms.

Wiener, Harvey S. "Collaborative Learning in the Classroom: A Guide to Evaluation." *College English* 48.1 (Jan. 1986): 52–61.

Williamson, Judith. "An Interview with Jean Baudrillard." Trans. Brand Thumin. *Block* 15 (1989): 16–19.

Wilson, Jill. "An Interview with Linda Flower: Helping Writers Build Mansions with More Rooms." *Writing on the Edge* 3.1 (fall 1991): 9–22.

Winkler, John J. *The Constraints of Desire: The Anthropology of Sex and Gender in Ancient Greece.* New York: Routledge, 1990.

Wittig, Monique. "One Is Not Born a Woman." *Feminist Issues* 1.2 (winter 1981): 47–54.

———. "The Trojan Horse." *Feminist Issues* 4.2 (fall 1984): 45–49.

Wolf, Christa. *Cassandra: A Novel and Four Essays.* Trans. Jan Van Heurck. New York: Farrar, 1984.

Wolf, Naomi. *Fire with Fire: The New Female Power and How to Use It.* New York: Fawcett, 1993.

Wolff, Janet. *Feminine Sentences: Essays on Women and Culture.* Berkeley: U of California P, 1990.

Worsham, Lynn. "Writing Against Writing: The Predicament of *Ecriture Féminine* in Composition Studies." *Contending with Words: Composition and Rhetoric in a Postmodern Age.* Ed. Patricia Harkin and John Schilb. New York: MLA, 1991. 82–104.

Young, Iris Marion. "The Ideal of Community and the Politics of Difference." *Feminism/Postmodernism.* Ed. Linda J. Nicholson. New York: Routledge, 1990. 300–323.

Young, Richard E. "Paradigms and Problems: Needed Research in Rhetorical Invention." *Research on Composing: Points of Departure.* Ed. Charles R. Cooper and Lee Odell. Urbana: NCTE, 1978. 29–47.

Young, Richard E., Alton Becker, and Kenneth Pike. *Rhetoric: Discovery and Change*. New York: Harcourt, 1970.

Zavarzadeh, Mas'ud, and Donald Morton. "Theory as Resistance." *Theory as Resistance: Politics and Culture after (Post)Structuralism*. New York: Guilford, 31–54.

——. "Theory Pedagogy Politics: The Crisis of 'The Subject' in the Humanities." *Theory/Pedagogy/Politics: Texts for Change*. Ed. Donald Morton and Mas'ud Zavarzadeh. Urbana: U of Illinois P, 1991. 1–32.

Zawacki, Terry Meyers. "Recomposing as a Woman—An Essay in Different Voices." *College Composition and Communication* 43.1 (Feb. 1992): 32–38.

Zeitlin, Froma I. *Playing the Other: Gender and Society in Classical Greek Literature*. Chicago: U of Chicago P, 1996.

Ziarek, Ewa. "Kristeva and Levinas: Mourning, Ethics, and the Feminine." *Ethics, Politics, and Difference in Julia Kristeva's Writing*. Ed. Kelly Oliver. New York: Routledge, 1993. 62–78.

Zizek, Slavoj. *Enjoy Your Symptom: Jacques Lacan in Hollywood and Out*. New York: Routledge, 1992.

——. *The Sublime Object of Ideology*. London: Verso, 1989.

Index

Adorno, Theodor W., 71
agency, 6, 23, 88, 185; political, 8, 20, 177; rhetorical, 5, 8, 20–21, 80, 81, 177. *See also* subjectivity; will
alētheia, 45, 49, 66, 77, 84, 111, 141
Althusser, Louis, 6, 124, 151
amor fati, 111, 113, 147
apatē: definition of, 70, 73; and Gorgias, 4, 11, 66, 75–79; and illusion, 86, 135; and seduction, 87; and Woman, 117, 144
Aphrodite, 54, 56, 58, 60, 87
aretē, 67, 68, 89, 191
Ariadne, 4, 27, 100, 118, 126
Aristotle, 38, 49, 50, 102, 127, 138, 176, 186, 189, 193; on audience, 83; and cause/effect, 102; and Gorgias, 70, 78; and *mētis,* 191; and the negative, 71; and political (deliberative) discourse, 89, 90, 124, 173; and principle of noncontradiction, 72; and Woman, 44, 55, 61
art, 11, 41, 111, 117, 120, 129; and Woman, 116, 118
artifice, 11, 81; and rhetoric and Woman, 42, 96. *See also* Baudrillard
Aspasia, 67, 126, 202n. 13; and Gorgias, 126
Athena, 189
Atwill, Janet, 43
Augustine, 18, 137, 138
Austin, Norman, 94, 96, 121, 201n. 2

Barthes, Roland, 89, 96, 186
Bartholomae, David, 8, 154, 183
Bataille, Georges, 6, 60, 90, 91
Baubo, 117, 118
Baudrillard, Jean, 5, 6, 24, 61, 128–52; and being (truth), 25, 27, 86–89, 130–31, 134, 135, 136, 140, 175, 176, 184; and dialectic, 2, 17, 21, 163; and the feminine, 4, 29, 31, 142–45, 147, 151; and pornography, 141–42; and seduction, 9, 10, 11, 30–31, 83, 86–87, 93, 95, 111, 129–30, 136–37, 142–52, 193; and signification, 86–89, 108, 133–36, 145–50, 185; and subjectivity, 12, 86–89, 91, 136–37, 141, 143–44, 145–47, 151, 158, 192
being, 14, 30, 32–64, 103, 120, 121, 130, 131; definition of, based on the negative, 6, 72; and Eleatics, 40–42, 65, 70, 72, 122; principle of the real, 3, 10, 134. *See also* Baudrillard; Parmenides; Plato; truth
Benjamin, Jessica, 153, 163, 166, 168, 169, 171
Berlin, James A., 8, 154, 155, 156, 192
Bizzell, Patricia, 20–21, 154, 155, 157, 174
Booth, Wayne C., 108, 139
Braidotti, Rosi, 22, 23, 24
Brockriede, Wayne, 81, 82
Burke, Kenneth, 153, 169, 183

Michelle Ballif is an assistant professor of English at the University of Georgia, where she teaches courses in critical and literary theory, rhetoric, and composition. She is coeditor, with Michael G. Moran, of *Twentieth Century Rhetorics and Rhetoricians* (forthcoming).

Rhetorical Philosophy and Theory Series

The Rhetorical Philosophy and Theory Series aims to extend the subject of rhetoric beyond its traditional and historical bounds and thus to elaborate rhetoric's significance as a metaperspective in provocative ways. Rhetoric has become an epistemology in its own right, one marked by heightened consciousness of the symbolic act as always already contextual and ideological. Otherwise known as the rhetorical turn, this dialectic between rhetoric and philosophy may lead to views transcending the limits of each and thus help us better understand the ethical problems and possibilities of producing theory.

The Rhetorical Philosophy and Theory Series seeks quality scholarly works that examine the significance of rhetorical theory in philosophical, historical, cultural, and disciplinary contexts. Such works will typically bring rhetorical theory to bear on the theoretical statements that enfranchise disciplinary paradigms and practices across the human sciences, with emphasis on the fields of rhetoric, composition, philosophy, and critical theory.

Queries and submissions should be directed to David Blakesley, Editor, Rhetorical Philosophy and Theory, Department of English, Purdue University, West Lafayette, IN 47907.